MW01630147

ALBERT MARQUET

Publishing Director: Paul ANDRÉ
Collaborator: Irina KHARITONOVA
Translator: Paul WILLIAMS
Design and Layout: DES SOURIS ET DES PAGES

Printed by Stamperia Artistica Nazionale in Turin (Italy)
for Parkstone Publishers
Copyright 3rd term 1995
ISBN 1 85995 116 3

ALBERT MARQUET

The paradox of time

Text
Mikhail GUERMAN

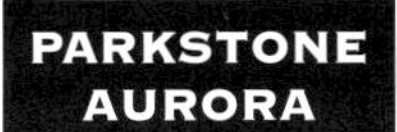

PARKSTONE PUBLISHERS, BOURNEMOUTH
AURORA ART PUBLISHERS, ST. PETERSBURG

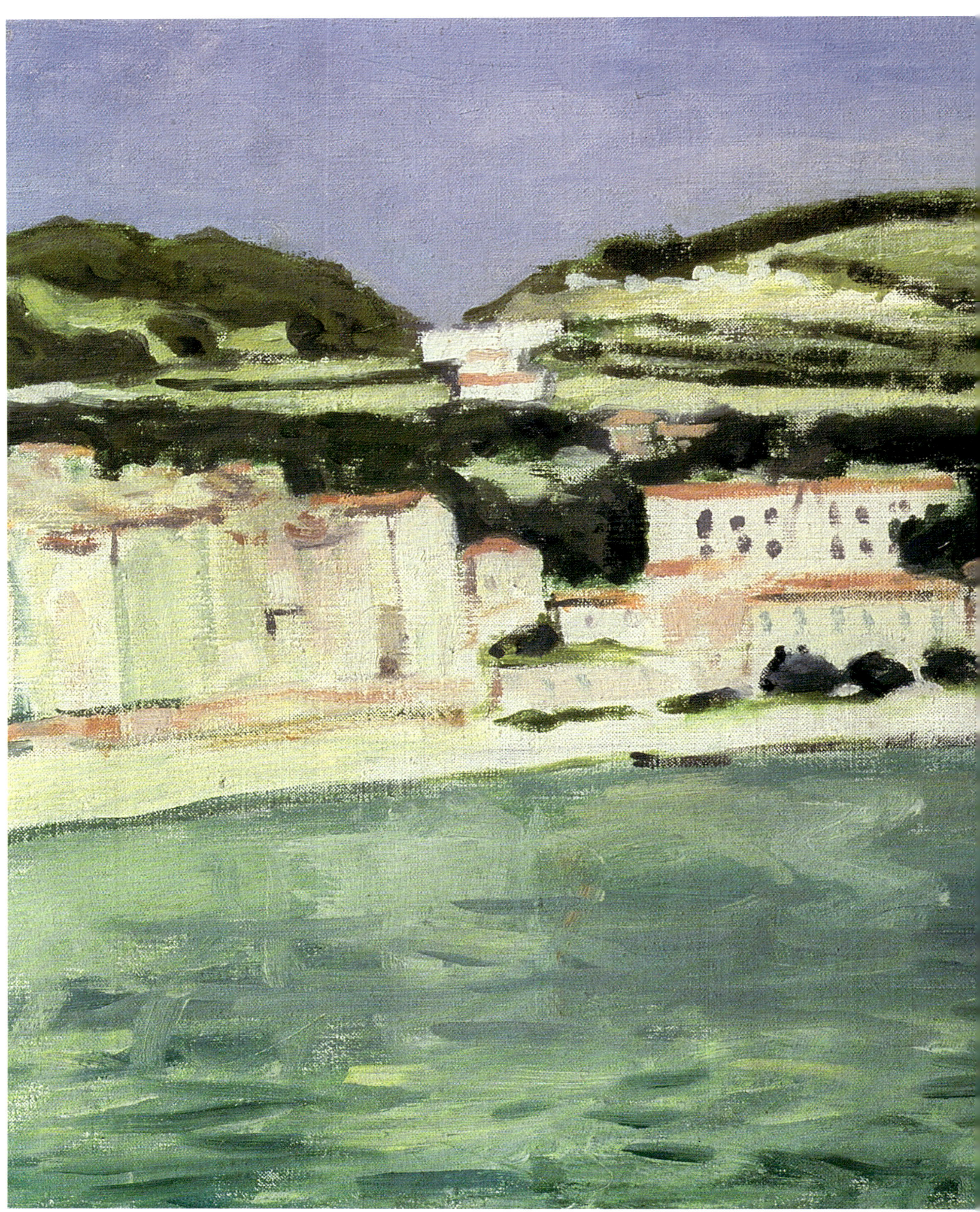

CONTENTS

MENTON HARBOUR
Detail.
The Hermitage, St Petersburg.

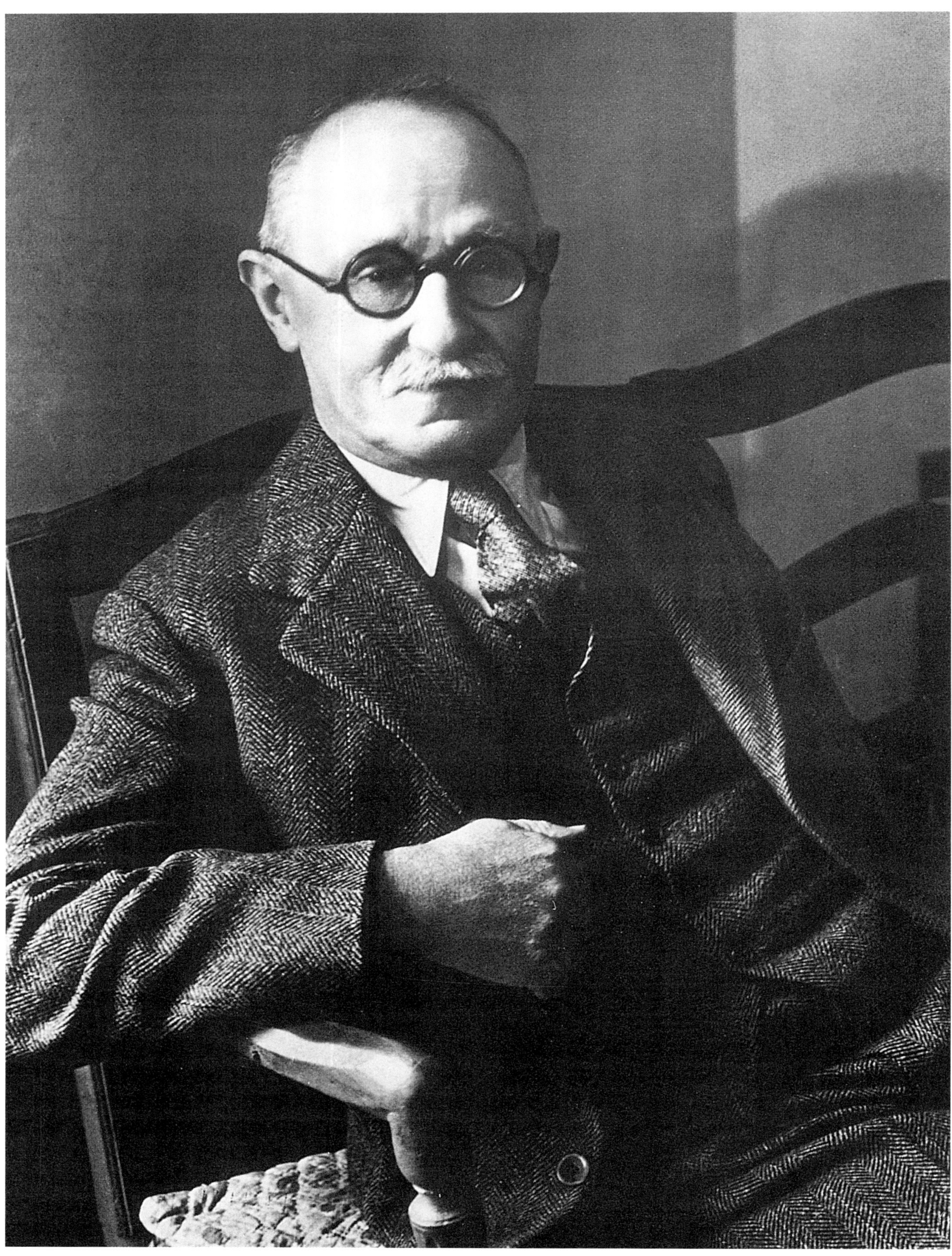

A T the end of the twentieth century, Albert Marquet may appear to be a rather mysterious character. For all their simplicity, his paintings can seem to contain as much mystication as post-modernist intellectual frolics. It is probably true that naturalness and the ability to be oneself cannot be explained, but simply exist as a fact. At least for the moment. Now all that remains is to look and to consider. It is said that great Frenchmen are born in the provinces and die in Paris. Marquet was no exception. He was born in Bordeaux in 1875, came to the capital as a teenager and never left.

When Albert Marquet began his studies in Paris, he was not yet sixteen years old. The only son of a humble railway clerk, he was, naturally, remote from the professional milieu and, still more, from a knowledge of the latest artistic trends.

The 1890s was the time when the closing century met with the one about to begin. The furore of the last Impressionist exhibitions had died away, but Monet, Renoir and Pissarro were at the height of their powers. Cézanne, still not fully recognized and known only to a very limited circle, was painting his finest canvases. At exhibitions, works by Bonnard, Signac, Henri Rousseau, Matisse and Gauguin hung side by side. Public taste was habitually outraged and retained its devotion to traditional visual verisimilitude. Many of the devices introduced by the Impressionists were already being used by the artists of the Salon, while in the schools of art the greatest respect was reserved for academic principles which dated back almost to the time of Louis David.

Marquet was lucky: soon after his arrival he became acquainted with men who were destined to create the new art.

His professional preferences formed quickly and unerringly — he joined the circle of most talented and independent painters. From his youth he displayed an inherent accuracy in the choices that he made and an ability both to learn from others without losing his self-reliance and to assimilate the most daring innovations while maintaining his fidelity to tradition. There is no doubt that of all the future Fauves Marquet was the most classical.

Marquet became close to Henri Matisse, studying together with him under Gustave Moreau at the Ecole des Beaux-Arts. Today it seems strange that this celebrated, fashionable and certainly not unpretentious artist was the mentor of Matisse, Rouault and Marquet. In point of fact, Moreau was anything but an technical innovator, and — to present-day eyes — his painting is fairly close to that of the Salon. But for his own time Moreau was an artist of a new persuasion: one of the Symbolists. His paintings charmed the public not because of their technical boldness, but through their refined artistry, their charming air of datedness. He had a capacity to create in his works an enigmatic world in which *fin-de-siècle* refinement combined naturally with motifs from exotic tales or mediaeval legends. Moreau's symbolism lay neither in spiritual drama nor in new creative principles as it had done with Baudelaire, Rimbaud or Gauguin. He worked in a wholly academic manner, carefully "crafting" paintings which are so overcharged with meaning that they verge on the banal, while his subtly "eroticised" mysticism remained entirely a product of its time. But, as was the case, for example, with Oscar Wilde, Moreau's excessive prettiness quite often concealed genuine feeling and subtle thinking. Moreover, he was a true master, a virtuoso adept of great professionalism.

It is well known that Moreau was a sensitive mentor with a love and gift for teaching. While not preaching the principles

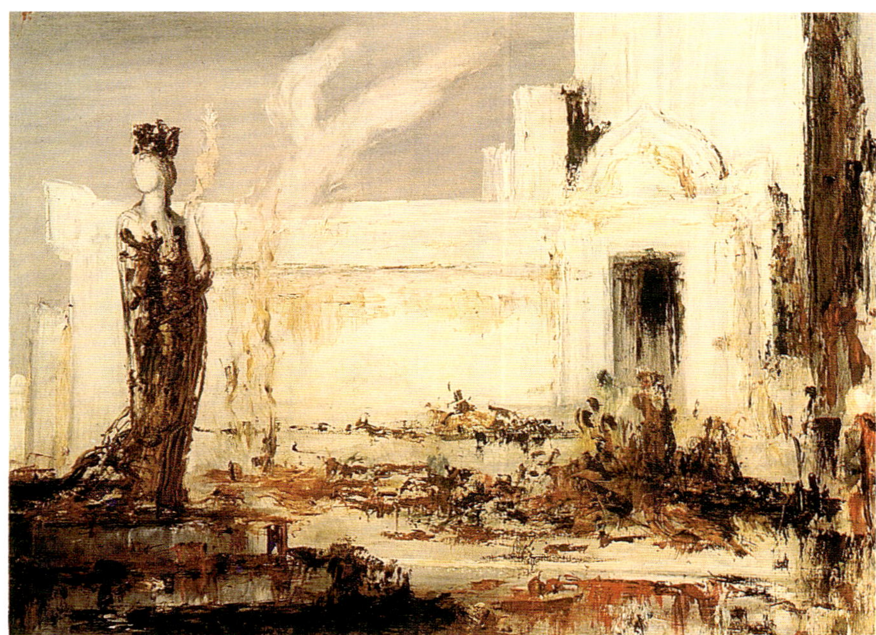

of the "modern" artists, he held them in respect, and, most importantly, he helped each of his pupils develop his own individuality (or at the very least did not hinder that process). He inculcated the "museum habit" in his pupils and they spent long hours working in the Louvre.

There can be no doubting that Moreau's devotion to symbols, things mediaeval and legends was developed — indirectly, yet perceptibly — in the work of his favourite pupil and another future Fauve: Rouault.

In Moreau Marquet found a mentor from whom he could indeed learn something and an artist with whom he might disagree, but even that disagreement would be productive. Moreau, moreover, for all his outgoing sociability in his mature years when he gave himself wholeheartedly to teaching, displayed a devotion to solitude and concentration when working which Marquet inevitably found attractive. The pupil

Gustave Moreau. ▶
Self-Portrait.
1850.

Gustave Moreau.
Helen at the Scaean Gate.
1880.

8

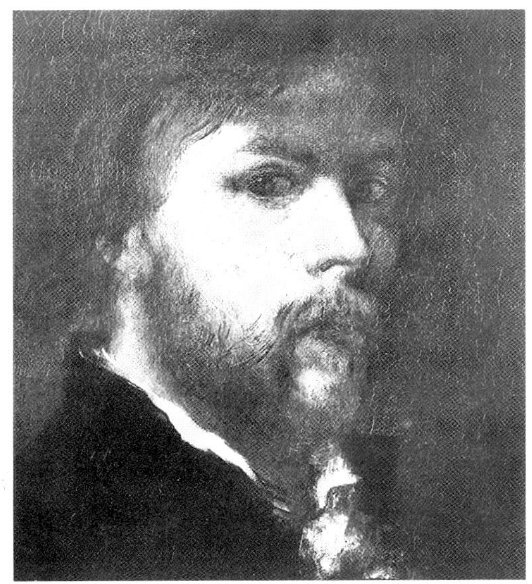

was also drawn by his teacher's mind, since Moreau was a widely educated man. It is possible that it was in Moreau's studio that Marquet acquired a lasting indifference to a meticulous finish and, even more, to the elaborate narrative subjects which characterized his teacher's work.

It is true that from the very earliest years of his studies Marquet, like the majority of those who were of his age and held similar opinions, rejected narrative painting. In contrast to Matisse, Rouault, Derain and many others Marquet *never* invented or composed a picture. He worked from nature.

The twentieth century can hardly have seen any other artist of standing who only painted the real world, without constructing a motif or creating some sort of "visual story". Marquet, like Cézanne, only selected and interpreted. He "gave physical expression to his sensations."

Surprisingly, he hardly experienced the influence of Impressionism, a trend which had already wholly demonstrated its vitality even in the most stagnant artistic circles and had opened up no small number of genuinely new possibilities for painters. Van Gogh and Cézanne were little known in Paris, if indeed they were known at all. Gauguin and the Pont-Aven school were also far from famous.

Yet Marquet, the born empiricist — more capable than anyone

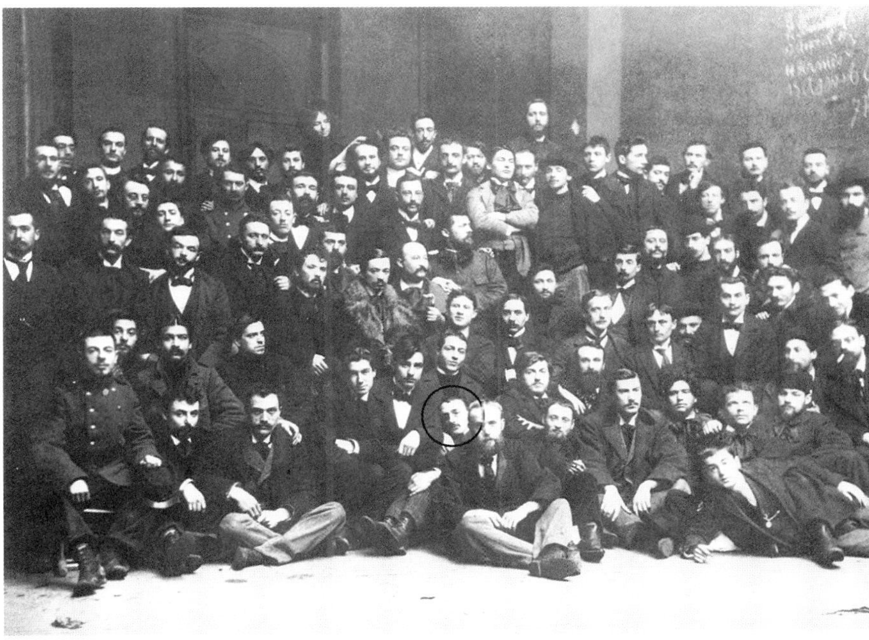

of delighting in the transitory states of nature, the instantaneous effects of lighting which transformed a landscape — and talented colourist, remained, as far as we can judge from his paintings, unaffected by the art of the Impressionists. The art of those who in such an inimitable and innovative way painted Paris, its fleeting effects of colour and light, and who revealed anew its painterly secrets seems to have been alien to him. The incidental was not of interest to Marquet. He did

Moreau's pupils
at the Ecole des Beaux-Arts.
1897.

9

not seek to capture with the brush the image imprinted for an instant on the retina. For all the affinity of their motifs, Marquet — like Cézanne — was opposed to Impressionism. He did not "reflect" reality. While remaining a loyal votary to nature, he nevertheless created it anew.

Therein lies Marquet's power to attract — and therein too, if you will, lies one of the paradoxes regarding his art.

Impressionism represented simultaneously both the climax and the crisis of the traditional nineteenth-century imitation of life. In the work of the Impressionists precise depiction culminated in something absolute — a portrait of an instant, the stopping of the unstoppable. That route was exhausted, and moreover a perception of a fleeting state of nature, passive and precise to the point of extreme concreteness, was already out of tune with the passion for profound cognition, for the creation of a new artistic world, one which would be the goal of the twentieth century.

It was now, when Impressionism was already a spent force, that artists appeared who tried to present not just reality perceived by the sensitive vision of the painter ("Monet is only an eye," Cézanne said), but reality deeply experienced and re-presented on canvas in a way which accorded with the artist's sense of the world and his own individuality.

Van Gogh, Gauguin, Cézanne and all the other artists who have gone down in history under the extremely imprecise term "Post-Impressionists", painted not so much the world

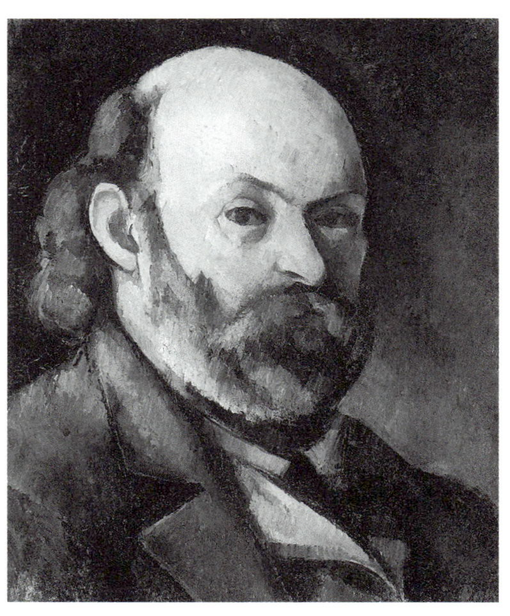

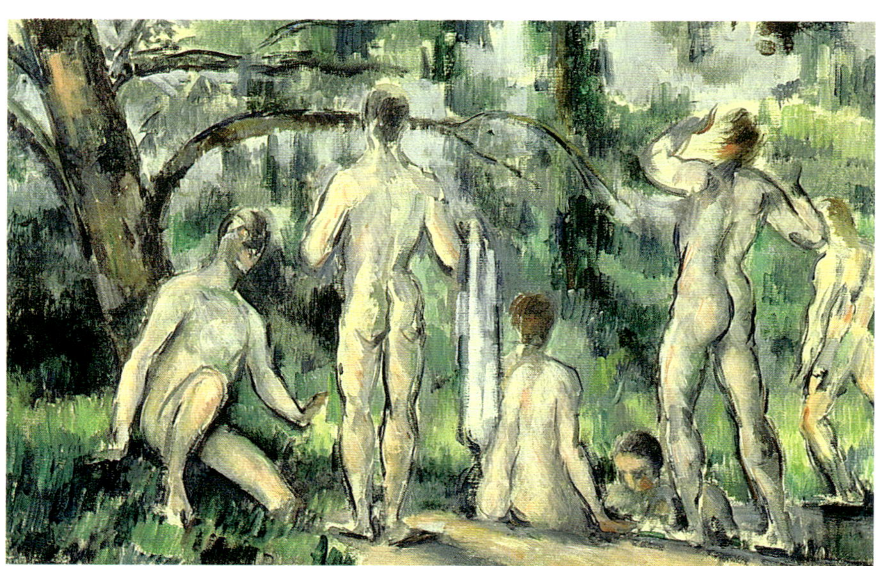

they saw as the world they experienced; a world re-created, suitable for the artist's "picture gallery of the soul", to borrow Hesse's phrase.

Marquet was not such. He was reticent, his brush restrained: The inner strivings of the soul would scariely find expression in his work. It is impossible to imagine him depicting physical

Paul Cézanne.
Bathing.
1892-1894.

10

matter acquiver with pain, as Van Gogh did, or presenting cosmic metamorphoses like those of Cézanne. Motifs drawn from real life always dominate in his paintings. But austerity of selection, lyrical asceticism, the ability to accentuate the essential and to attain a peculiar sense of stability, not simply to arrest the moment (as the Impressionists did), but to endow it with a kind of permanence, even a sense of eternity — *that* Marquet did have on a par with the greatest achievements of the twentieth century.

All this appeared at an early age. Marquet's formation as a painter was almost instantaneous and evolution is barely detectable in his work. One can, of course, trace the development of practical skills, of confidence, of the gradual abandonment of bright colours and the emergence of the large, free brushstroke, but there is little basic change in Marquet's art. He found his niche almost instantaneously.

In his youth he experienced a short-lived but intense fascination with Pointillism. At the end of the 1890s he often painted

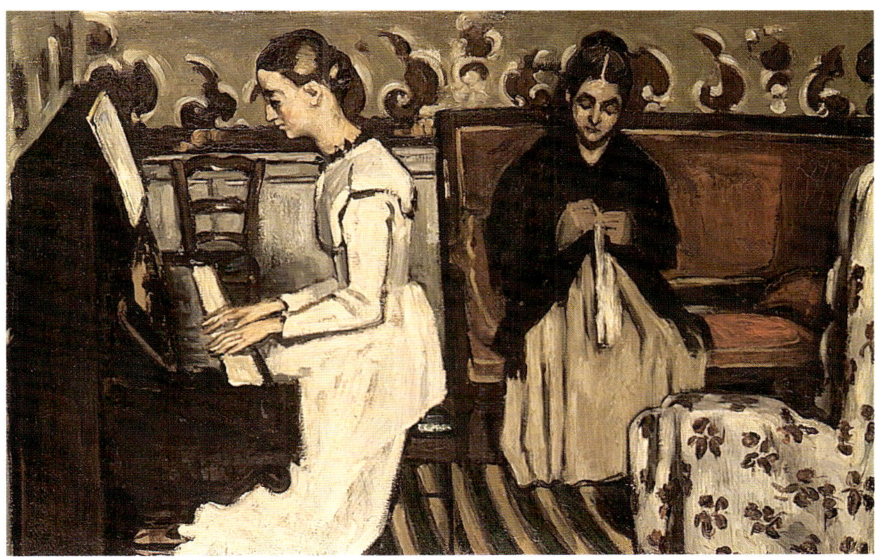

the backgrounds of academic studies in tiny dabs of pure colours. His "pointillist" works are above all impersonal; the artist was concerned with the manner itself, which to a significant extent precluded a personal perception. Marquet's fascination soon passed, but his adoption of a strictly rational system like Pointillism was significant: the search for logic and simplicity was not a chance occurrence. Nor was it a coincidence that Marquet made so many copies of Poussin (of whom Cézanne, once again, was so fond): many years later he spoke of the hours he had before that artist's paintings: "I was certain that they would never bore me."

Marquet was thirty-two years old when, in a rare excursion into portraiture, he painted *The Sergeant of the Colonial Troops* (1907; Museum of Fine Arts, Bordeaux). The auster-

Paul Cézanne.
Girl at the Piano
(Overture to Tannhaüser*).*
Ca. 1868-1869.

11

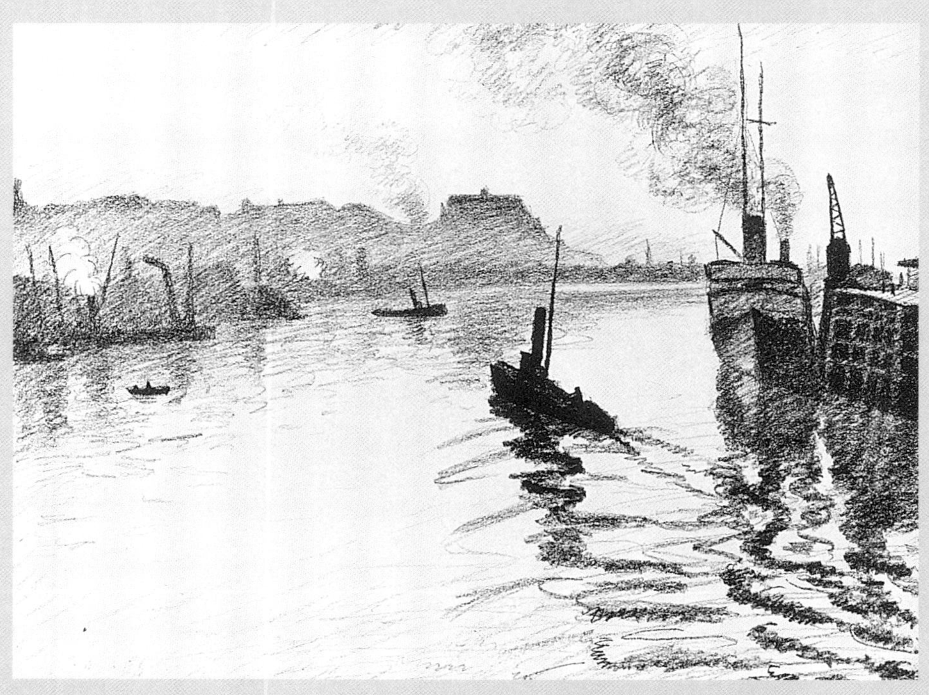

Albert Marquet. *The Port of Boulogne. Early Morning.*

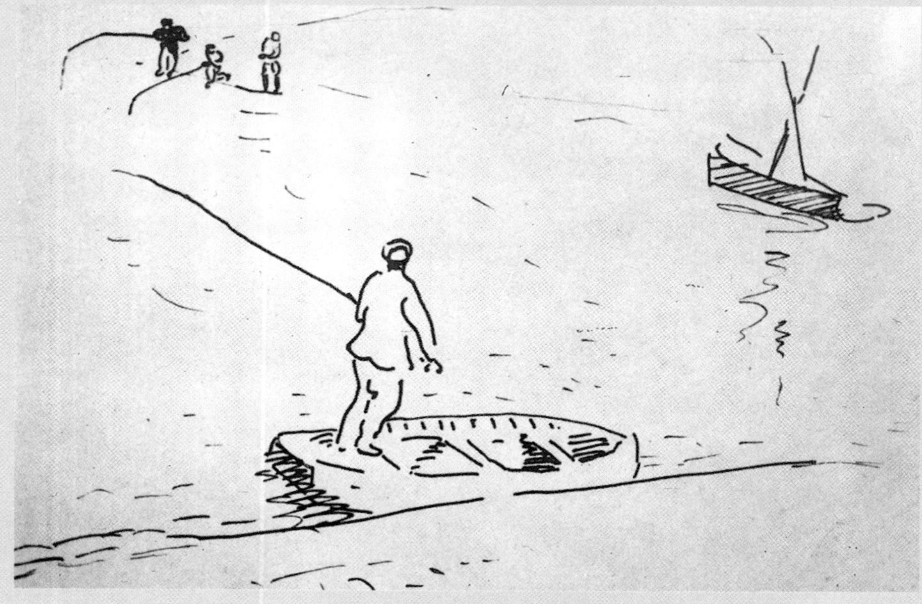

Albert Marquet. *Angler in a Boat.*

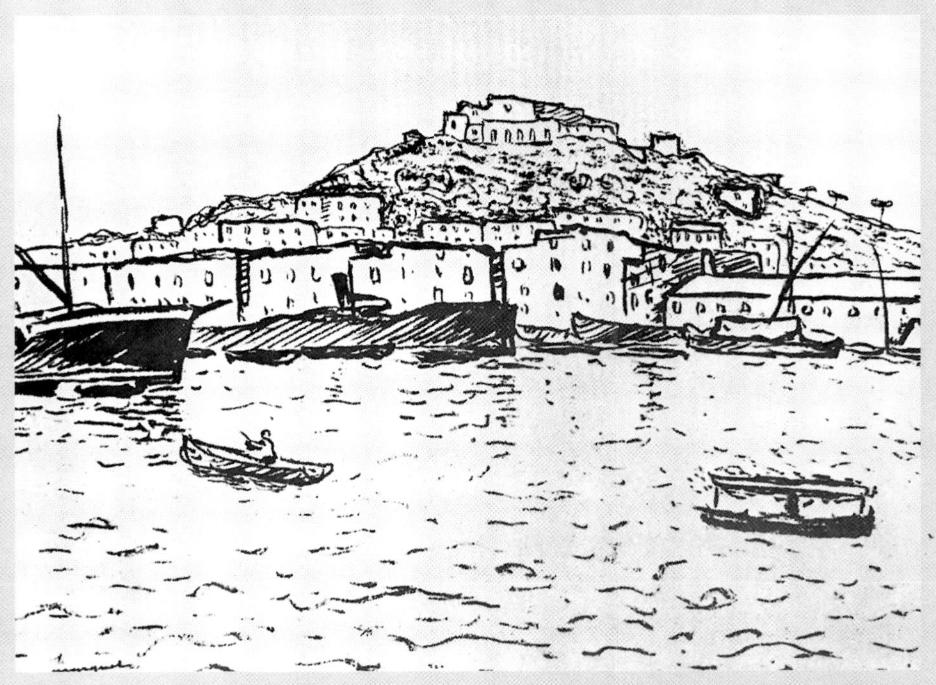

Albert Marquet. *Estaque.*

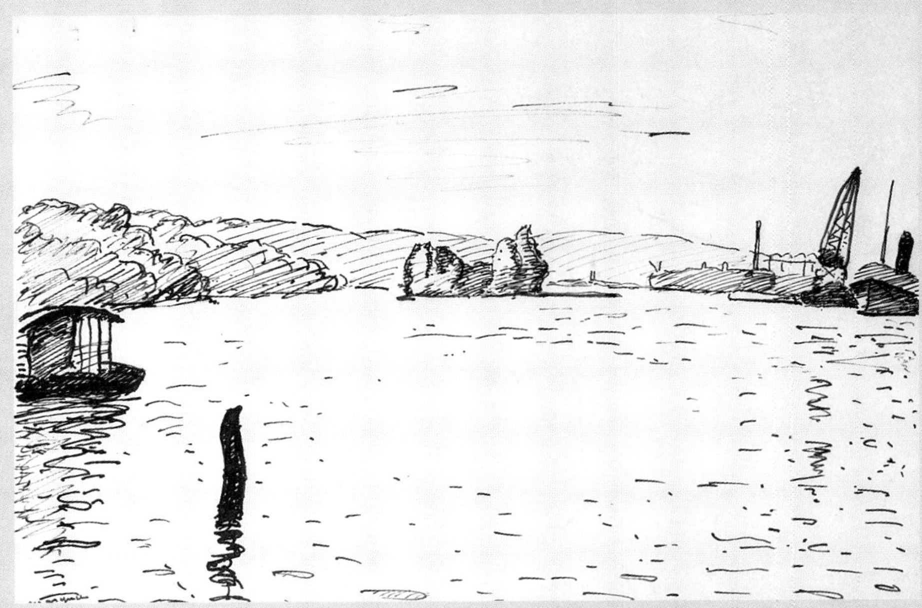

Albert Marquet. *View in the Vicinity of Rouen.*

ity of the work is surprising for a beginner: an almost smooth background, no accessories, a figure with no depth. Space is expressed only by precisely inspired planes of colour. Modelling is reduced to a minimum, with the artist's brush sharply distinguishing only the deep shadows. The dense materiality and pronounced immobility of the figure cause us to think once again of the principles of Cézanne (Marquet would, of course, have seen the large Cézanne exhibition at Ambroise Vollard's gallery in 1896).

Even then, in all probability, Marquet sought individuality not so much in facial features as in the silhouette, the pose, the way of moving (later this would become the distinctive quality of his portraits and depictions of models). This is again typical of Marquet — he was always more concerned with the relationship of parts, the effect of the whole. Possibly for this reason the figures he painted were usually stronger "likenesses" than the faces; possibly it is this quality which makes his nude studies so interesting.

A number of such works by Marquet have survived. They are

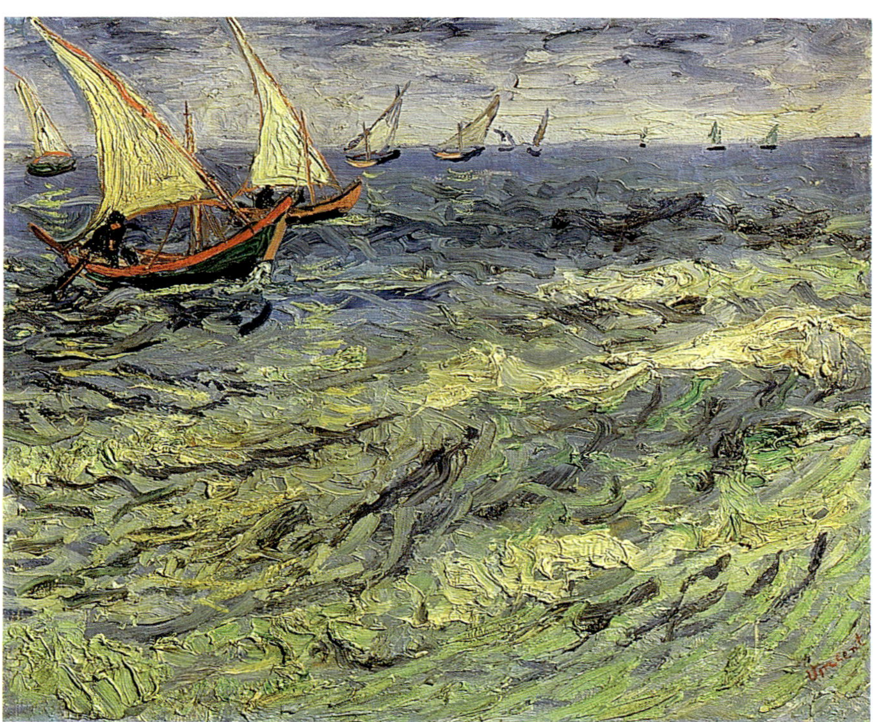

not the usual figure studies but true "portraits of the human body". Perhaps, if the artist's interest in the depiction of figures had lasted longer, it would be possible to talk about Marquet's "*nus*" as a phenomenon just as interesting as those of Degas, Renoir or Modigliani. But his models are not numerous and little known.

Nevertheless, this sphere of Marquet's creative activities is a good deal more important than it might seem. The somewhat olympian lyricism inherent in Marquet the landscapist

14

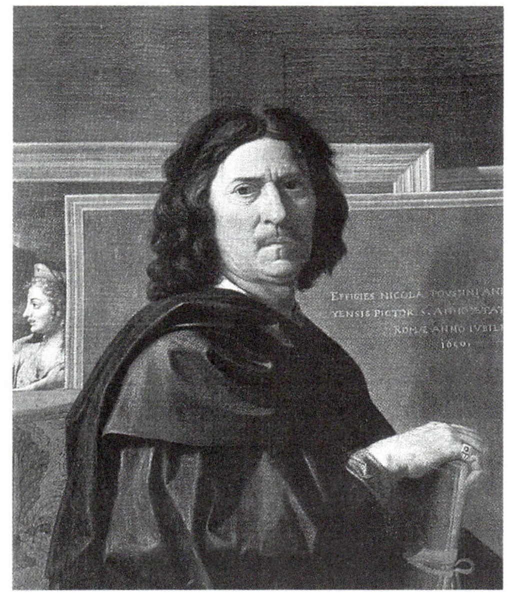

unexpectedly gives way in these canvases to an impassioned expression of severely individualized, seemingly highly personal, emotions. It would be no exaggeration to say that Marquet's deeply private temperament found such powerful expression here, that it provides anyone familiar with Freud's works with food for thought. Here, again, there are links with the emotional and artistic world of Cézanne, who was miraculously able to combine severe asceticism and strong sensuality. There is no need to conduct psychoanalytical experiments on Marquet's paintings, but it would be prudish not to mention the obvious.

In Marquet's studies of nude figures we can clearly trace a persistent concern above all with the individuality of a body, its construction, dynamics and distinctive forms. Each and every one of Marquet's nudes is characterized by the combination of a precise, resilient line and sensitive modelling with a somewhat unsparing depiction of bodies that are far from beautiful yet mysteriously attractive, thanks to aesthetic emphasis on the private, the intimate, the personal.

We can begin with the early study painted in 1898 in the studio of Gustave Moreau (this painting, now in the Museum of Fine Arts, Bordeaux, has the alternative title *Nu fauve* which was probably suggested by the unexpectedly intense colours, since there were seven years to go before the first Fauve exhibition). For all its analytical objectivity, this work is already marked by disturbing concrete contours, a feature which breaks away from the overall somewhat generalized style. This can be sensed even more keenly in the 1905 canvas *Nu dans un atelier de l'ami du peintre. Deuxième nu fauve* (Museum of Modern Art, Paris).

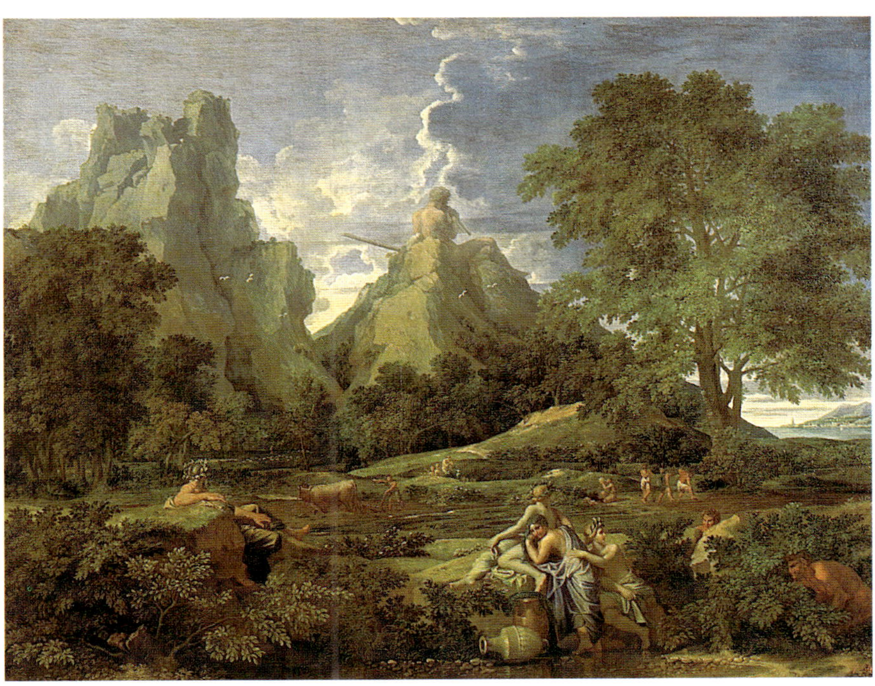

Nicolas Poussin.
Landscape with Polyphemus.
1649.

These qualities expressed themselves more fully in a superb
study from 1909 now in the Museum of Fine Arts, Bordeaux.
The standing figure of the model is painted in backlighting.
Marquet's brush seizes greedily on the slight angularity of
the shoulders, the peculiar bend of the knee and the steep
drop of the hip. The curves are at times reduced to a broken
succession of straight lines in order to bring out the impression more intensely and to give that impression stability and

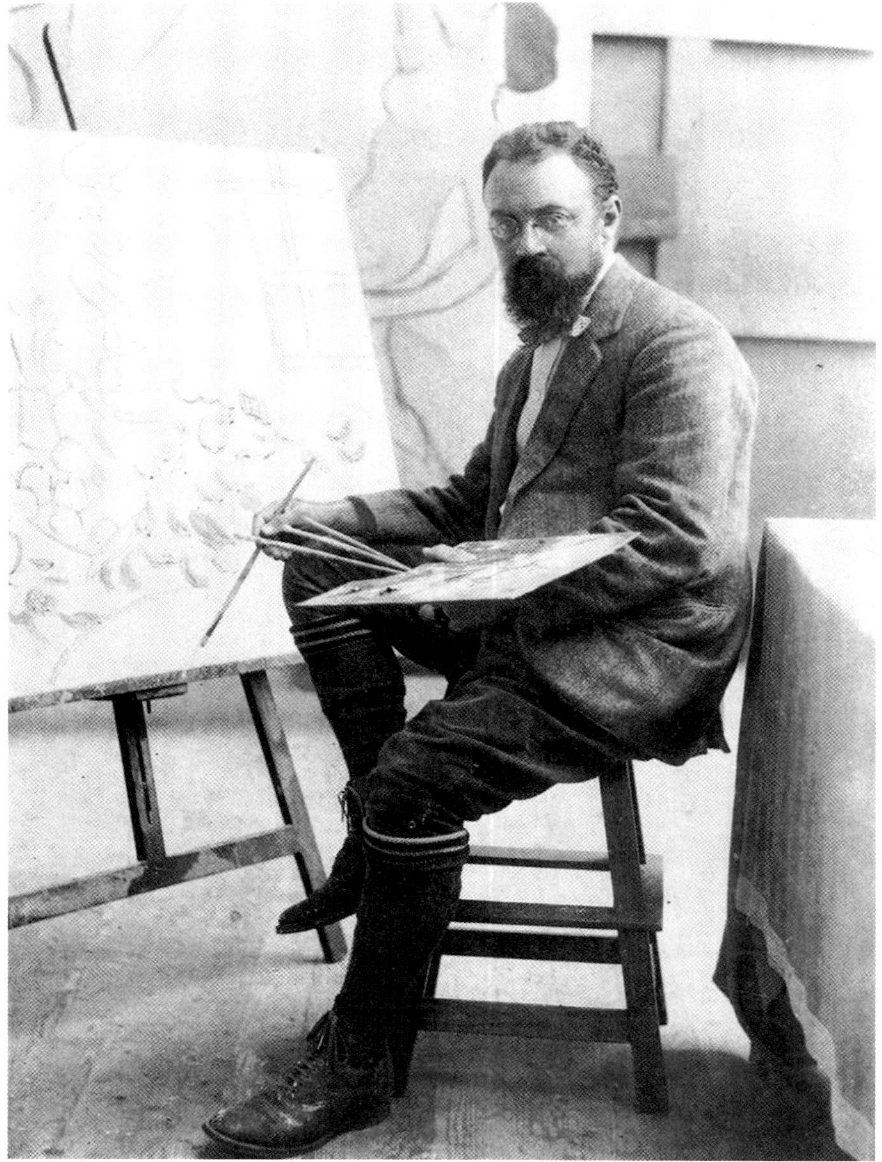

extension in time. The compositional arrangement is unusual
and significant for Marquet: the acute lines of perspective
immediately retreating into the depths of the painting, the
contrast of the corners and the high horizon which is raised
even further towards the edge of the canvas.
Marquet even then, in his youth, was making increasingly
frequent use of a black line which, as in Daumier's painting,
shows through the layer of paint, giving a harsh outline to

NUDE. KNOWN AS "NU FAUVE"
1898
Oil on paper applied to canvas. 73 x 50 cm.
Signed and dated bottom left:
Marquet 1898.
Museum of Fine Arts, Bordeaux.

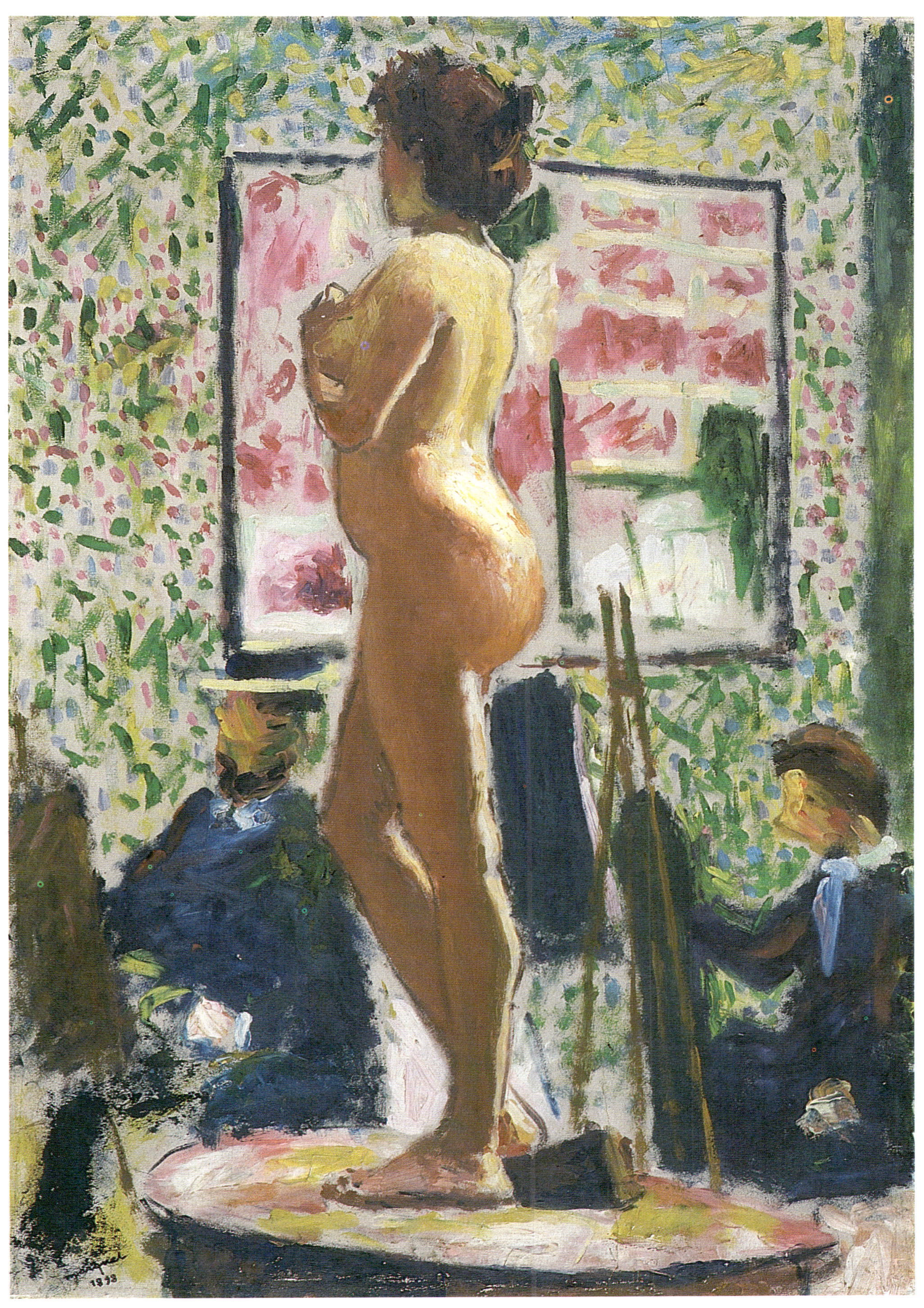

tender and powerful patches of colour and introducing an unexpected, recognisably constructional element into the painting.

If we try to discover prototypes which Marquet might have followed in his painting of the nude then the works which most readily spring to mind are those of Degas and, perhaps,

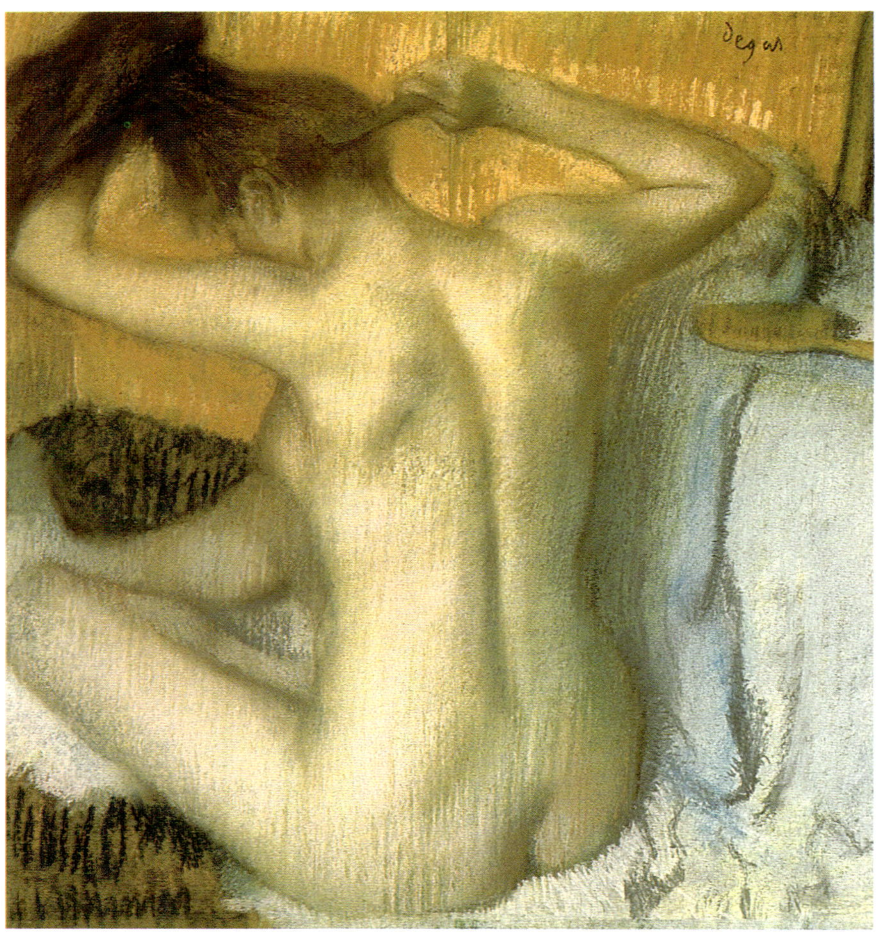

Toulouse-Lautrec. But these influences are fairly remote and his profound link with Cézanne undoubtedly prevailed.

Of his contemporaries Marquet was closest of all to Matisse. The two had more than just tastes in common. They were friends who shared the traditional poverty of artists starting out in Paris. Together they searched for casual jobs in order to get by, one of which was moulding the sculptural cornices in the Petit Palais.

At a time when Marquet was working in a calm, concentrated manner, not paying much attention to the disputes of the genuine and the supposed "iconoclasts" of the foundations of art and not involving himself in theories to which he had a lifelong indifference, Matisse was flitting from one extreme to another. He experienced an ardent fascination with the painting of Van Gogh, then he met Signac, one of the creators of Pointillism, and tried his own hand at that technique (one

18

of his earliest known works, *Light. Peace and Contentment* (1904, private collection, New York) was created in this manner). After that came the fabulous world of Oriental art which captivated Matisse with its bold and overt stylization of forms, the purity of its bright surfaces of colour and its daring expressivity of line. He studied Gauguin and travelled to London to gain a thorough knowledge of Turner's paintings. Matisse's energy and talent, his ardent, conscious desire to find a new course in painting distinct from both the passive observation of the Impressionists and the spiritual complexity of Van Gogh and Cézanne, drew kindred spirits to him. A group of artists formed around Matisse who were very different, but

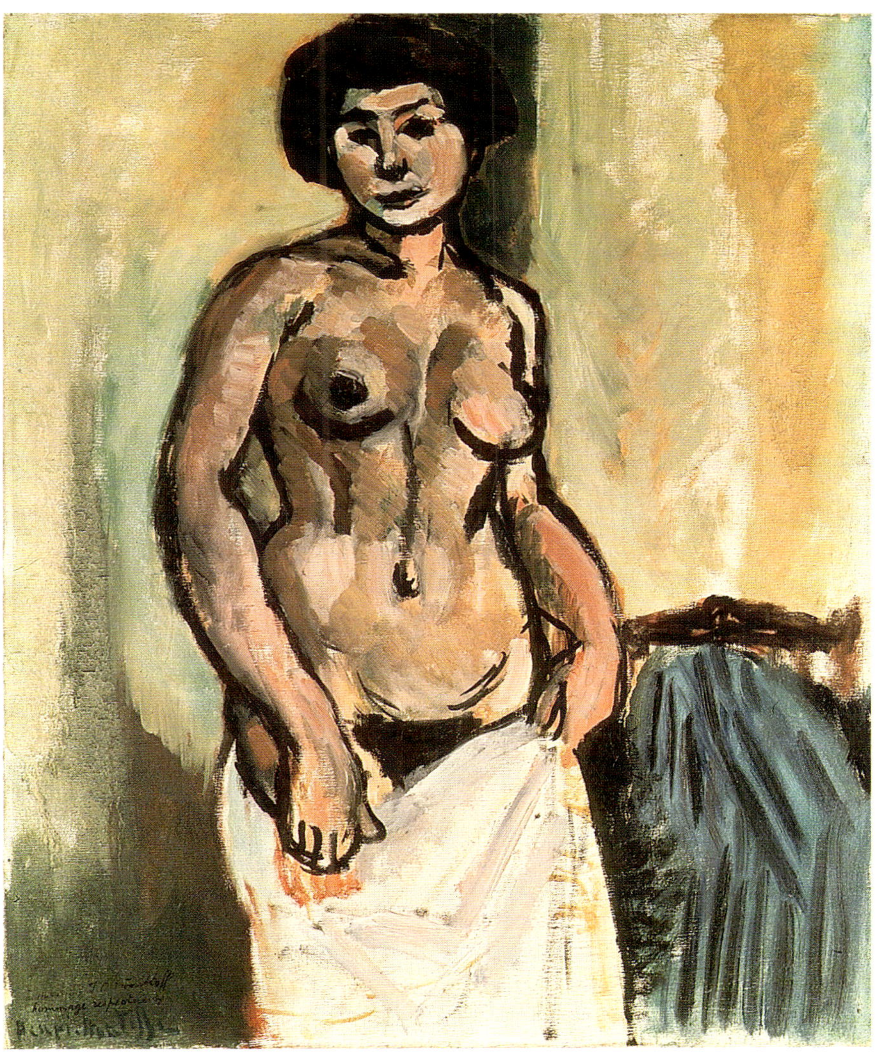

who were united in their desire to create a form of art which would be entirely new, daring, capable not so much of reflecting the world as of expressing the feelings of its creator.

With the possible exception of Pointillism, the significant trends in French art in the late nineteenth and early twentieth centuries had no serious or consistent theoretical background. What Zola wrote about Edouard Manet or Théodore Duret

Henri Matisse.
Nude. Study.
1908.

19

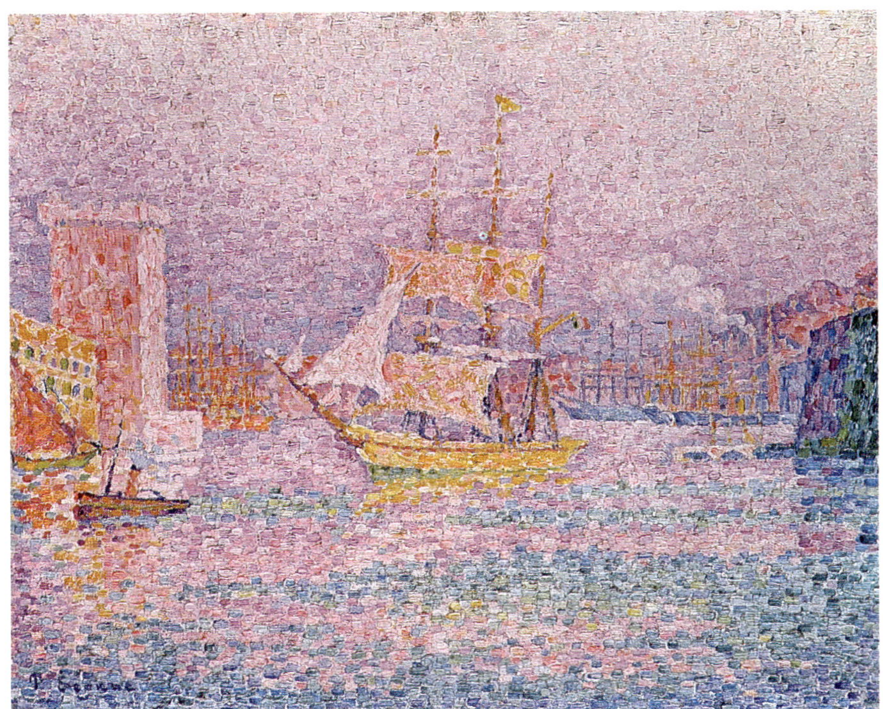

about Impressionism was more an explanation of something that had already occurred, rather than an artistic formula.

That is how it was with Matisse's group too. There was no theory, but there was a set of attitudes which the young artists held in common, a striving to paint in a new way, powerfully and emotionally, to assert the value of pure colour unattenuated in numerous, chance effects of light, to create their own world and not to reproduce nature impassively.

Fauvism, like an instantaneous burst of light, is a remarkable phenomenon and — even for the confused artistic life of the beginning of the twentieth century — a rather mysterious one. A furious passion for self-expression, the extreme "liberation" of colour, glowing angular patches of paint — this all represented an exceptional mixture of a brave experiment and a desire to escape the morbid problems of the age, to escape the seed that gave birth to alarming Cubist experiments, redolent of intellectual aggression, to escape the dark passion of the German Expressionists. A splendid choir in which — for a while and apparently deliberately — the voices of the soloists almost ceased to be distinguishable: that was perhaps the impression created by the first group exhibition of those artists who were destined to be labelled *"fauves"* ("wild beasts") at the 1905 Salon d'Automne.

This nickname, tossed out by the critic Louis Vauxcelles with that same casual aptness with which thirty years earlier the journalist Leroy had hit on the word Impressionists, defined fairly precisely the distinctive feature of these young men's art, or at any rate the impression which their paintings made on the viewers.

The Fauves — Marquet, Matisse and Rouault — had already exhibited at the Salon d'Automne in previous years. Their works were mostly received with indifference, but occasionally more positively: Marquet's landscapes had even been praised by the well-known critic Roger Marx. But when the whole group was placed together in one hall, the Fauves became a sensation. Paris, it seemed, was used to everything and it was hard to imagine that after the scandals at the *Salon des Refusés* and the First Exhibition of Impressionists, anything of the kind could ever happen again.

Nevertheless, it did! Evidently the Fauves' unrestrained freedom of self-expression was perceived as the sinister harbinger of the total destruction of traditional stereotypes. Public taste, for all its conservative nature, possesses an exceptionally fine sense of danger, and it unerringly detected the moment when modern art proclaimed its complete and final autonomy.

Beyond the superficial desire of the young artists to "*épater le bourgeois*", to demolish tradition, there was something new and savagely blunt in this way of painting. After all, even the Impressionists, for all their novelty in the eyes of the average exhibition-goer, had painted nature and, although, from the point of view of the spectator unaccustomed to innovations, their work was careless and ugly, nature could still be recognised; it had, in some respects, a resemblance to real life. But this was where the Fauves' proclaimed independence came into its own — independence from nature, and from any sort of tradition, with submission only to the artists' ownstrivings. These artists gave expression to their emotions outside the medium of objects: with a colour, a line

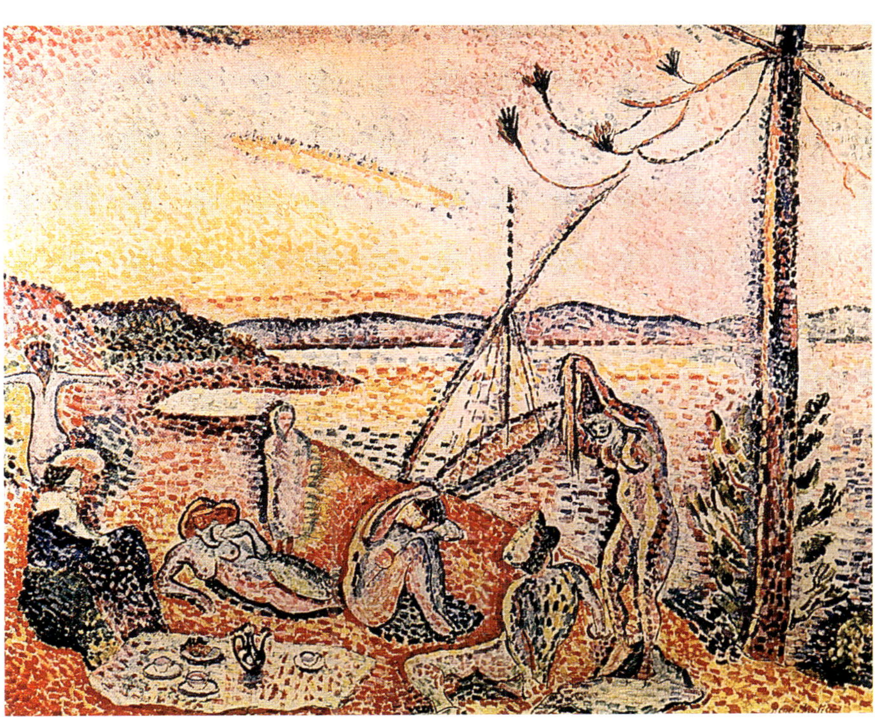

Henri Matisse.
Luxe, Calme et Volupté.
1904.

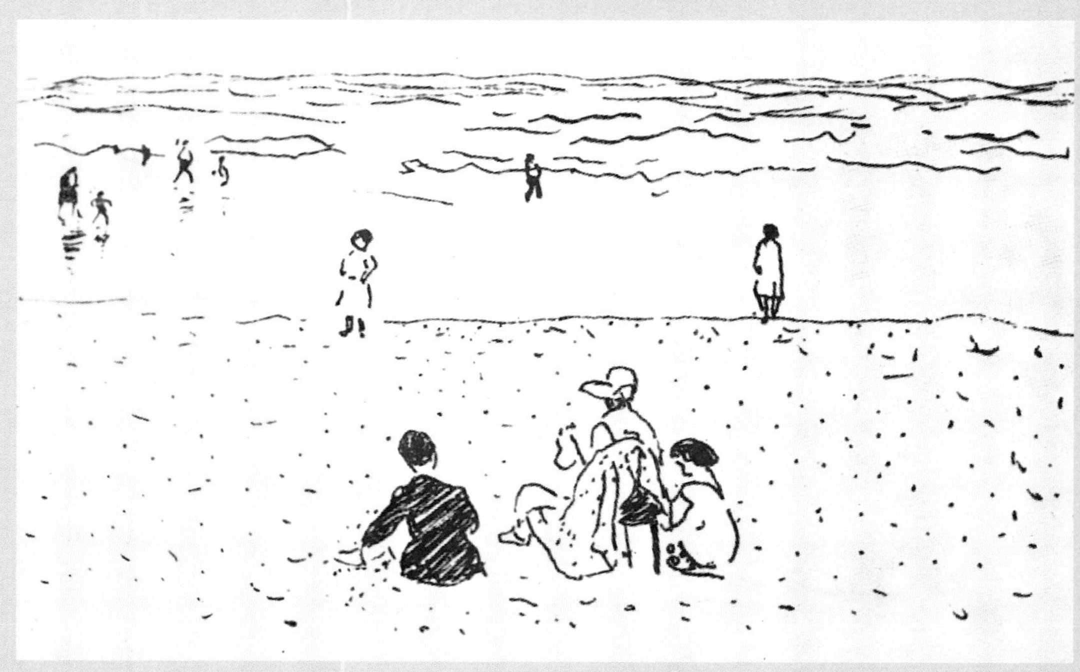

Albert Marquet. *By the Sea.*

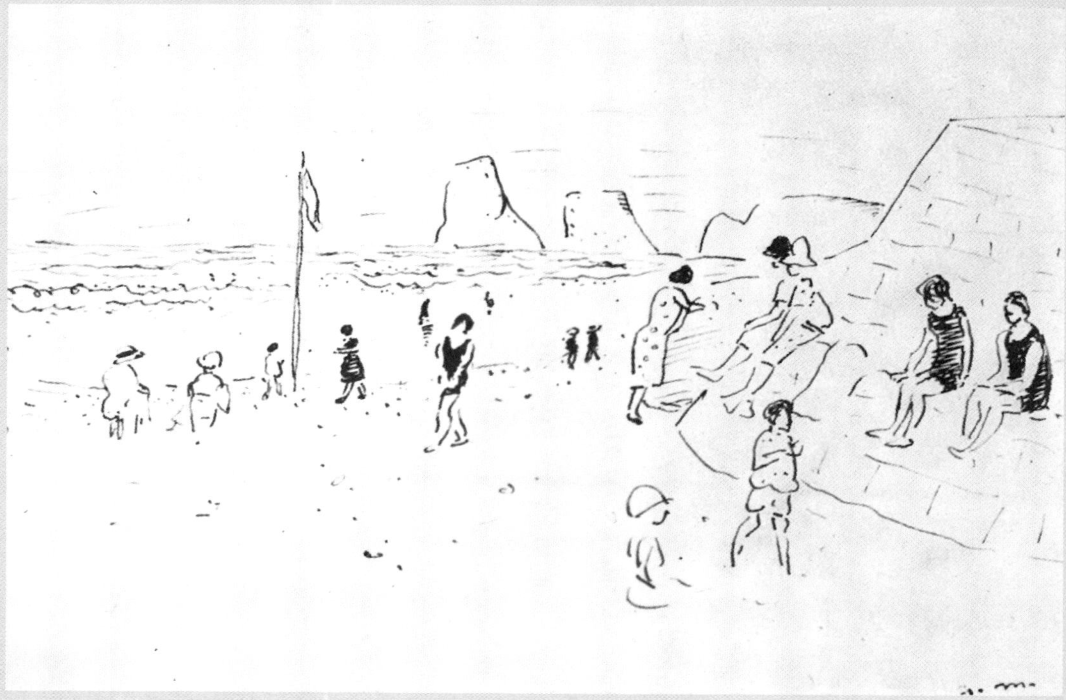

Albert Marquet. *On the Seashore.*

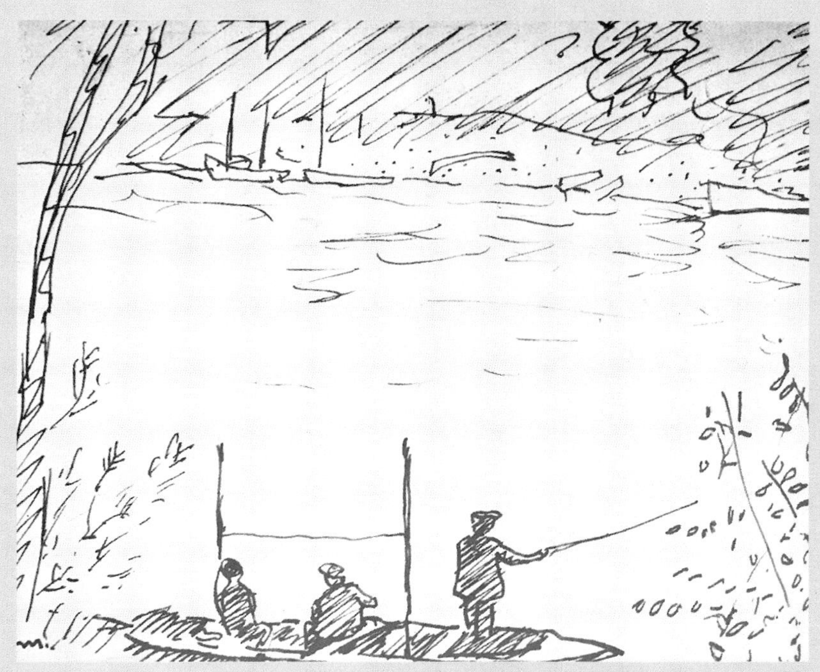

Albert Marquet. *Triel-sur-Seine*.

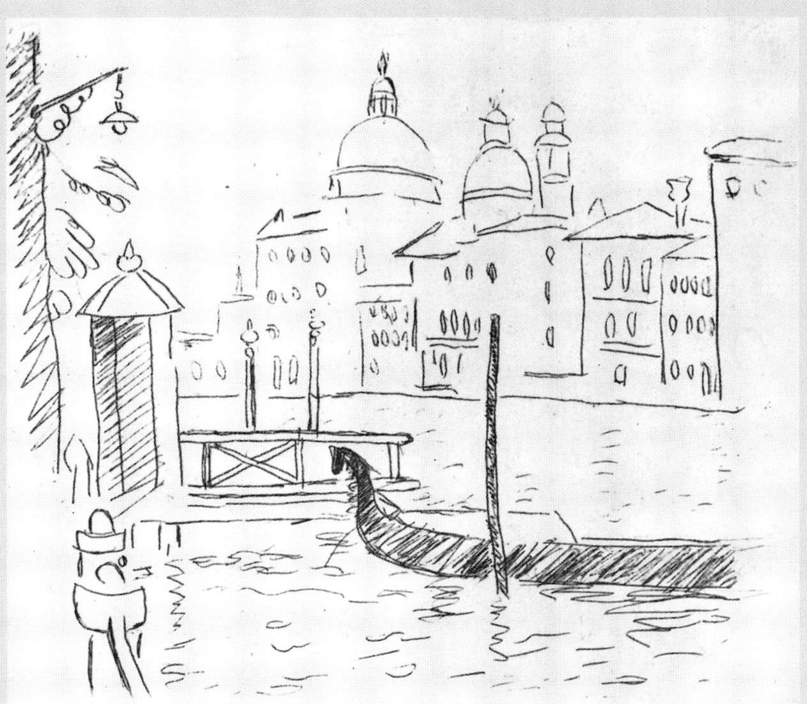

Albert Marquet. *Venice*.

or a patch. The Fauves created some new world, impulsive and, to the unaccustomed eye, chaotic, in which it was not the depiction of reality that reigned supreme, but simply the realization in paint of the artist's fantasy.

Of course, now at the end of the twentieth century, the Fauves do not seem independent of the objective world. But then, in 1905, the bond seemed to have been conclusively broken. Furthermore, the extravagance which the artists themselves displayed in manners and dress, deliberately demonstrating their mistrust of conventional decorum even at highly formal vernissages, evoked disquiet and annoyance. A spirit of the

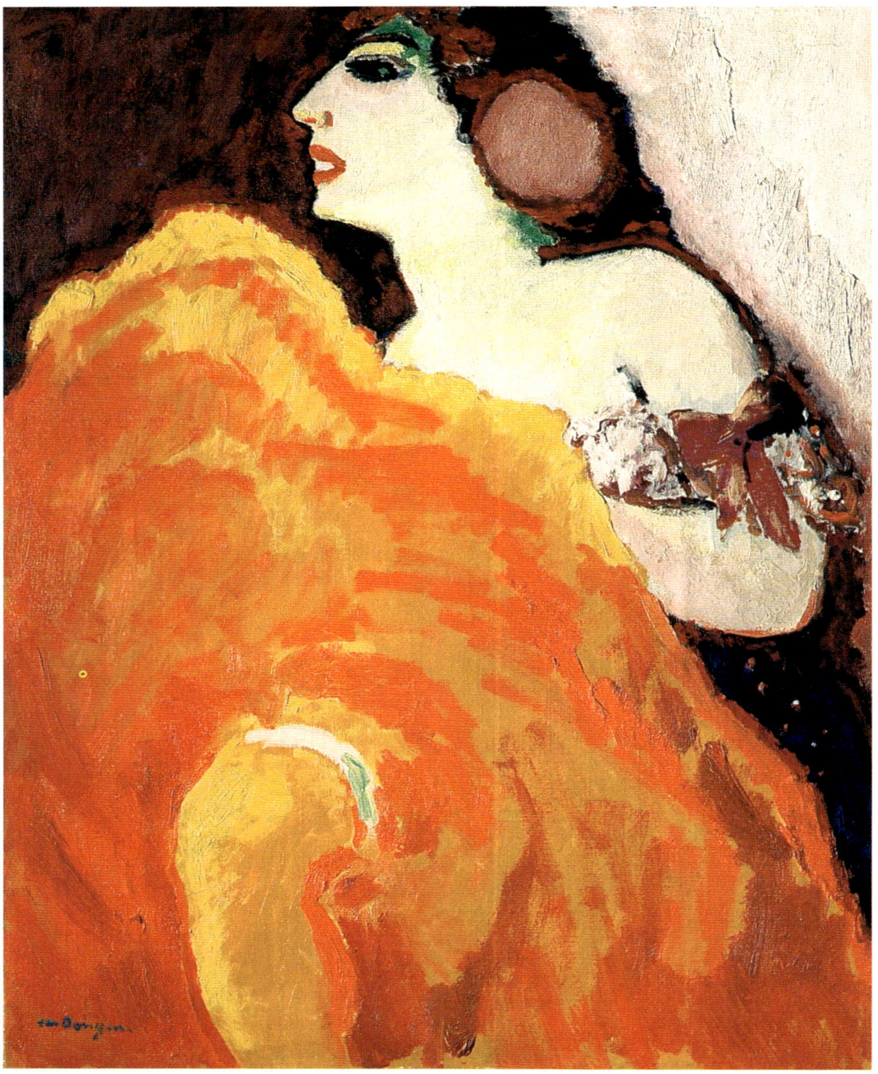

times was coming into being which in Russia was imprecisely but tentatively styled "Futurism" — an age of deliberate attempts to shock and of acts of aesthetic provocation in which art itself quite often took second place and at times disappeared altogether.

Now, almost a century on, when each of those who belonged to the group is known as a great and original creative spirit,

Kees van Dongen. ►

24

it is difficult to imagine that they were perceived almost as clones. The olympian phantasmagoria of Matisse, the gloomy splendour of Rouault, the angular, icy nature of Derain concentrated to the point of exploding, the lyrical Hoffmannesque grotesquerie of Dufy, the violent colours of Vlaminck, the tragic slapstick of Van Dongen and, eventually, the laconic, austere landscapes of Marquet — how different they seem today! But then, at the 1905 Salon, a fascination with colour shared by all these dissimilar artists inspired them with equal enthusiasm to turn to the unprecedented brightness of "overt" colour. Hitherto unseen combinations of colour surfaces with deliberately careless outlines astonished the eye and disturbed the mind.

Marquet was evidently not too easily influenced by the militant subjectivism which the Fauves proclaimed by way of an artistic programme. In general for him a formula was something alien and tedious. Yet the extremely interesting experiments with powerful and pure colour, the free and precise expression of individual sensation — characteristics of many of his companions' work — did represent a new school. It was something basically different from Moreau's school or even the Louvre. It was at this very time that Marquet gained individualism as a painter, an individualism that he never lost. The works Marquet produced in the period of the first Fauve exhibitions stand comparison with the most garish canvases by Vlaminck or Matisse, both in the vigour of the colour scheme and the abstraction of forms. It is sufficient to take a look at the small painting *Posters in Trouville* (1906, private collection, Paris) to see direct links with the Fauves' experimentation. In itself the very choice of motif — a flat wall flooded with sunlight, the contrast of pure patches of colour not softened by distance with straight, sharp edges — enables Marquet virtually to forget about conveying space or volume and to concentrate on a purely decorative, surface effect. The paints, almost unmixed, have been laid on the canvas in broad impasted strokes, while the figures in the foreground are barely delineated.

As a group the Fauves did not last long, but the trend to which they gave birth became a lasting and highly significant phenomenon for European art. It in many ways determined, as is well known, the subsequent creative course of its members, who became the greatest representatives of the "Parisian school"; it noticeably influenced not only the emergence of Cubism, but also the development of German Expressionism. As for Marquet, Fauvism gave him much, as it did all the members of the group, but did not penetrate to the core of his artistic being.

He remained "a knight of the real world". But Fauvism was a school of independence for him, teaching him to be fearless

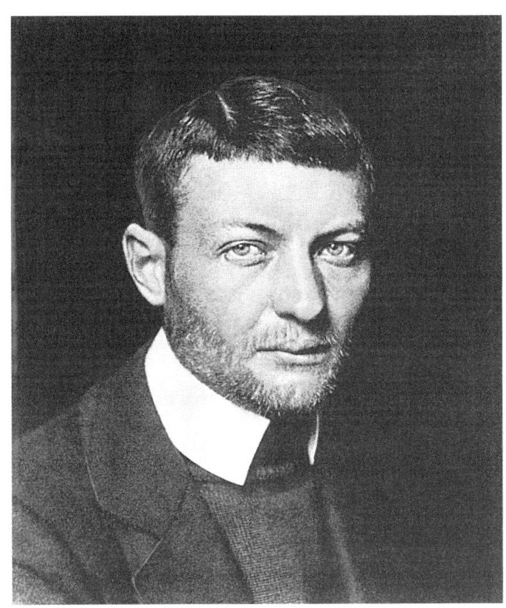

in the search for self-expression. It gave him an ability to use absolutely overt colour, broad surfaces and a hitherto unseen degree of abstraction.

In this period of instantly forming and just as instantly dissolving artistic groupings, of lively and frequent contacts between many of those active in the arts, at a time when the cafés of Montparnasse became virtually the centres of world art, a time of countless exhibitions and the first appearances

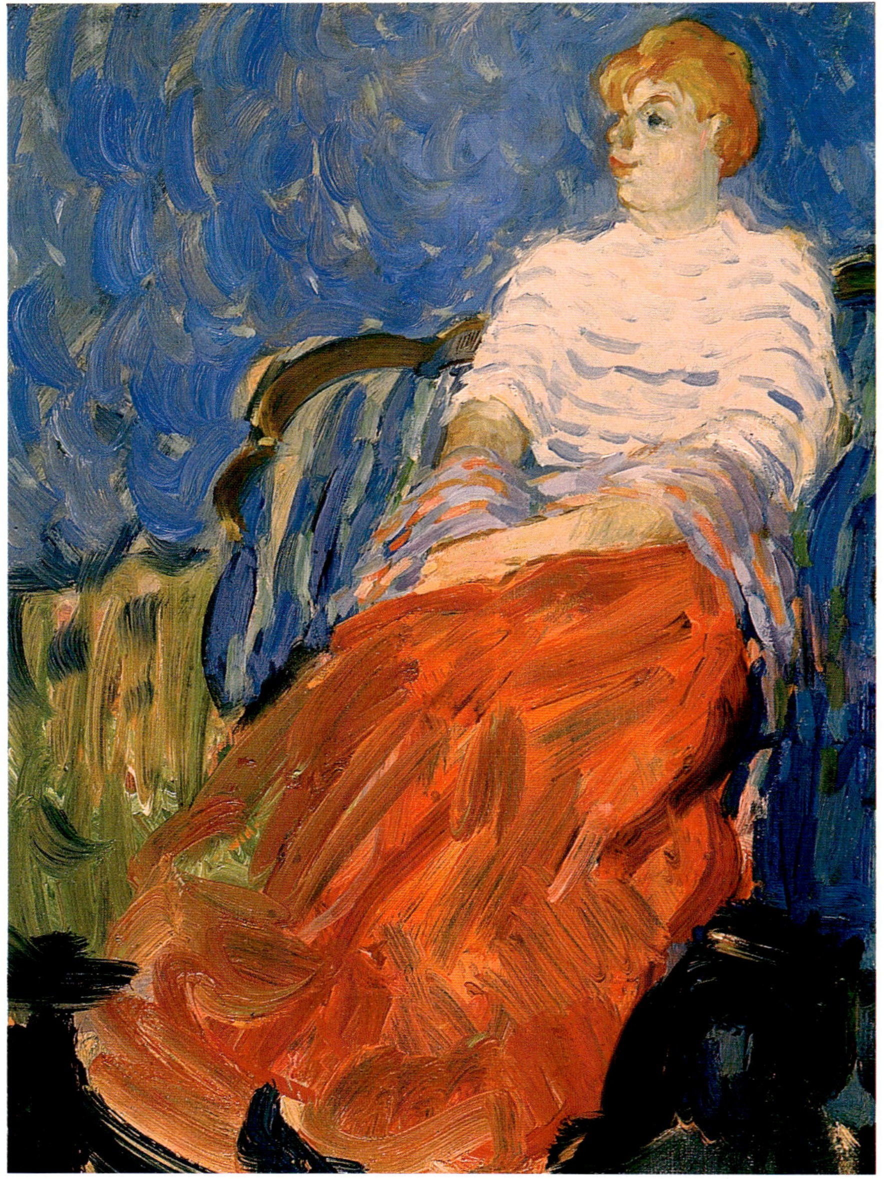

of the "classic" avant-garde, Marquet formed his creative personality in near isolation. At the age of thirty-five he went to draw at life classes in the so-called Académie Ranson. He sat for hours at a time on café terraces, engaged in an activity no longer fashionable: making rapid sketches of passers-by, instant street scenes, barely managing to capture with pencil or pen what his eye seized on ed with exceptional acuity. His drawings were most often done in Indian ink. At times the

Raoul Dufy.
Woman Seated.
1904.

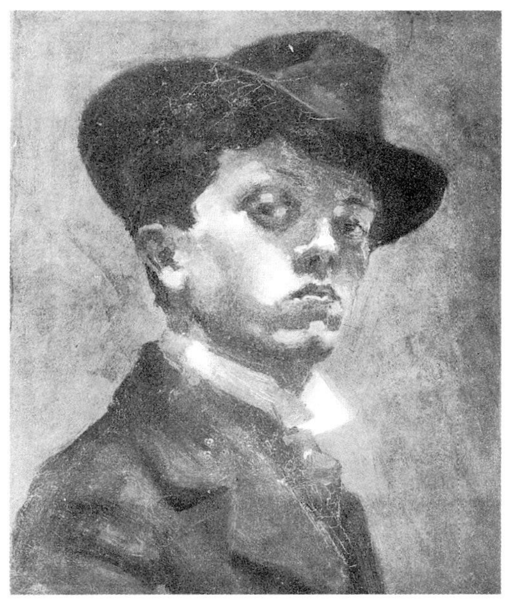

line expresses nothing but motion — the folds of a raincoat blowing about as its owner walks, the tilt of a head. Shape appears only dynamically in the sketches — at rest it seems not to exist for the artist. In a few strokes of the pen or brush the quintessence of one motion or another appears, purged of the casual and the transient. Drawings of this kind could be given the title *Running*, *Heaviness* or *Effort*; they become a dynamic formula, almost a pictogram. But at times he also produced genre-type sketches, ironical, even sarcastic, capable of competing for sharpness of characterization with the drawings of Guys or Daumier himself. And it seems entirely natural that the artist was passionately fond of Chaplin's films. He loved them at a time when the "Little Tramp" was perceived not so much as a great actor, but simply as an amusing clown.

Marquet's gift as a impetuous and acute draughtsman revealed itself early on, back in 1903 when he produced drawings to illustrate Charles Louis Philippe's *Bubu de Montparnasse*. His line can be crude, retaining the elegance and vitality of improvization. It perpetuates the movement of his hand; the viewer's eye unerringly perceives with pleasure the beginning and end of each stroke, where the pen or pencil was put down and where it was picked up. It was in Marquet's drawings perhaps earlier and more noticeably than in his paintings that the maturity and artistry emerged which few achieve so young.

Nonetheless, Marquet did not enjoy widespread success or fame until practically the mid-1910s. His works did not begin to sell quickly. It is true that Eugène Drouet, a very well-known dealer at the time who kept a large "salon" on the Avenue Matignon, took his canvases on commission. But, even at the age of fifty, Marquet recalled his younger days without pleasure — they were tainted with poverty.

Despite his financial problems, Marquet travelled as much as he could: the Côte d'Azur, Normandy, London, Naples, Hamburg, Tangiers... He had a definite preference for maritime cities, although it would be incorrect to call him a marine painter. The artist had such a perception of landscape as an integral whole that he, as it were, renounced the genre (here too we are forced to recall Cézanne, who practically never depicted people in his landscapes).

For all his variety of artistic occupations and enthusiasms, all the wide range of motifs and themes that we observe in his life, there is a single line in Marquet's creative biography which appeared as early as the turn of the century and determined the overall character of his work.

It is, of course, the Parisian landscape. It is surprising how many of Marquet's celebrated canvases were not painted in Paris at all, but depict foreign shores and exotic cities. But, it would appear, his painting is so important a part of the process every thinking person goes through in order to comprehend Paris, that his art is simply inseparable from the city. If Marquet had painted nothing else but Paris, he would still have become the artist that he was.

He painted Paris when he was studying and when he was exhibiting with the Fauves. And after his trips to Brittany, Normandy and North Africa, he invariably returned to the same embankments and streets.

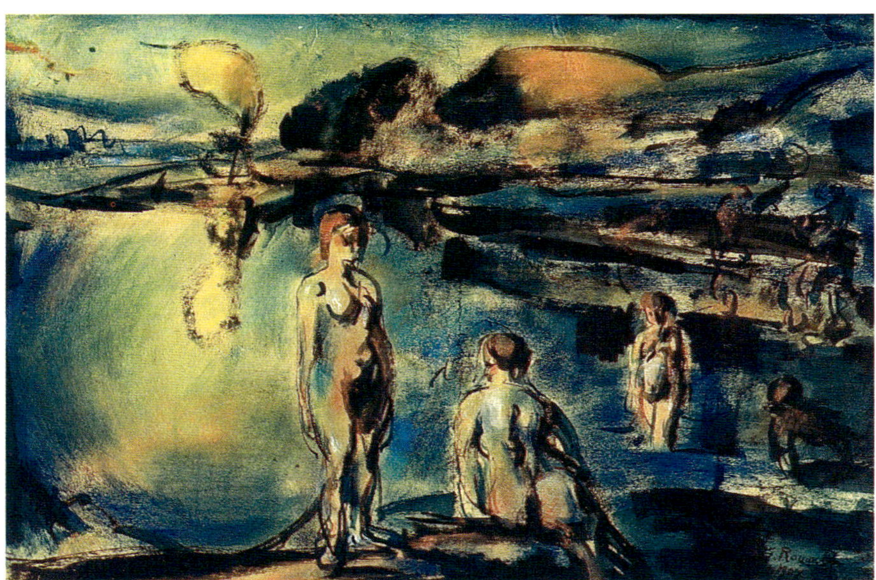

For all the undeniable, striking picturesqueness of Paris, all the great number of artists, French and foreign, living and working there, it can boldly be said that no-one ever painted the city with such constancy and understanding, so devotedly, so lovingly and so often as Albert Marquet.

In general, the tradition of the Parisian urban landscape is not so great nor so significant as it might otherwise seem. Artists had been depicting the city for centuries, since the time of "Yves the Monk" and the Limbourg brothers. Yet, in essence, if we overlook a few etchings by Jacques Callot, the Parisian landscape in pure form is a child of the nineteenth century — Granet's watercolours, the works of Corot, Turner, and, finally, the Impressionists. But for all that there was still not a single artist for whom Paris became the main theme of his life. It was only with Utrillo, the subtle poet of Montmartre, that an artist dedicated his brush to Paris. Marquet was among the first.

Looking at the changing face of Paris, Marquet's work, like it or not, inevitably brings to mind the Impressionists. Not because of the vision of space, nor the composition of the painting, nor even the perception of the Parisian cityscape, but because of something entirely different — the sense of the exceptional poetic identity of the city. This strange point of contact is more like an opposition: with Marquet Paris is as steady in its most transitory states as with the Impressionists it is mobile. The Impressionists turned everything into a fascinating illusion; if Marquet does not make the illusion material, he at least endows it with a temporal stability. There was nothing unusual in a young artist painting the Paris embankments. A hundred others around him were doing the same thing, from his friend Matisse to foreigners whom no-one knew. The important thing is that Marquet remained loyal to the subject all his life and managed to create his own Paris, without which it is now impossible to picture the city, just as Argenteuil is unimaginable without the Impressionists or Provence without Cézanne.

The very first Parisian landscapes established the main motifs: embankments, bridges, the Ile-de-la-Cité. For all his great affection for the city, Marquet sought variety not in different viewpoints or in different localities, but in the changing states of a view, in its "melodies". Like Cézanne seeking out great plastic ideas and images in the roundness of Provençal apples, Marquet constantly looked for something new in the familiar without leaving the banks of the Seine.

At the time of the Fauve exhibitions, his Parisian landscapes noticeably displayed a characteristic Fauve tendency towards deconstruction. The deliberate coarsening and generalizing of the contours of the houses, the calculated use of patches of colour for effect are undoubtedly testimony to his brief but perceptible flirtation with Fauvism.

But both Marquet's own talent and the special poetic logic of Paris — that "plastic cartesianism" which invariably penetrates through any fogs, wreathes of smoke or other attributes

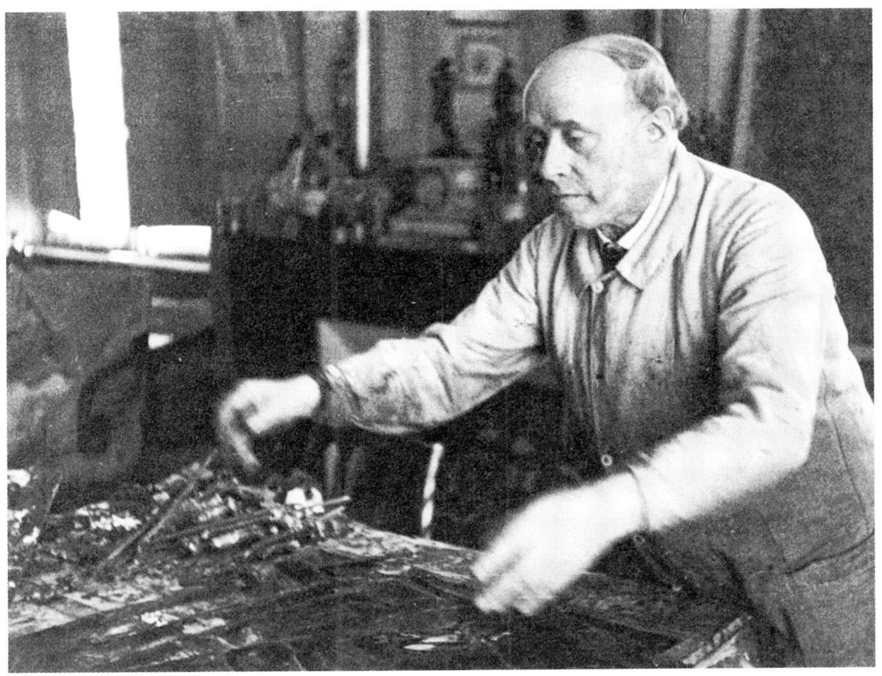

Georges Rouault.
1932.

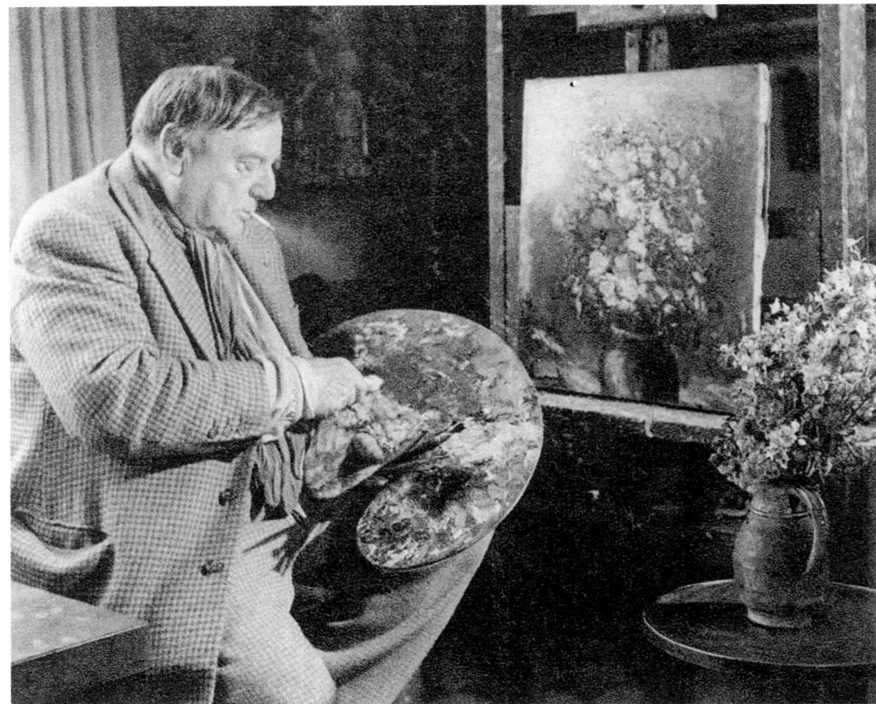

of the lyrical landscape — protested against excessive decorativeness and intense colour. In that same period Marquet painted far more severely; he was finding his own clear, precise "Parisian code": solid forms, slightly softened by distance, but always definite, a strong expression of space, but not one which conflicts with the canvas, energetic perspective and a powerful sense of the unity of sky, water and ancient buildings.

By the turn of the 1910s, Marquet was undoubtedly a fully fledged artist. He could now permit himself an experiment in the spirit of some interesting or simply fashionable trend. His nude studies of the 1910s have an unmistakable touch of the *Art Nouveau* about them — the refined fragmentation of nervous lines, the somewhat morbid decorativeness. This touch is very weak, but nonetheless detectable. The *Art Nouveau* style had become an integral part of the environment. These new trends in architecture, the decorative arts and, ultimately, in home furnishings, in workshops and in the design of magazines influenced vision and perception. Marquet was far more dependent on the real world than, for example, Matisse. He never, either in his youth or in his mature years, created an isolated painterly world. And now he saw all around him — in shop windows, fabrics, paintings and books — tired, languid "Beardsleyesque" lines, whimsical ornamental patterns on furniture and carpets, that strange heady combination of indeterminacy and distinctly calculated forms. This all had an influence on Marquet's work as well. But his artistic idiom was not too strongly affected. The *Art Nouveau* in painting was not so much the style of the artist himself as the milieu of his models, their manner of department, their "belonging" to the *Art Nouveau* space.

But the fashionable angular langour of the models and the rhythm of the lines with its *Art Nouveau* resonance clash with the austere, energetic manner of painting. The bold colour scheme and confident, classic balance of masses emerge triumphant. The artist's individuality was not insensitive to the tastes and experiments of the day, but in a necessary way it was independent of them.

Already by the late 1910s his nude studies were displaying a classic simplicity of outline, although the individuality of the body was not lost. An example is the 1918 study now in the Paris Museum of Modern Art. Marquet, however, was tackling figures less and less often. He almost stopped painting portraits. He recognized his true and, probably, only vocation — the landscape.

In time Marquet's material circumstances improved, at least sufficiently to give him independence. He gained the precious opportunity to be himself. And the older he became, the more

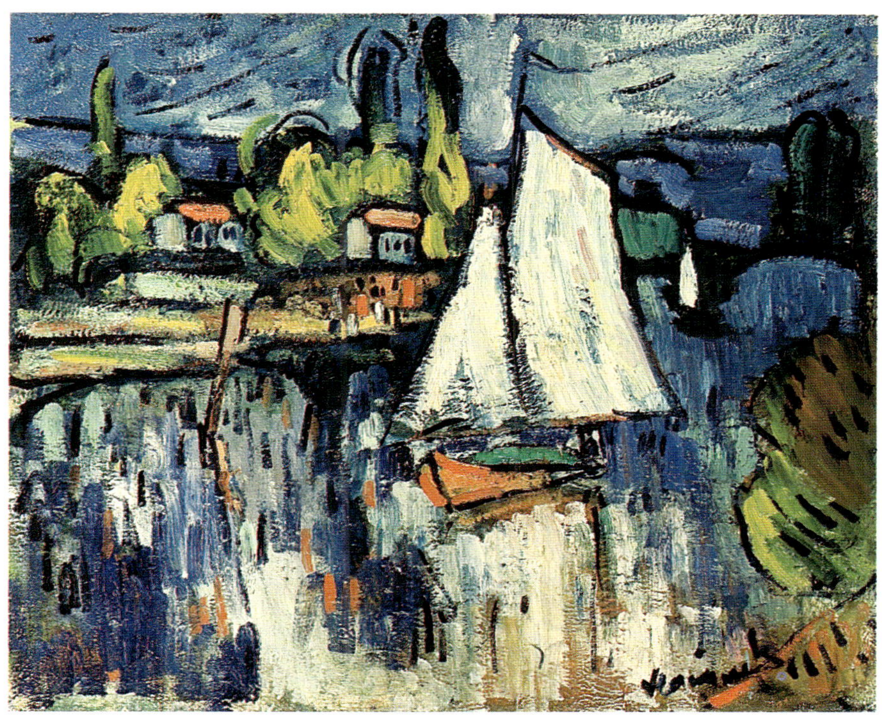

he travelled. Of course, these were not simply journeys for their own sake: each trip produced dozens of canvases, whole cycles devoted to a city, the sea, a province, a country.

At first it seems surprising that such a profound artist, capable of seeing so much in one and the same long familiar and long explored corner of Paris, capable of painting Notre Dame dozens of times, would constantly travel the world in search of new and at times exotic impressions. But therein lies an important feature of his art. Like a lyrical poet he wants to

Maurice de Vlaminck.
View of the Seine.
Ca. 1904-1905.

31

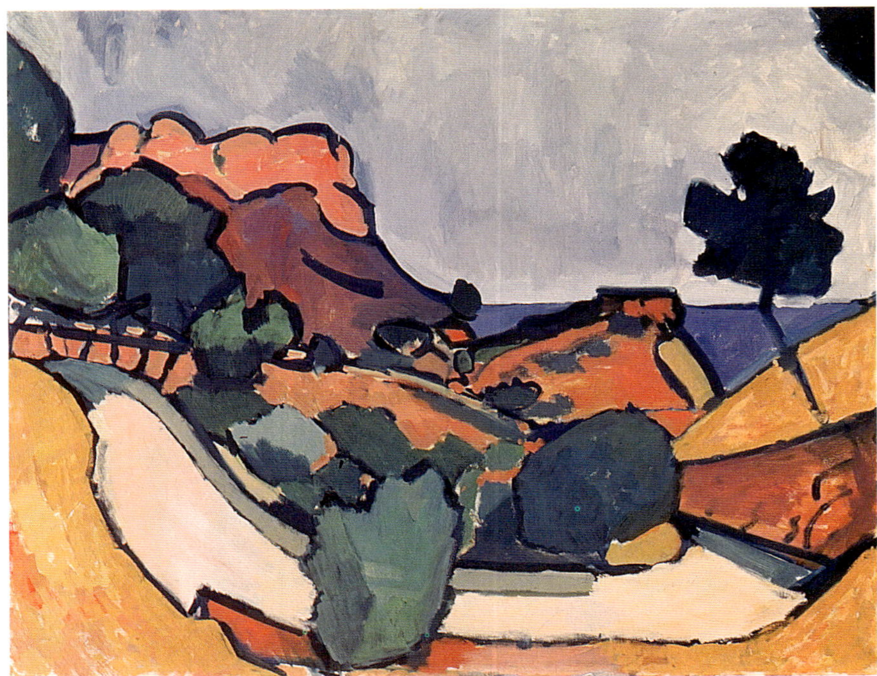

André Derain.
Road in the Mountains.
1907.

PINE TREE AT ALGIERS
1932
Oil on canvas. 65 x 81 cm.
Signed bottom right: *Marquet*.
Museum of Fine Arts, Bordeaux.

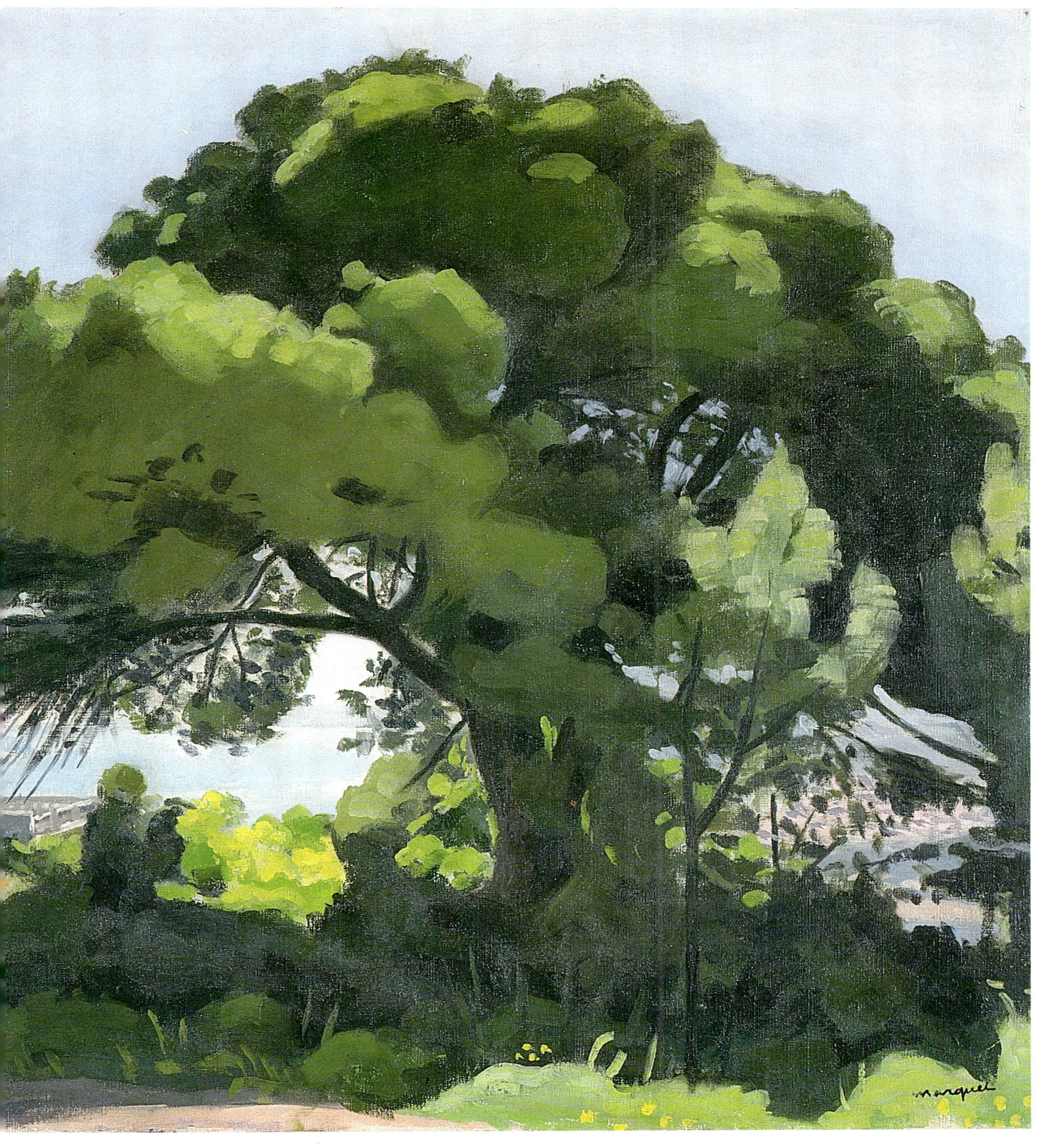

find in life not simply events worthy of description, but phenomena which generate a lofty response in the human soul. In Norway or Algiers, in Egypt or Germany, he was searching for more than subjects to reproduce on canvas. Here is Marquet in Hamburg (1910). Anyone who knows that stern city, full of the rumble of cranes and the smell of the fog and the sea, with its lakes, towers and canals, will have no difficulty in identifying it in the artist's works. But Marquet did not travel to Hamburg just to paint a "portrait" of another city. He found there something eternal, beautiful and new: how splendid the black, tarred sides of the boats seem, the black palisade of jetties against the background of the dully glistening Elbe, grey smoke in the fog, the gilded spire of St Michaelis the bright red lead on the ships, sides and the black funnels of the steamers. Hamburg brought something unfamiliar to Marquet's palette, one more aspect of reality. And that helped him to understand the visual beauty of the world, and of Paris in particular.

Apart from his painter's case and a supply of canvas, Marquet invariably took with him on his travels a sketchbook, Indian ink, a reed pen and later (from 1925) watercolours as well. He could hardly wait to arrive at his destination and start work. But long ago it was quite rightly said that happiness is not a destination, it is a means of transport. And Marquet began working while still in his railway carriage.

That means that from the train window he saw a world asking to be set down on paper. Hundreds of little sketchbook pages were filled with instant drawings, capturing fleeting visual impressions. It might seem that Marquet drew as fast as he could look and see — his lines are that impetuous, the sensation recorded with such indisputable precision. One could, perhaps, compare his drawings with frames from a film travelogue.

The only difference is that Marquet was constantly making a selection: a selection not only of objects — most important and vital to the sketch — but also of lines, which are as economical as they are expressive. At times it seems that the

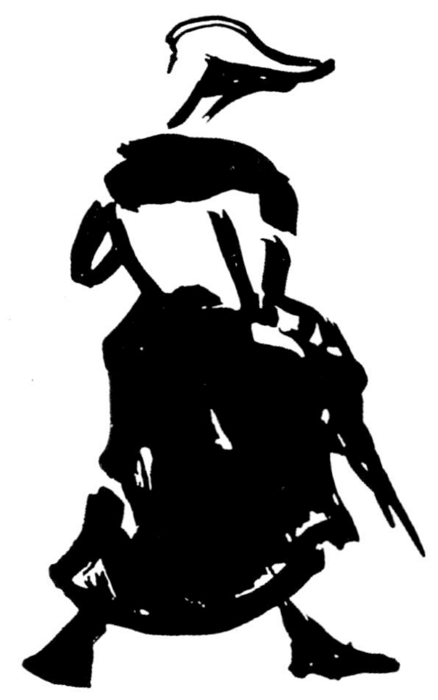

Albert Marquet.
Woman in a Black Skirt.

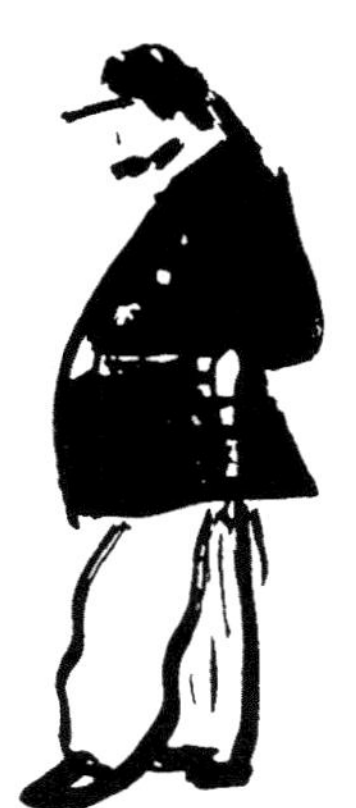

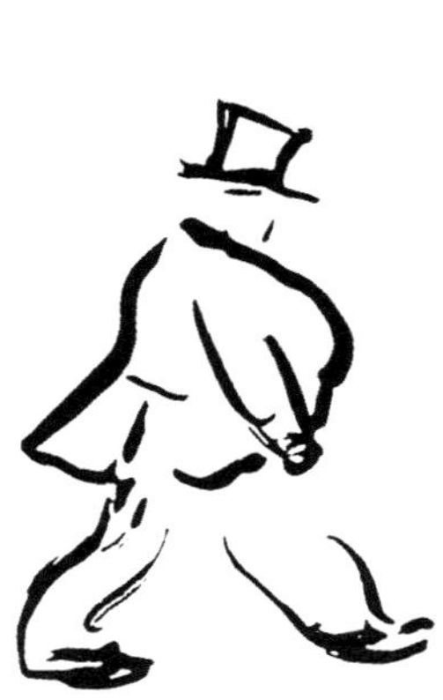

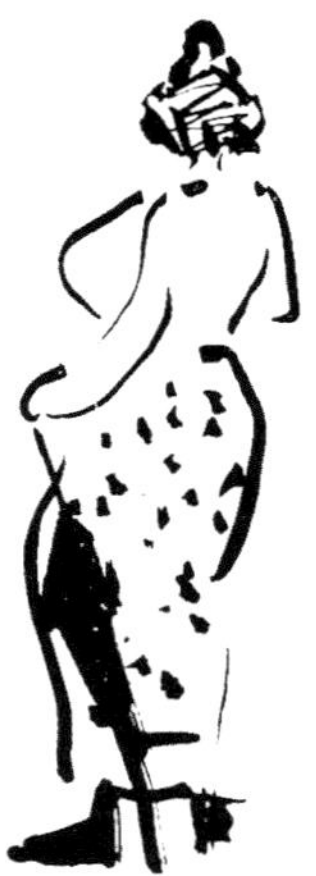

Albert Marquet.
Street Sketches.

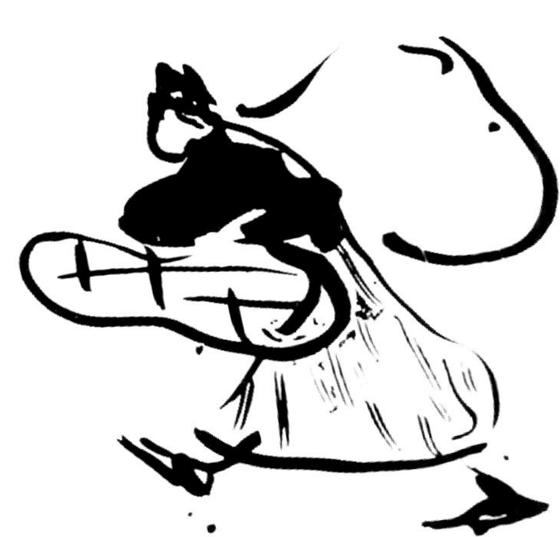

Albert Marquet.
Woman with Bundles.

artist combined several impressions in one, gathering and condensing them.

Mileposts, the crowns of trees, telegraph wires, houses — it is as if their contours have been broken by the motion of the train and the celerity of the artist's hand. The transparent, elusive horizons are graphic mirages that appear for a bare instant in the distance. Speed becomes a sort of collaborator in this truly new graphic depiction of the world: Marquet sets down the vision of a twentieth-century artist hurtling across the face of the Earth, an artist for whom motion reveals new aspects of reality. And these several impressions, these several disjointed images are fused by the movement of the pen into a single whole: a refined, powerful hieroglyph which is in itself a work of — almost abstract — art.

An innumerable series of drawings is extended by water-colours produced with the same astonishing speed and immediately establishing the fundamental: the relationship between the main patches of different shades, the chord of colour, through which an impression is rendered permanent, even monumental.

It goes without saying that Marquet, with his ability to mercilessly dispose of secondary features in his rapid sketches, his ability to bring out the artistic effect, did not need to work over a painting for a long time in the studio. There is no essential difference with him between a study and a finished painting. Each of his studies is already a painting, while his paintings retain all the immediacy of studies made from life. That is only natural: the artist painted a picture on the basis of a direct impression from the real world, but that impression was from the very start formulated and structured in a particular way. At the moment of looking at the world, Marquet already eliminated the superfluous and sought out the essence, "condensing" what he saw. It was probably a function of the artist's very consciousness to concentrate what he saw, to "translate" it into his own laconic "language".

This is not simply a concrete quality of his talent. Marquet was also distinguished by exceptional taste, a sort of "artistic

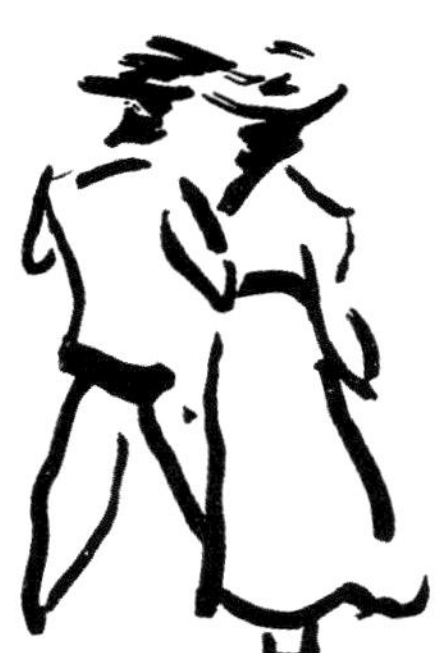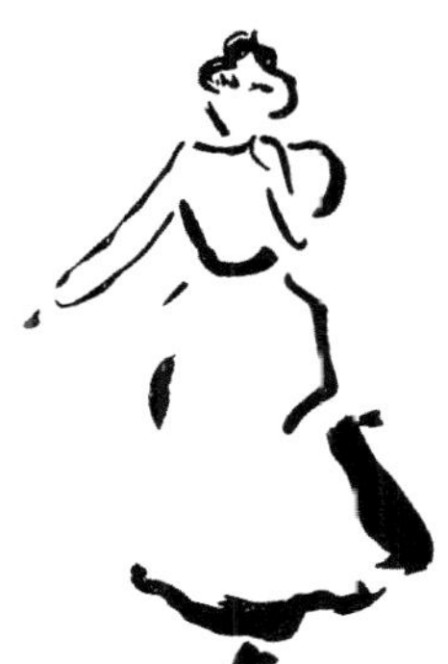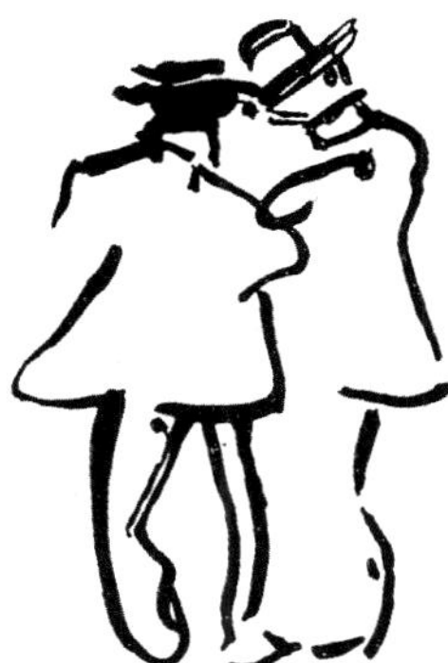

Albert Marquet.
Illustrations for Charles Louis-Philippe's
book *Bubu de Montparnasse.*

bashfulness", which ruled out the use of any sort of superficial effect, any coquetry with regard to the motif, any attempt
to shock or tantalise.

Marquet's taste was almost ascetic, based on the consistent
rejection of anything that could be sacrificed.

One might think that among the landscapes beloved of artists
there are none more banal than Vesuvius and the Bay of
Naples. Yet Marquet looks at them with the eyes of a discov-
erer: the dimly emerald, mirror-smooth water, the bay, the
"blossoming sails" as Cato called them. In *The Bay of Naples*
(1908; Marcelle Marquet collection, Paris) the artist not only
managed to see the bay in a way it had never been seen before,
but also to convey that astonishment to the viewer. He is sur-
prised by the very lack of similarity between this landscape
and the usual conception of it. The contrasts of gloomy and
saturated colours are unexpected and disturbing — the dark
grey sails on the glowing water and the dense green shadows
on it, the scarlet patches of the tiled roofs, the ochre boards
of the decks, and ashy lilac Vesuvius. The colours are unexpected and harsh, the contours reduced to some primary formula. The impression is evinced in its very essence and has
almost become a visual aphorism.

Here too Marquet's uncompromising taste helped him to
avoid theatricality and the vulgarly exotic. He painted a landscape, which in real life is oversaturated with colour and an
abundance of extremely delicate nuances of shade, with an
elegant economy of paints and shapes that excluded any
superficial effect.

The same applies in equal measure to the well-known Hermitage landscape of 1909, also called *The Bay of Naples*,
although in this work Marquet was tackling a more precise,
local task. While in the preceding canvas the artist was record-
ing a persistent impression, experienced many times and thus
extended, as it were, in time, here he is interested in a briefer,

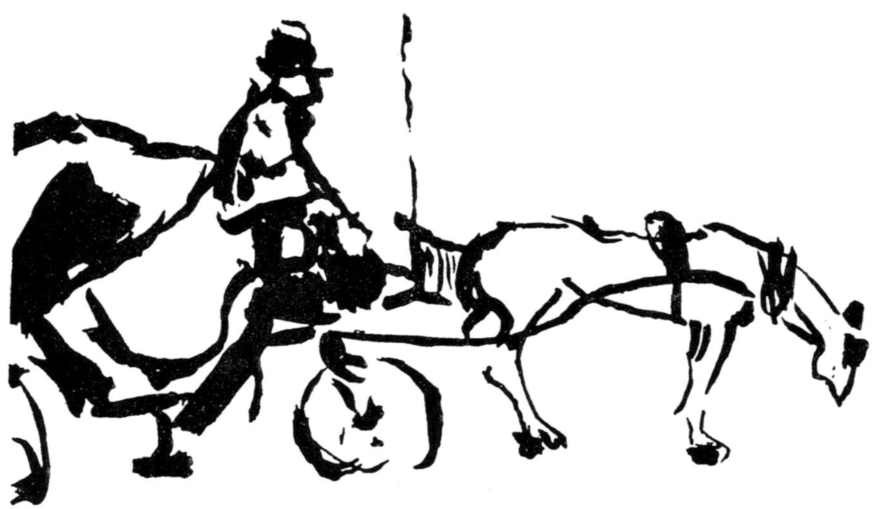

Albert Marquet.
Cabman in Paris.

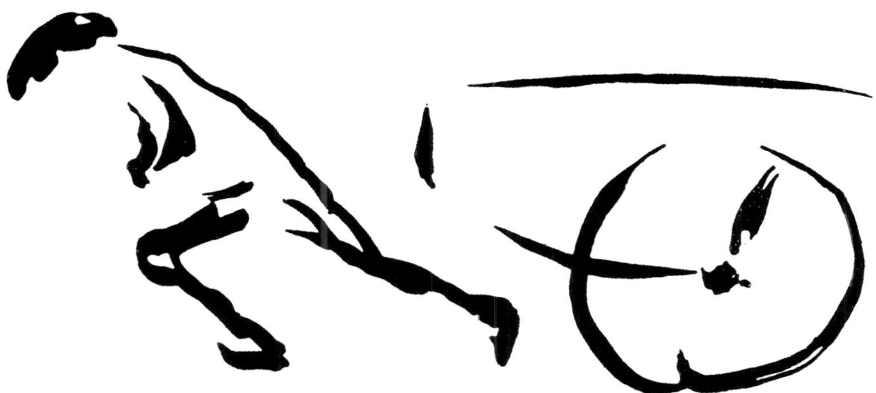

more fleeting image: the sea glistens with a cold, milky green sunlit brilliance and the black patches of boats appear to have been glimpsed for an instant. The canvas is so blindingly full of bright tones that one can believe that the artist barely glanced at the view before screwing up his eyes and recalling only a general sensation of dazzling brilliance.

The large surfaces of colour, almost devoid of nuances, confidently and economically construct a sense of space, while a slight, barely detectable alteration of tone within a patch of colour helps the eye to sense almost physically the way the surface of the glistening sea recedes towards the horizon.

And yet there is more to this painting than the reflection of a casual, yet fascinating impression of the world. The rhythmical, even ceremonial succession of the black silhouettes of the boats, the calm combination of numerous diagonals (the slanting sails of the yachts, the oars, the slopes of Vesuvius), the broad, powerful brushstrokes, which in themselves form a strict rhythm — all of this brings an unexpected monumentality to an outwardly casual composition reminiscent of the studies of the Impressionists. The nature of this significance, this stability in Marquet's paintings, once again brings them close to Cézanne. Marquet saw and painted the world as a planet in which rounded spaces receding into the distance invariably reign, where the sky and the earth are perceived as a joyful and logical unity.

It is curious that in his southern landscapes Marquet also used a fairly restrained range of colours and rarely resorted to bright tones. Even in those canvases which are marked by an especially pure and bright palette, there is not much truly bright, overt colour. Both the landscape just mentioned and *Menton Harbour* (1905; also in the Hermitage) are painted in a fairly sparing manner. Only the bold contrasts between the turquoise of the sea and the pinkish ochre of the houses creates any impression of the Midi, the southern landscape and the still, sun-warmed air. Marquet's colour scheme is rendered sharper by the frequent, masterly use of black paint in dense, dull patches, and at times also in the contours. In

37

Maurice Utrillo.
The Rue du Mont-Cenis in Montmartre.
Ca. 1914-1916.

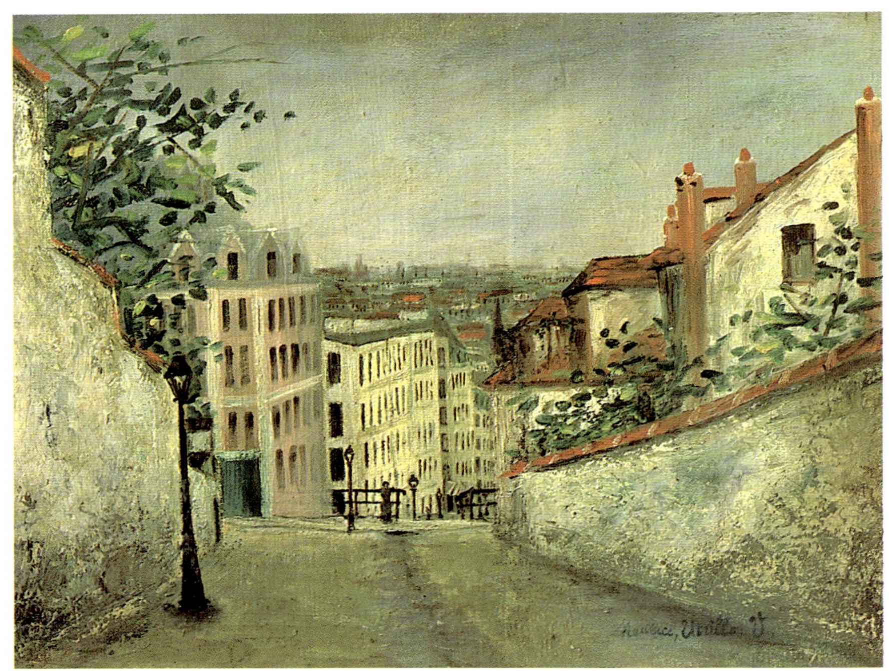

THE LUXEMBOURG GARDENS
1902
Oil on canvas. 46 x 55 cm.
Signed bottom left: *Marquet*.
Museum of Fine Arts, Bordeaux.

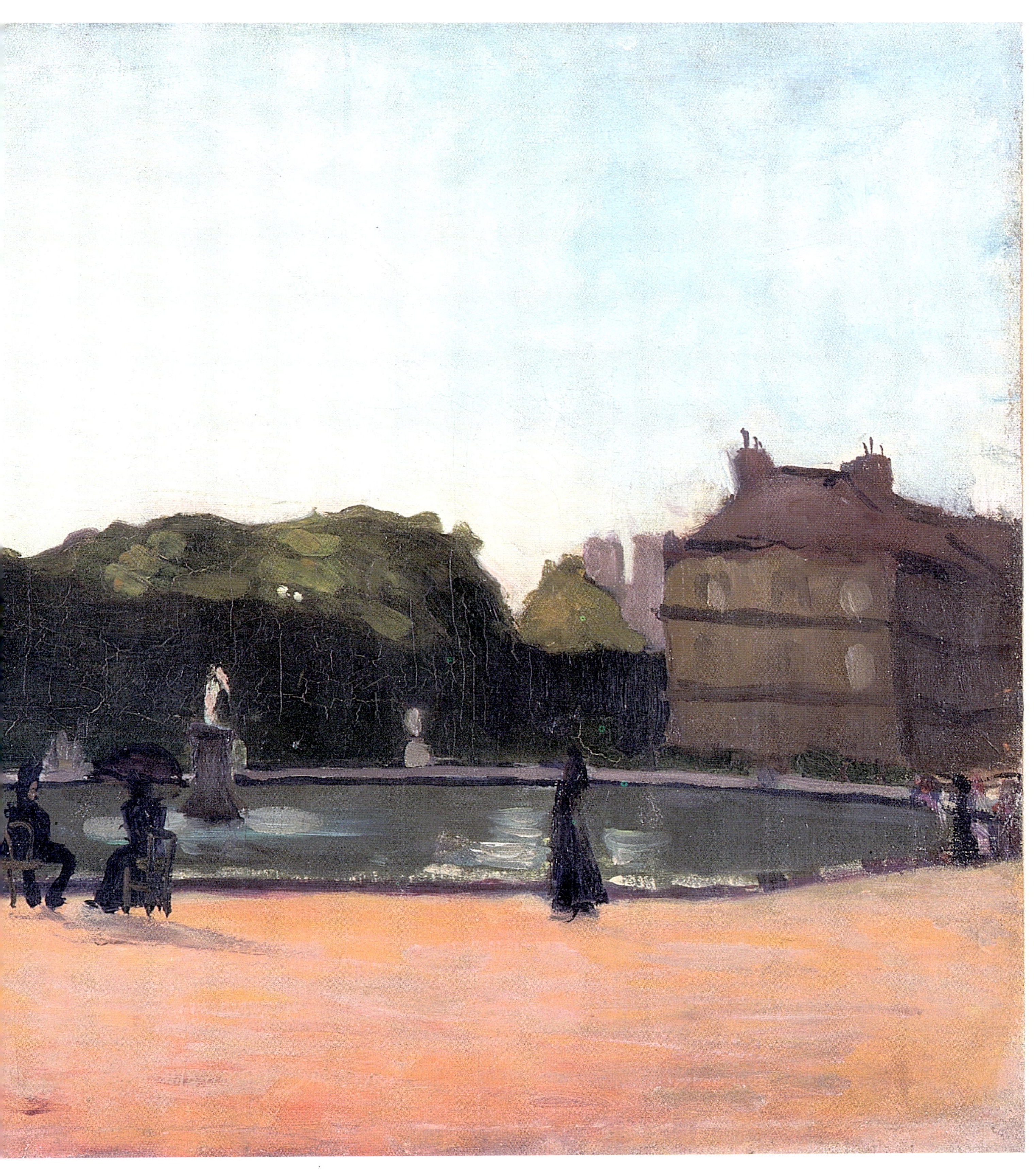

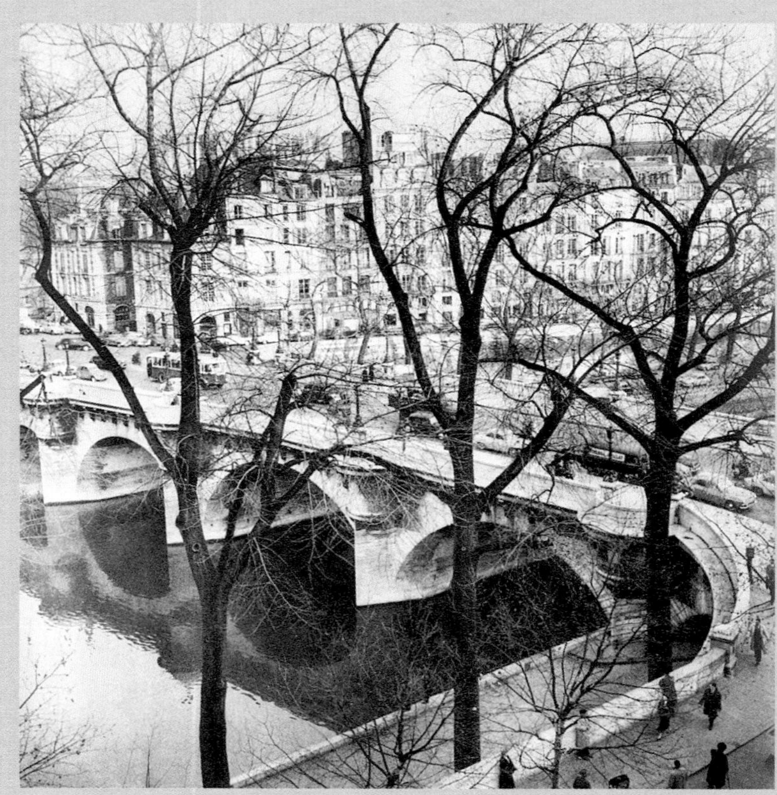

The Pont Neuf.

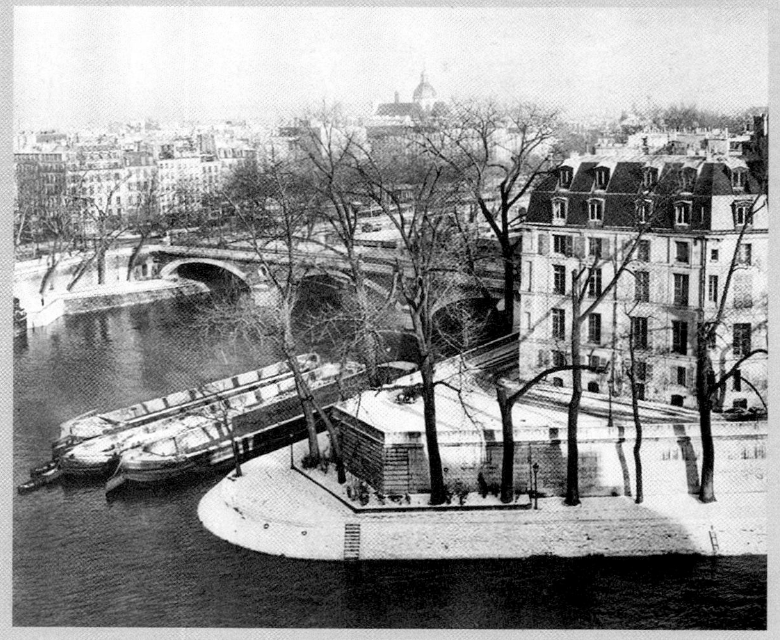

The Ile Saint-Louis.

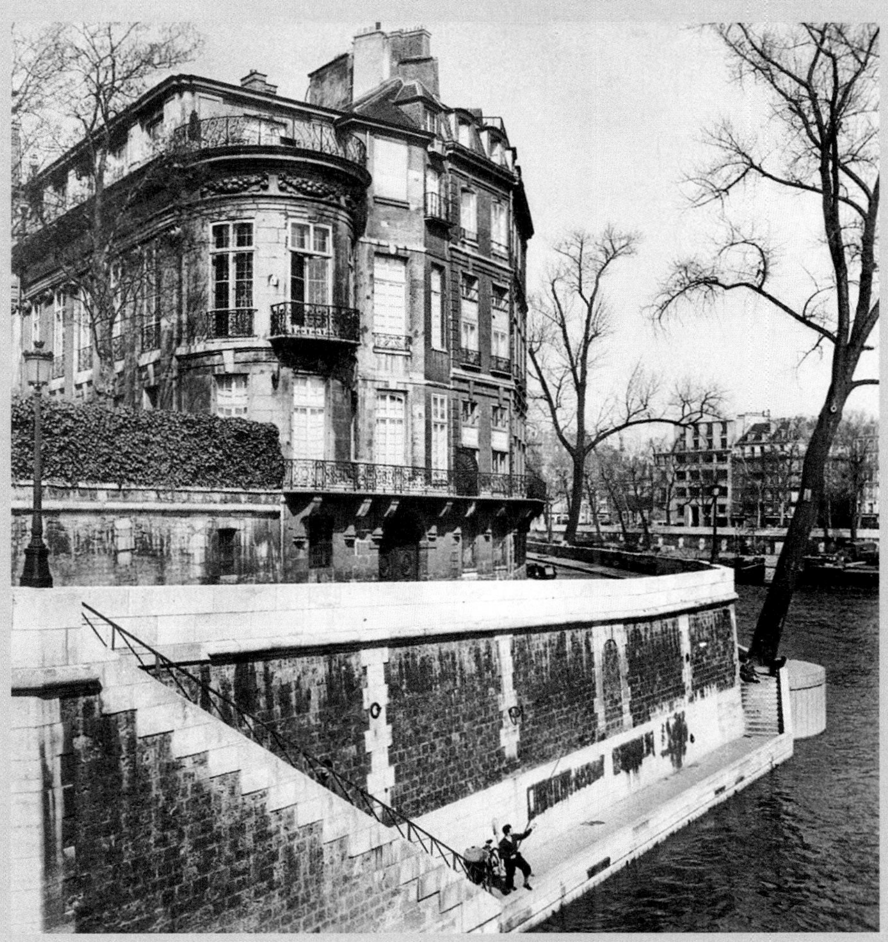

The Hôtel Lambert.

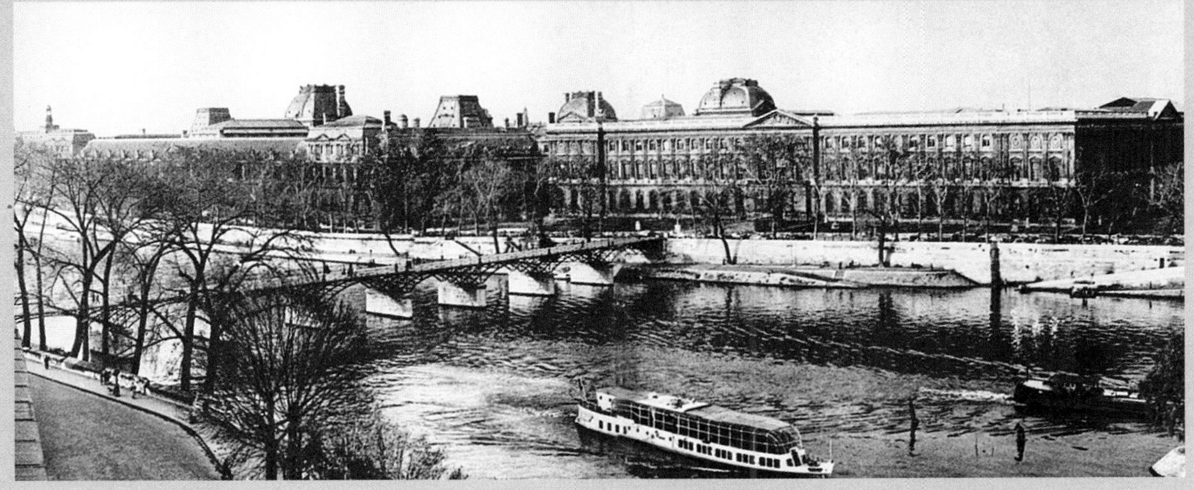

View of the Pont des Arts and the Louvre.

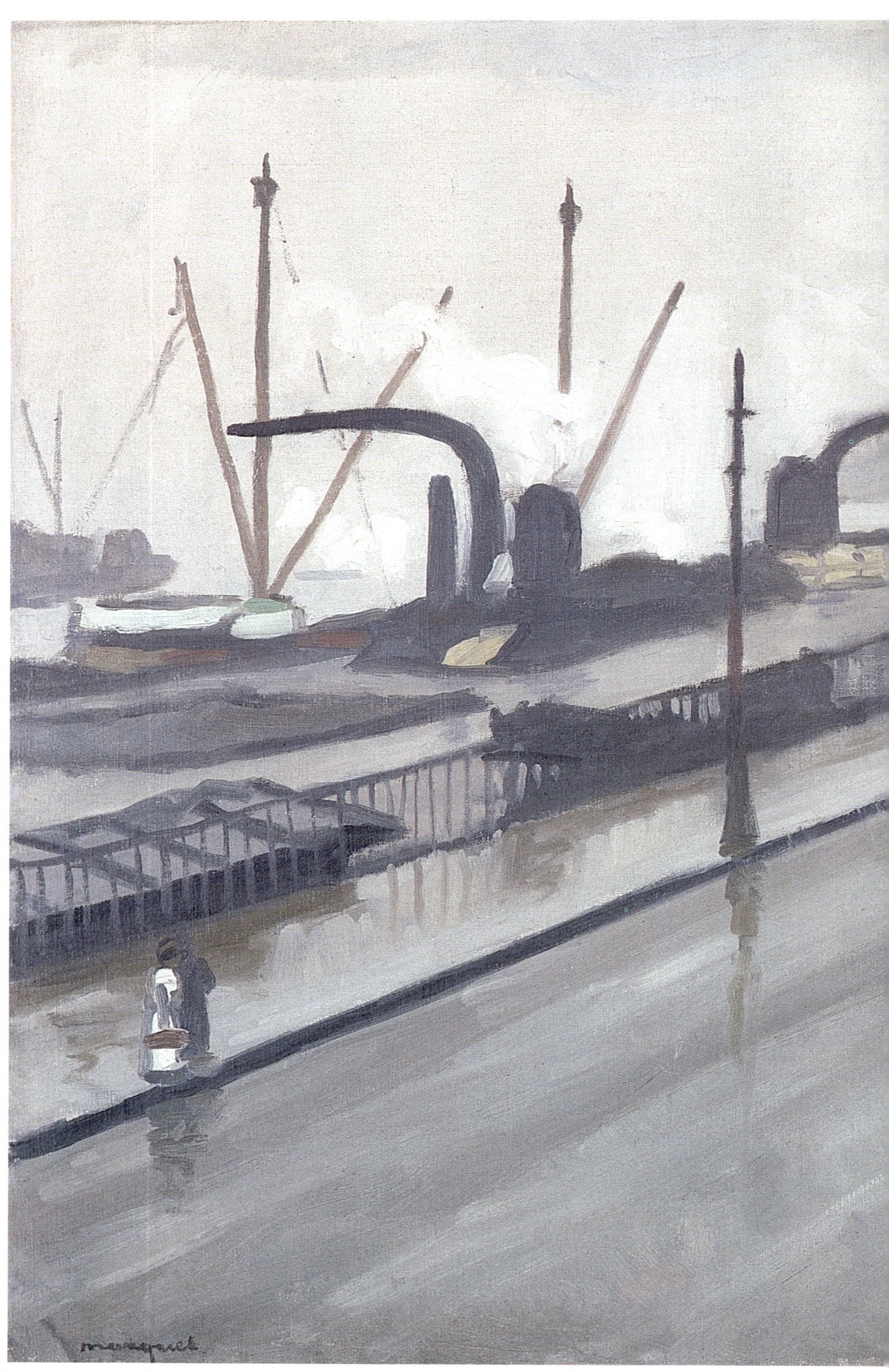

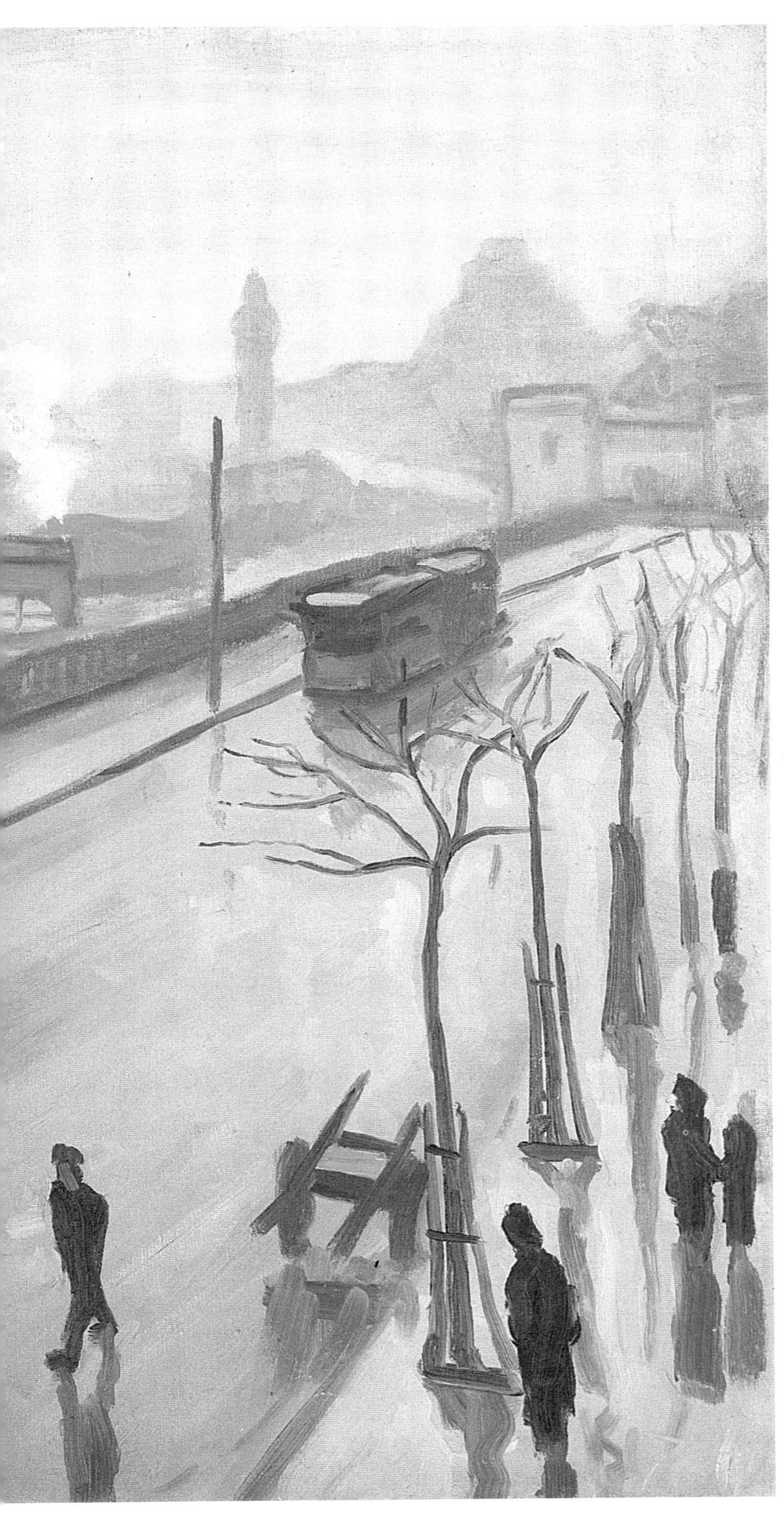

HAMBURG HARBOUR
1909
Oil on canvas. 65 x 81 cm.
Signed bottom left: *Marquet*.
Museum of Fine Arts, Bordeaux.

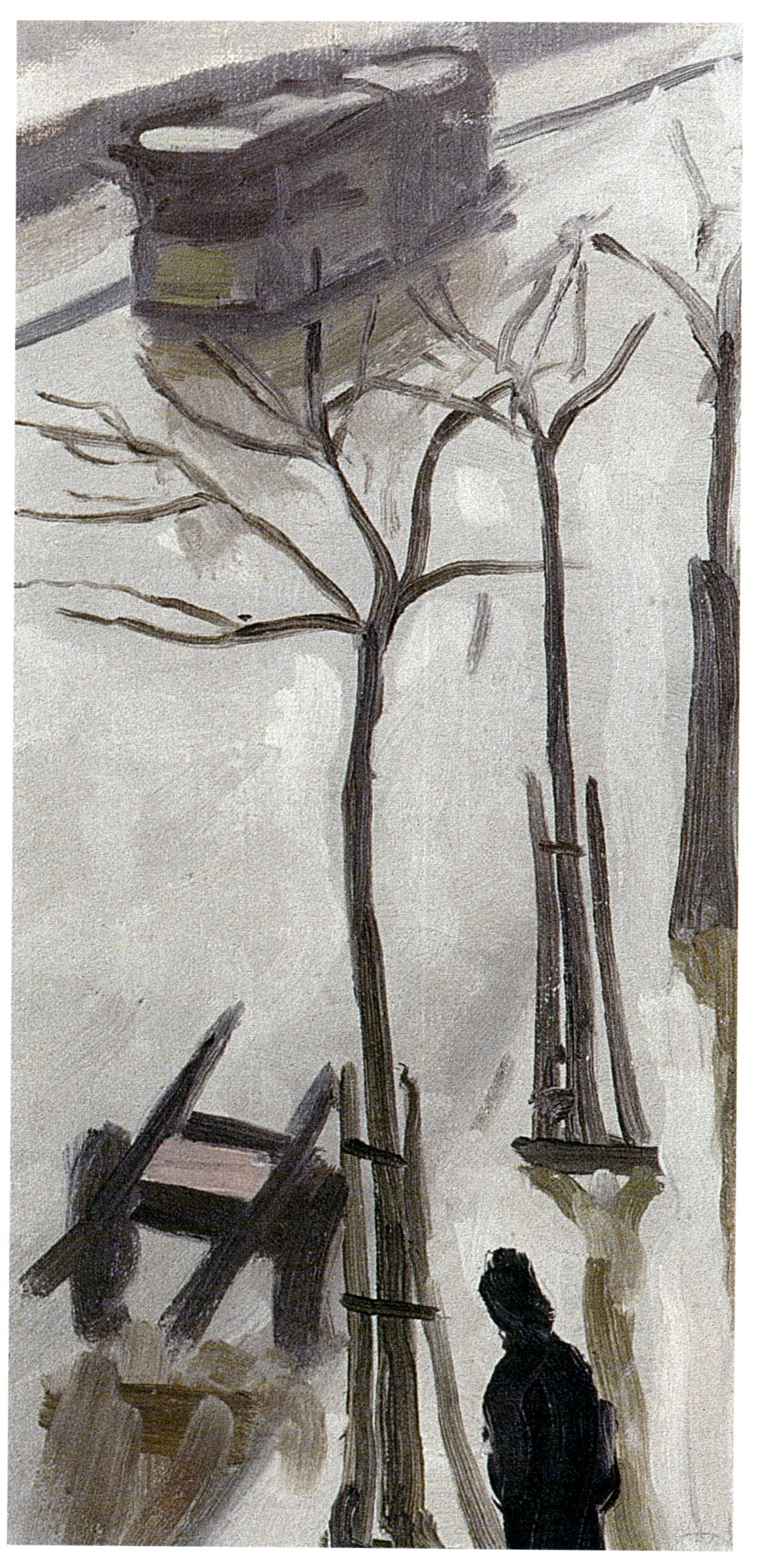

HAMBURG HARBOUR
Detail.
Museum of Fine Arts, Bordeaux.

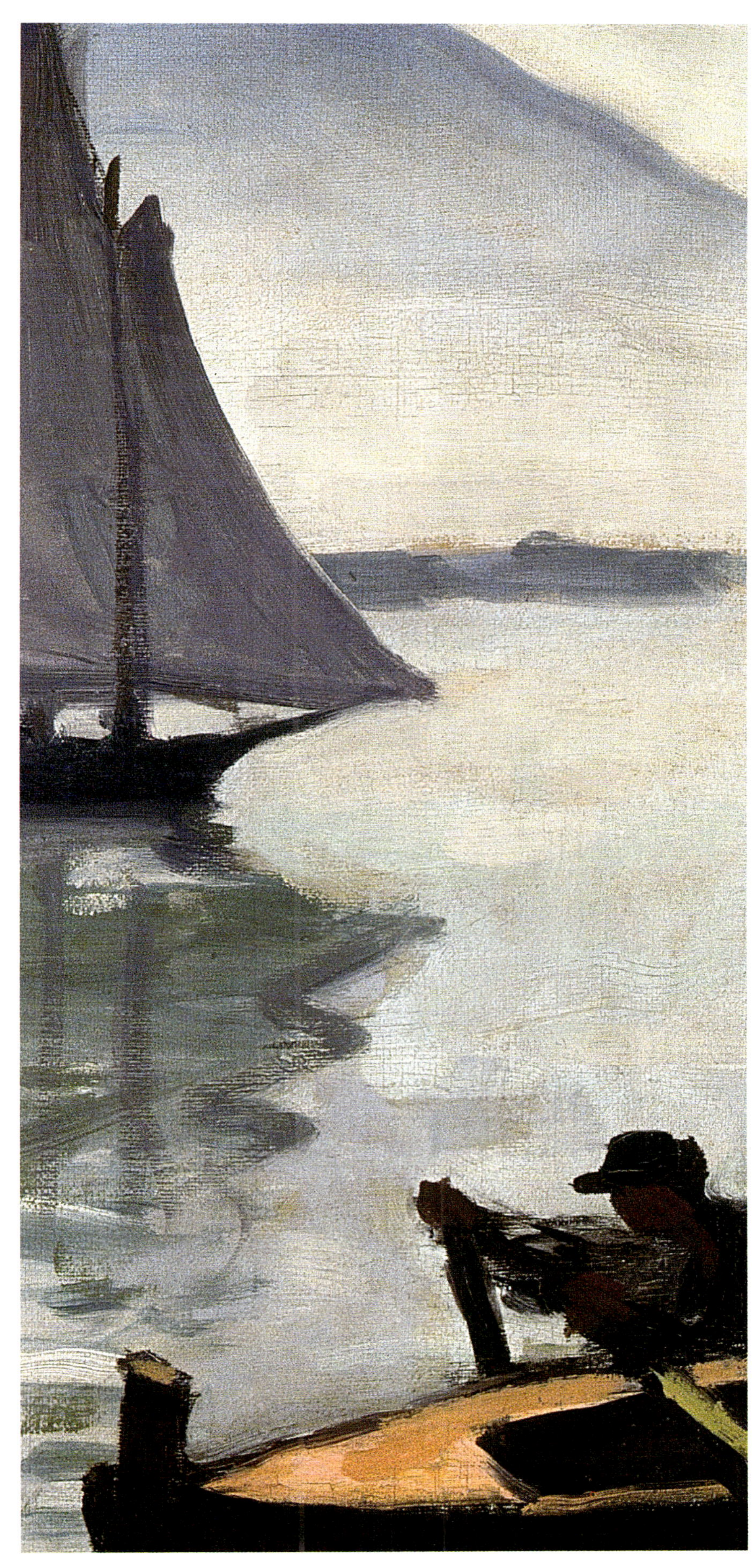

NAPLES, SAILING BOAT
Detail.
Museum of Fine Arts, Bordeaux.

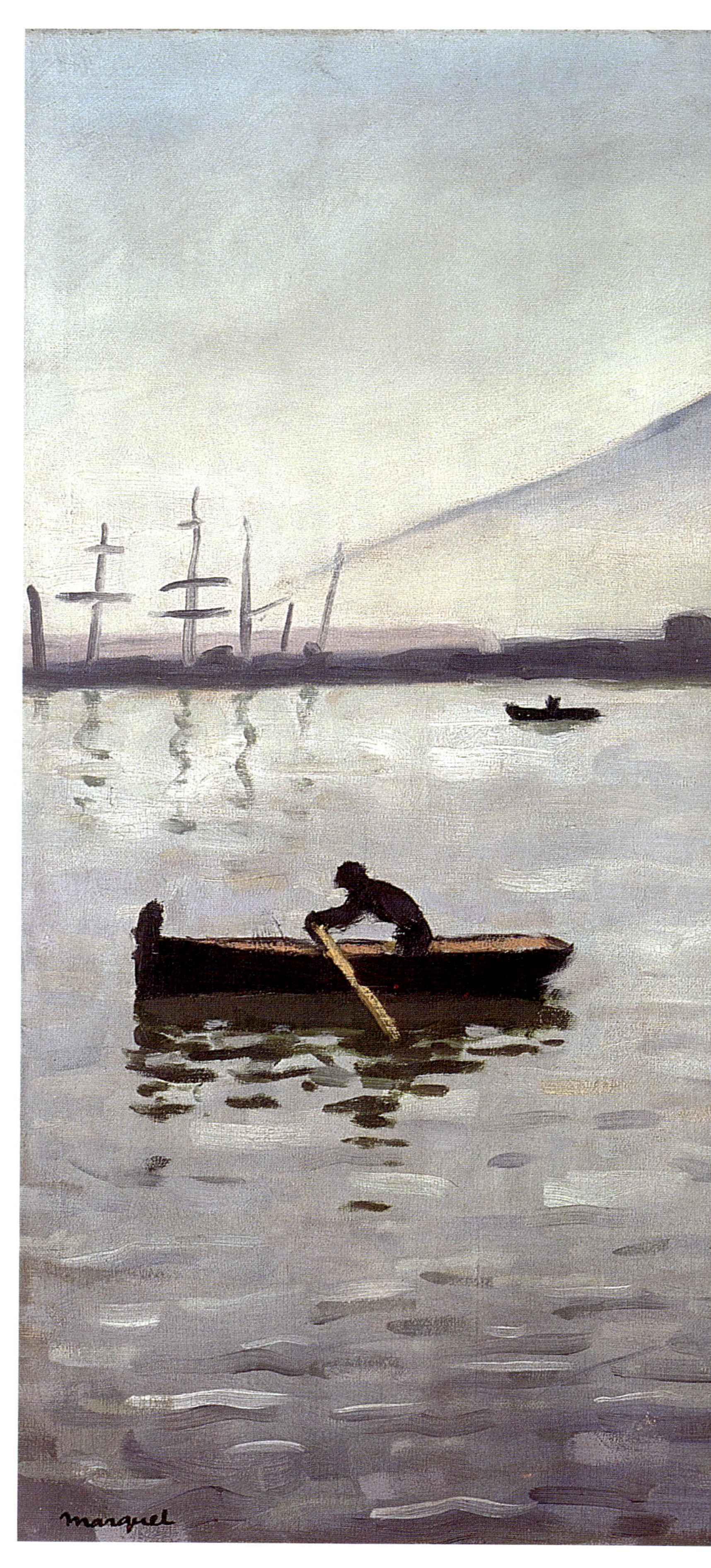

NAPLES. SAILING BOAT
1909
Oil on canvas. 65 x 81 cm.
Signed bottom left: *Marquet*.
Museum of Fine Arts, Bordeaux.

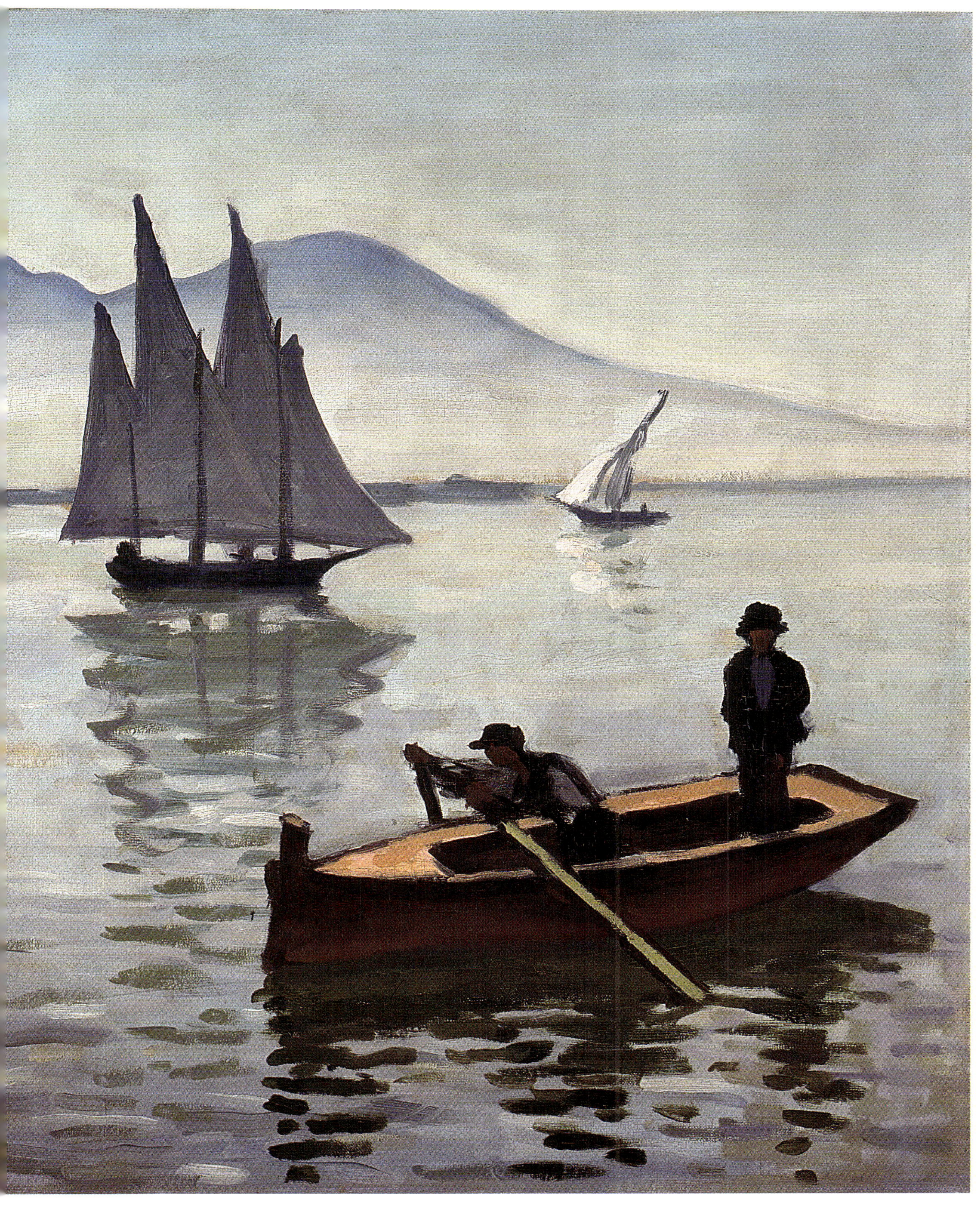

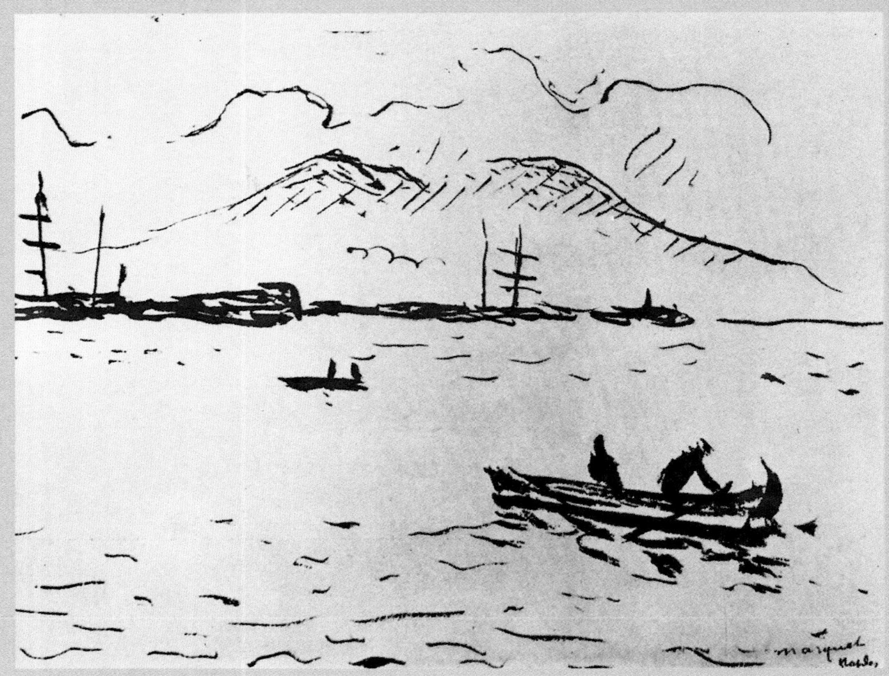

Albert Marquet. *The Bay of Naples.*

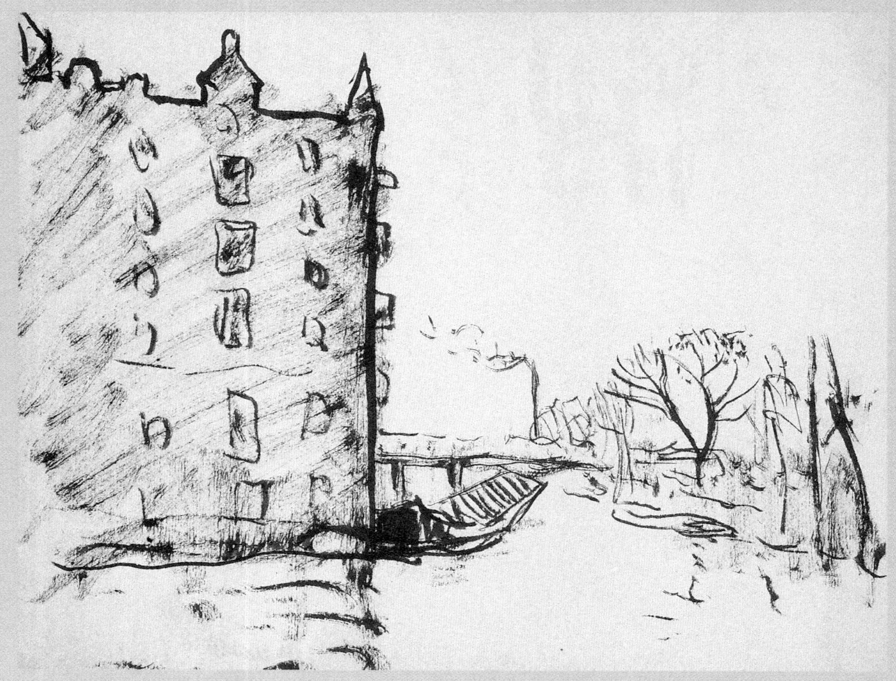

Albert Marquet. *Embankment.*

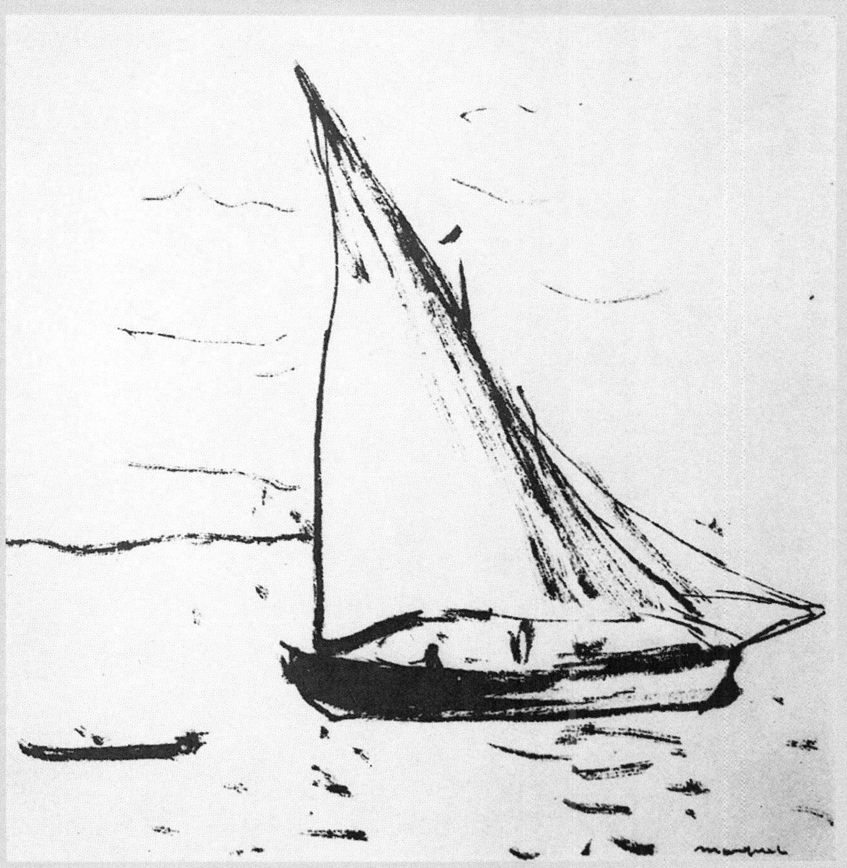

Albert Marquet. *Sailing Boat.*

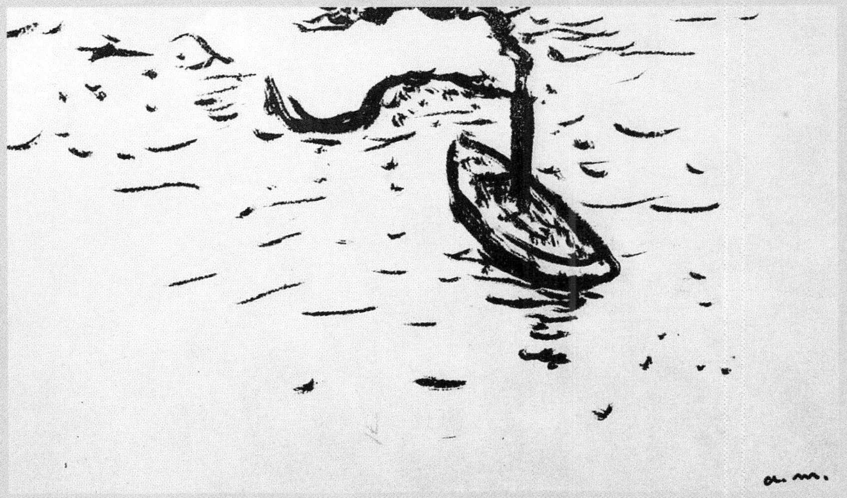

Albert Marquet. *Tug.*

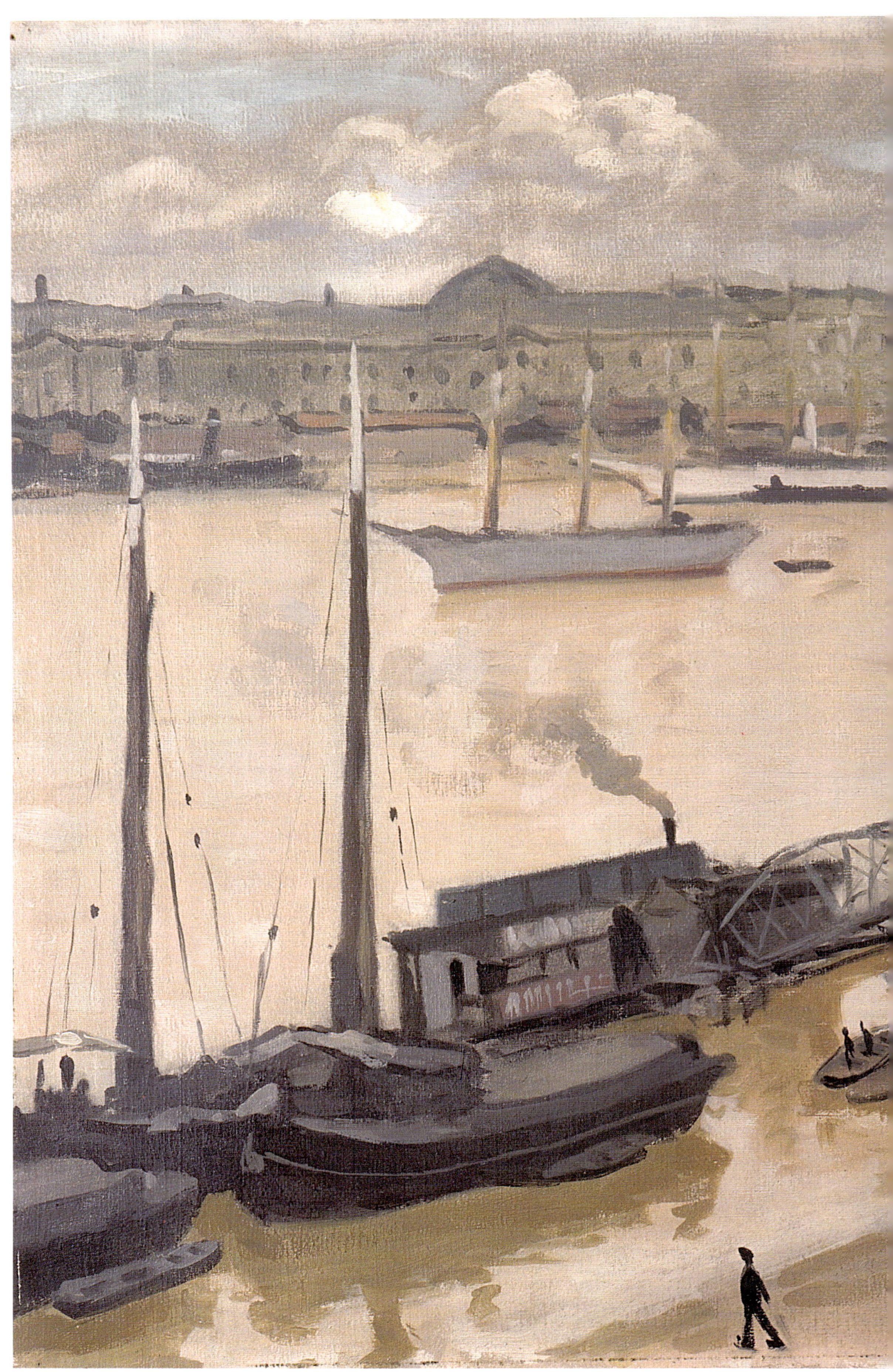

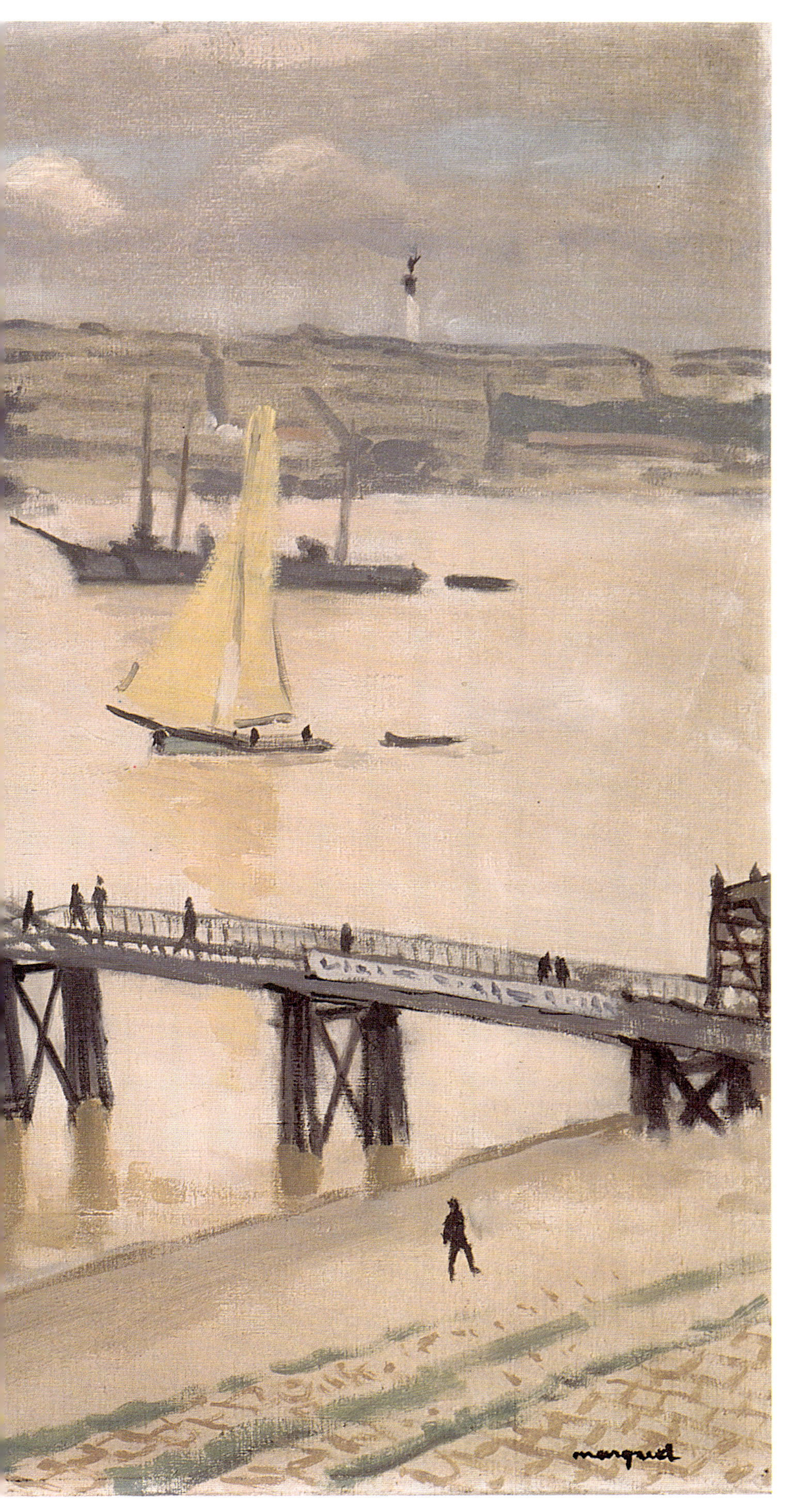

BORDEAUX HARBOUR
1924
Oil on canvas. 64.5 x 80.5 cm.
Signed bottom right: _Marquet_.
Museum of Fine Arts, Bordeaux.

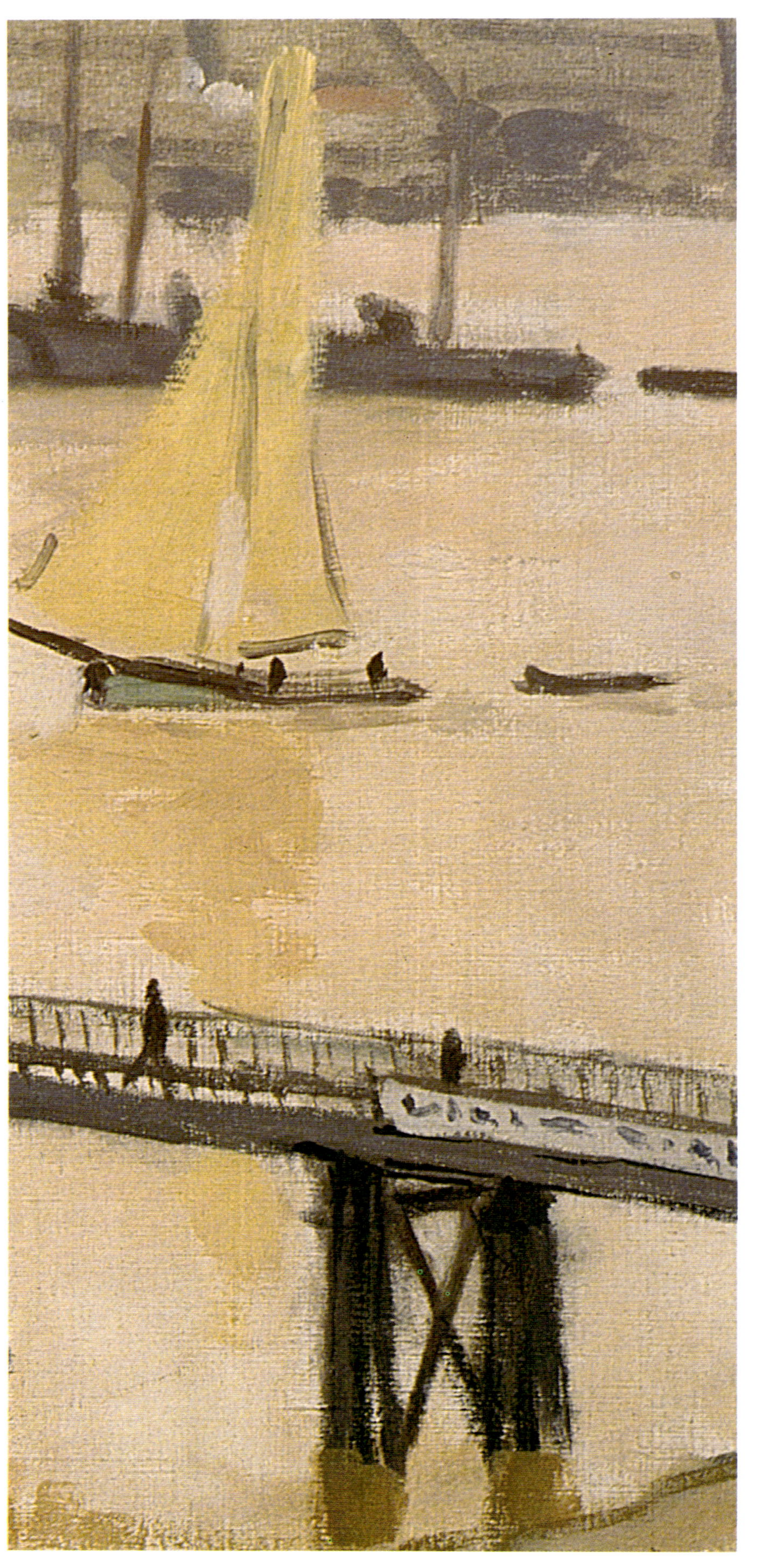

BORDEAUX HARBOUR
Detail.
Museum of Fine Arts, Bordeaux.

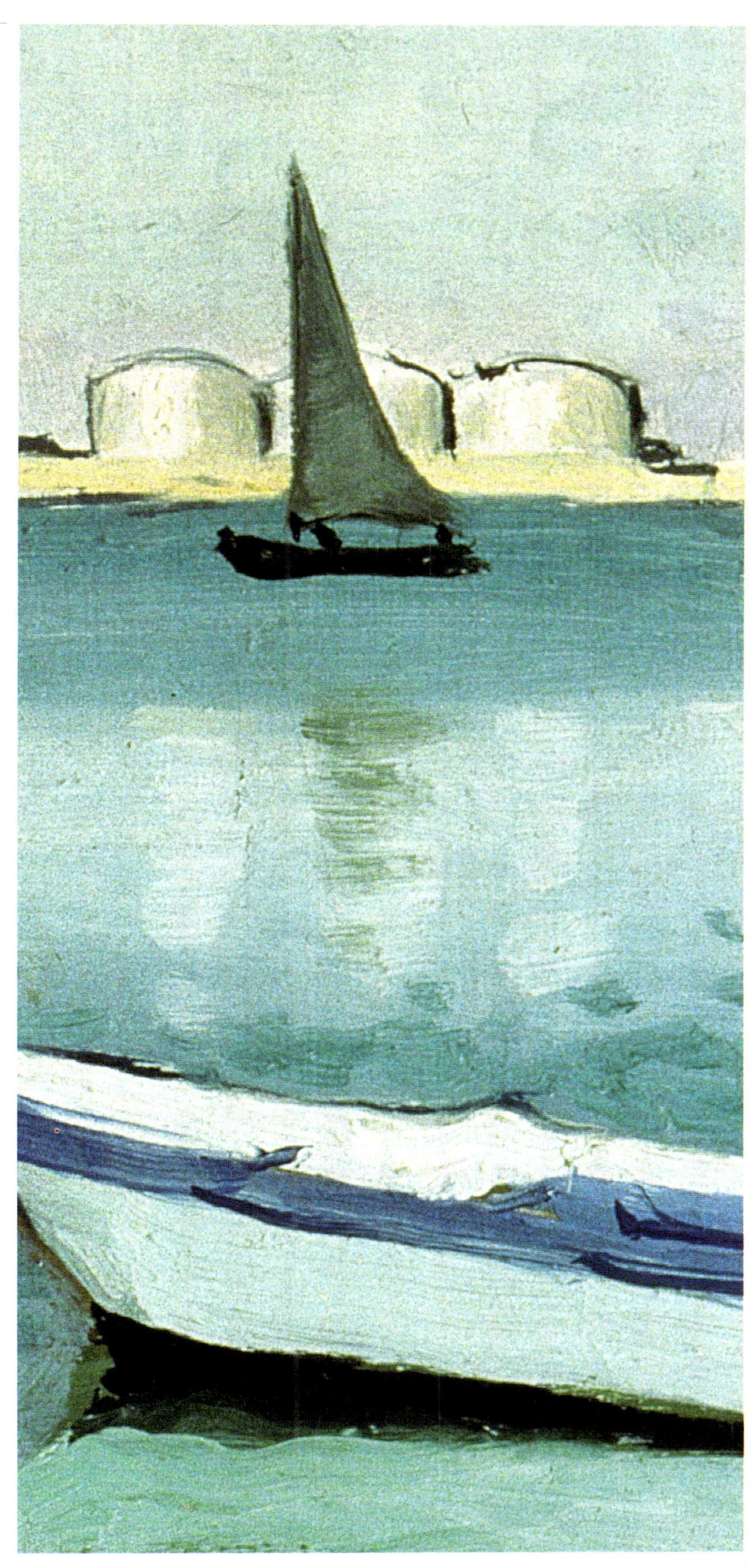

Detail.
Museum of Fine Arts and Archeology,
Besançon.

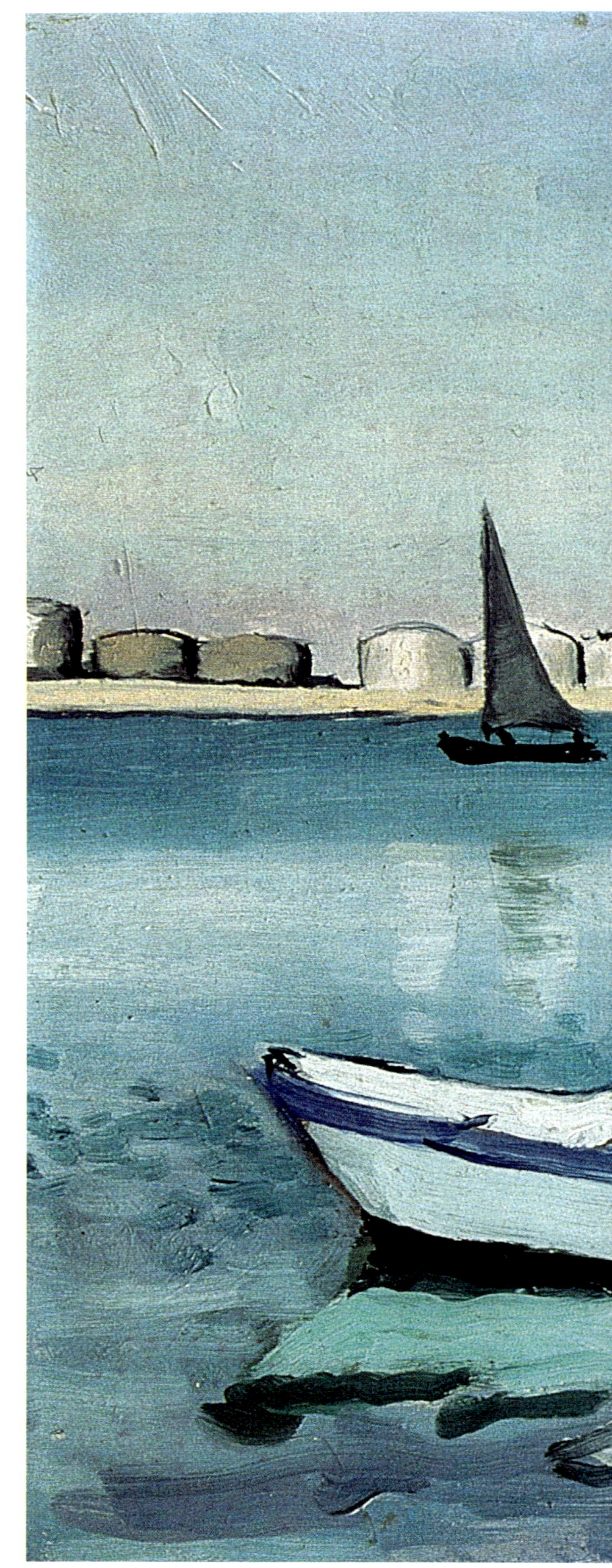

THE HARBOUR AT SÈTE
1924
Oil on plywood. 31.5 x 39 cm.
Signed bottom right: *Marquet*.
Museum of Fine Arts and Archeology, Besançon.

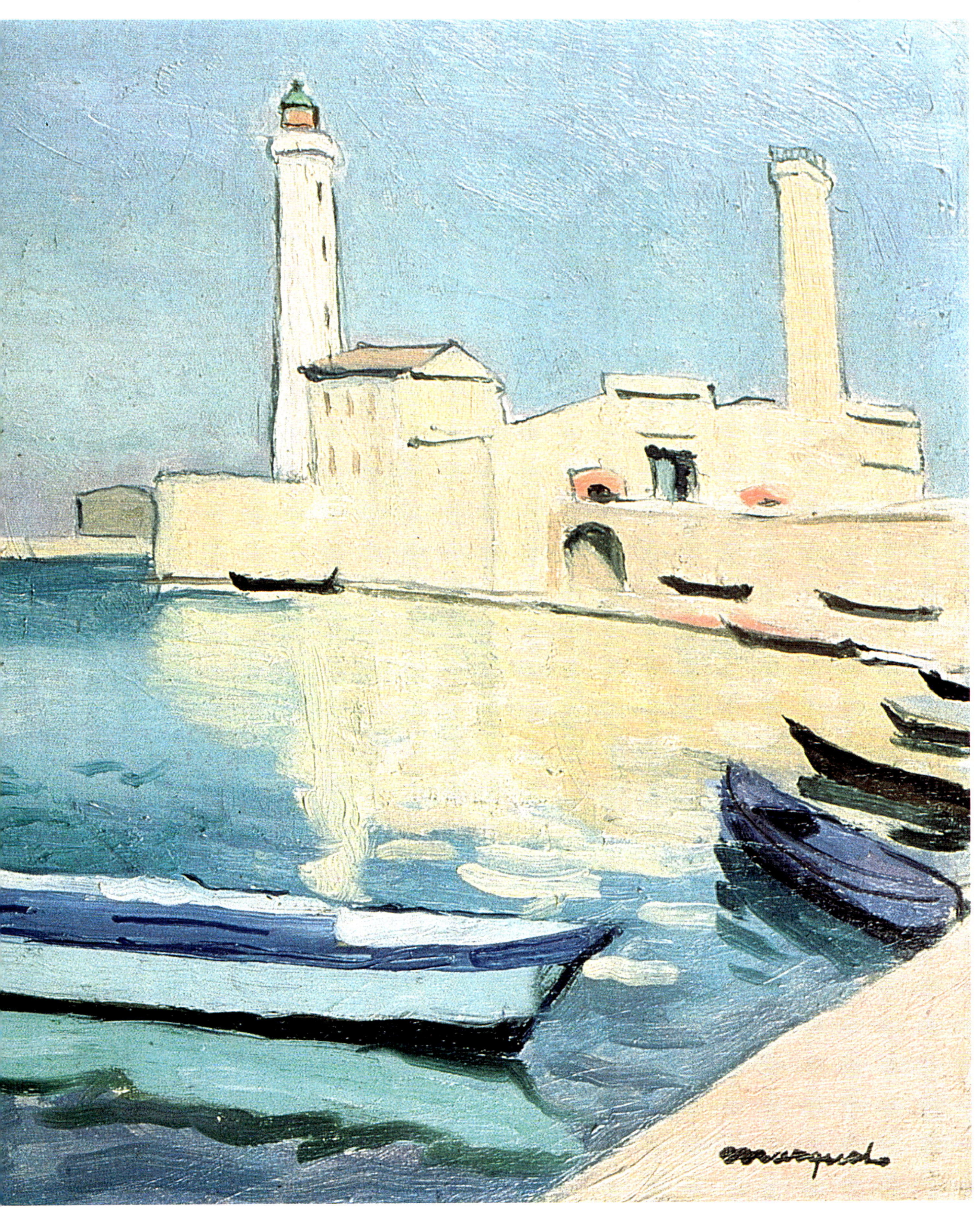

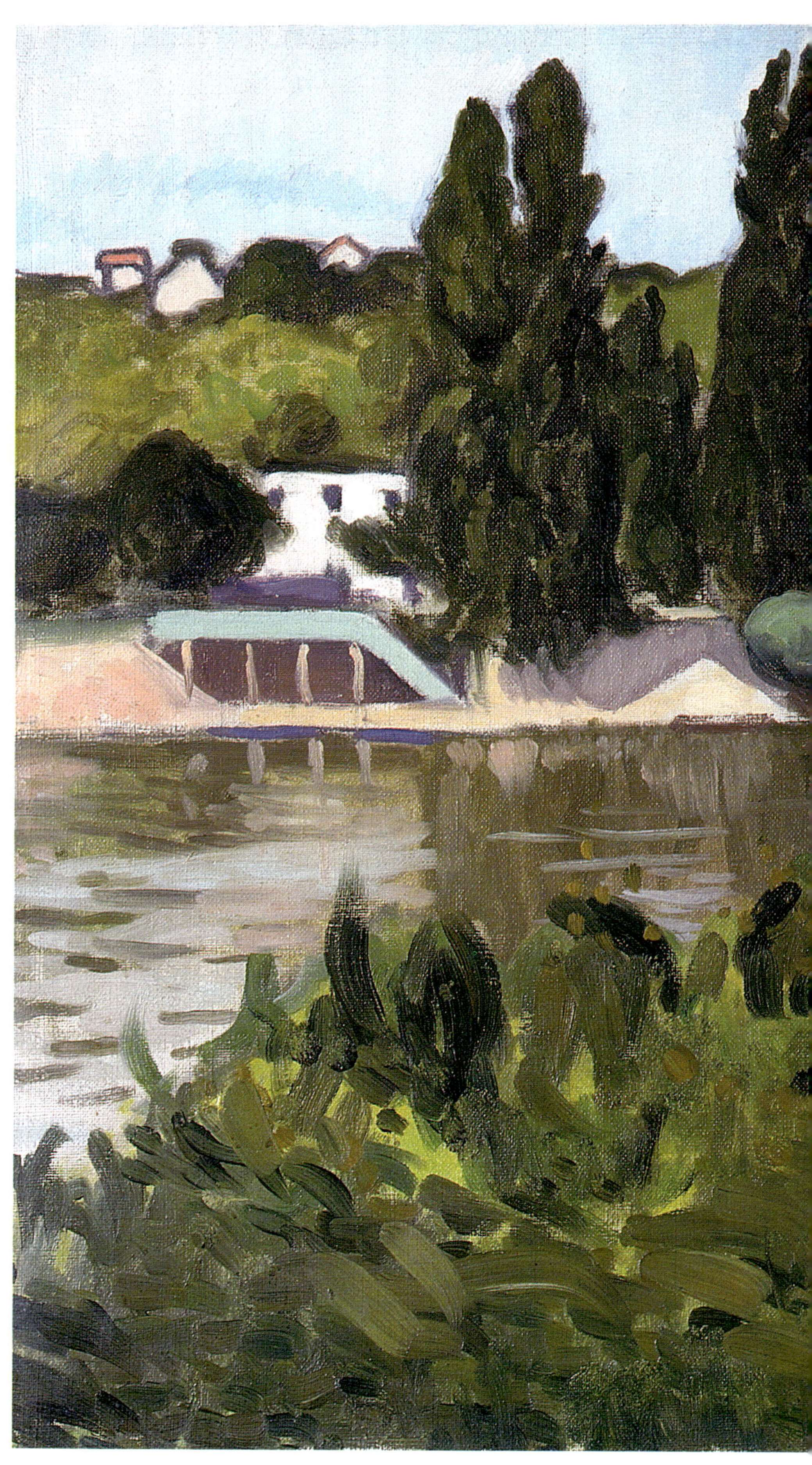

SAMOIS
Ca. 1917
Oil on canvas. 50 x 61 cm.
Signed bottom right: *Marquet*.
Museum of Fine Arts, Bordeaux.

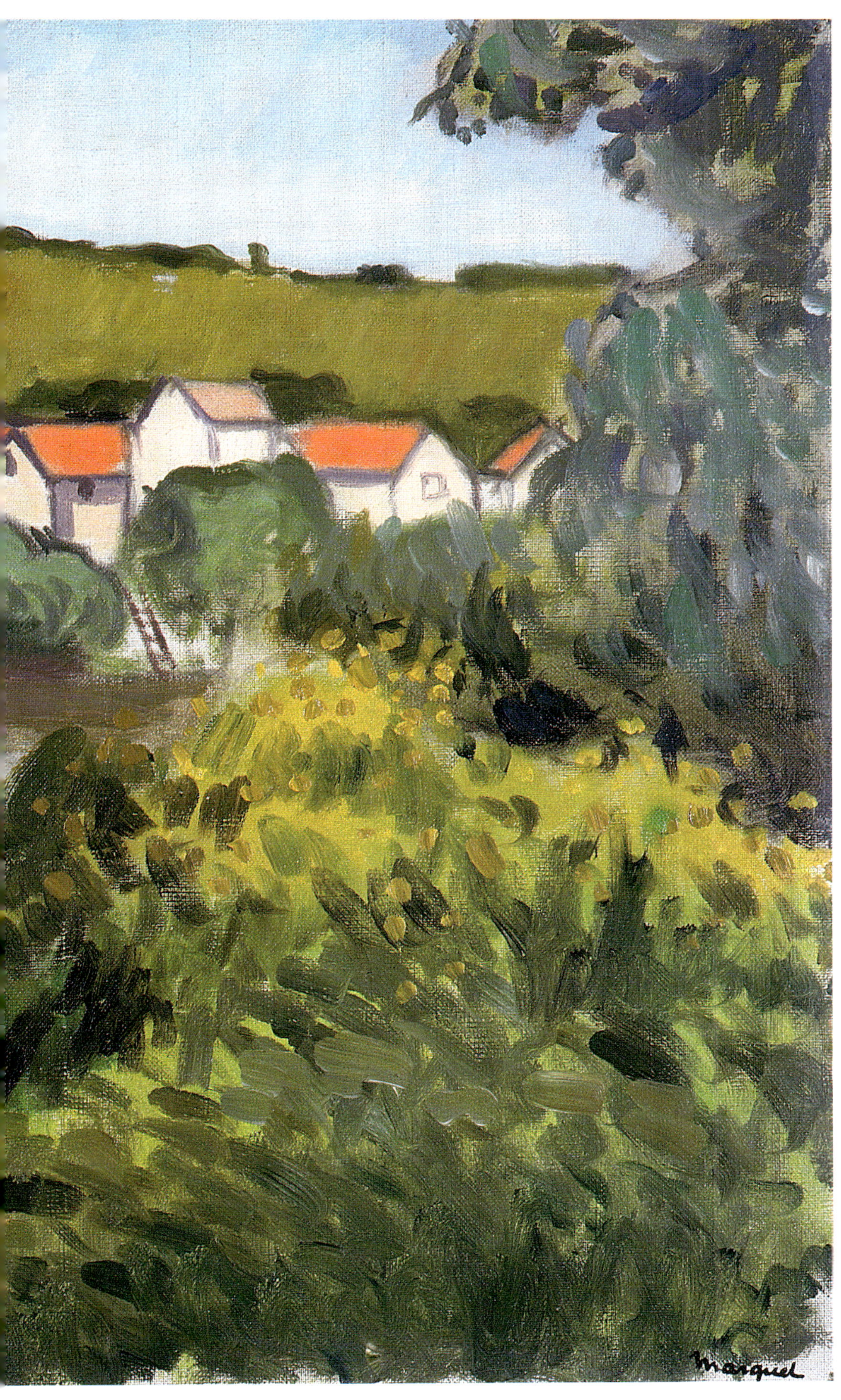
Marquet

the sunny southern landscapes the use of black is particularly
effective, disturbing the eye with its severity.

Nevertheless it seems beyond doubt that whatever Albert
Marquet did, wherever he travelled, whatever experiments he
ventured to make, his sole aim was to add something new to
his vision of Paris, his chief and basically only character.

In 1908 he took up residence on the Quai Saint-Michel on
the Left Bank opposite the Ile-de-la-Cité. He looked out on
Notre Dame, a succession of bridges and the quiet Ile Saint-
Louis. In this studio he painted a large number of landscapes,
seen practically from one and the same point and repeating
the same set of motifs.

Yet again we are forced to recall Cézanne. From his youth
Marquet, who (in contrast to Cézanne) was hardly a stay-at-
home, who knew and loved many streets and buildings in
Paris, was inclined to severely restrict his range of motifs.
He returned time and again to one and the same thing, yet
he had not the slightest inclination to do what the Impressionists did in painting only the shifting colour on unchanging
surfaces. No, Marquet, like Cézanne, sought the maximum
precision in conveying his sensations with the aid of a limited
group of motifs which from painting to painting became more
and more "themselves". Of course, Marquet was no dogmatist:
he delighted in painting the different states of nature, varying
light, sun, rain, fog, but the main thing remained the mysterious process of bringing forth the hidden formula in a motif
and that global planetary comprehension of space, two things
which had formerly preoccupied Cézanne. For that reason he
calmly repeated a motif, without ever repeating himself.

The group of Parisian landscapes now in the museums of

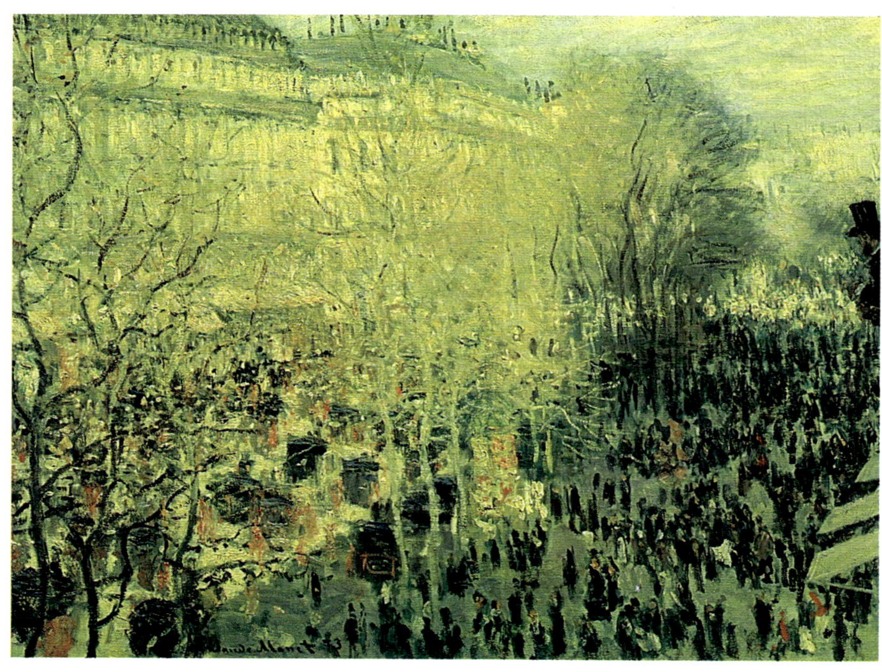

Claude Monet.
The Boulevard des Capucines in Paris.
1873.

58

Camille Pissarro.
The Avenue de l'Opéra in Paris.
1898.

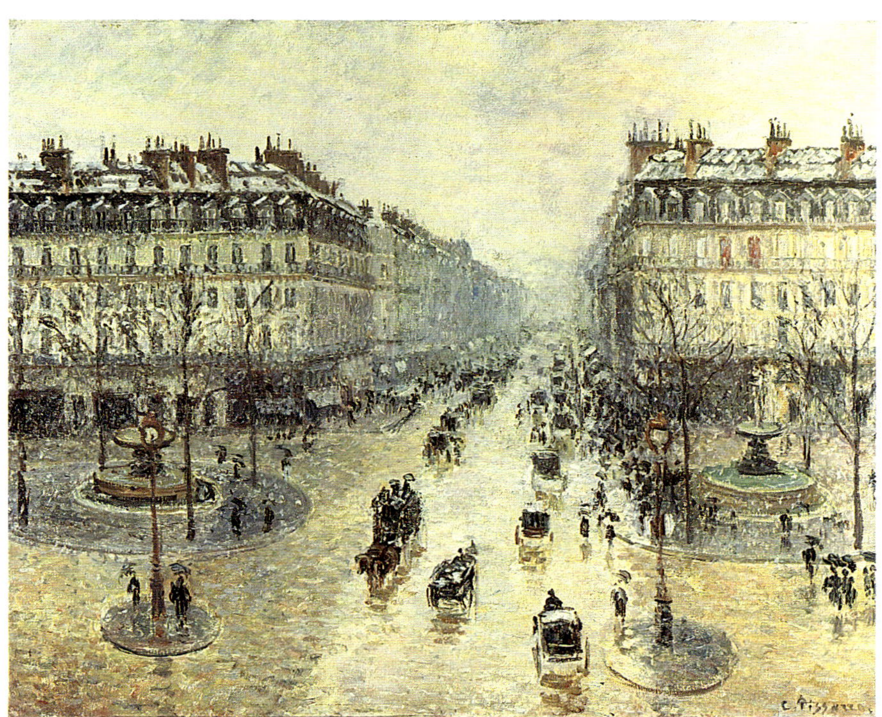

Moscow and St Petersburg are highly representative and could by themselves give a complete picture of Paris as seen through the eyes of Marquet.

But we must take into account here a factor of what one might call "inverse perception".

Just as any experienced viewer at the end of the last century was simply no longer capable of seeing Argenteuil or Louveciennes other than through the prism of the landscapes of Monet and Pissarro, Mont Sainte-Victoire other than through Cézanne's "aesthetic lens", and so on, so the present-day person has long since (consciously or unconsciously) attuned his or her perception of Paris to the "note" struck by Marquet. It is Marquet who even now enables us to see through the sparkling, fascinating trivia of Parisian reality to the splendid but concealed rhythms, colours and dimensions of the city, its majestic presence and solemn sadness.

One of the earliest Parisian landscapes in the Russian collections, the 1906 painting *The Quai du Louvre and the Pont Neuf* (Hermitage, St Petersburg), was painted with very great precision. The viewer is confronted by a spacious panorama of the city: from the embankment by the Louvre dotted with dapples of hot sunlight where it has penetrated through the dense plane trees, towards the Pont Neuf and the stone-clad banks of the Ile-de-la-Cité. Further on are the time-scarred walls and towers of the Conciergerie, the delicate spire of the Sainte Chapelle, the proud outlines of Notre Dame, while to the right, far off on the horizon, obscured by the heat-haze of summer, is the dome of the Panthéon.

Paris has more faces than perhaps any other city. It really

59

does contain a host of those charming, very "Parisian" little features, details that are extremely tempting for the artist. It was these details that captivated Daumier, Gavarni, Guys, Toulouse-Lautrec, Degas and many of the Impressionists. Parisians are incapable of missing these delightful, entertaining or engaging trifles.

It required a rare, as it were philosophical view of things, a sort of perceptual courage, to see the general and overlook all these "molecules of Parisian charm" and at the same time to remain an adherent of strict objective forms, not deviating for a moment into those experiments which alone, as it then seemed, could bring an artist success. Marquet was tackling a task which in its way was more complex even than that chosen by Cézanne. Cézanne was searching for some universal formula for the sufficiently (and deliberately) depersonalized object. An apple or a jug in his work is an image generalized to the extreme — an "apple *per se*". Marquet, however, was setting down on canvas the "painterly formula" not simply of a specific city, but of a city which is, first, endlessly individual and which he greatly loved, and, second, a city long since debased by cheap pictures and hosts of banal preconceptions and associations (incidentally, in 1907 Marquet saw the tremendous retrospective exhibition of Cézanne in Paris and that event could quite possibly have revealed to him yet again a long-familiar and beloved artist). It is for that reason, probably, that Marquet's Paris always has an air of some sort of bashful severity about it. Almost always the artist and the viewer are somewhat aloof from the city, they are observers and not participants in Parisian life. Indeed Marquet rarely recorded the fleeting lustre of the city: the sparkle of sunlight on the leaves of the plane trees, the reflection of the dull sky on the wet roofs of the carriages. There is virtually nothing of that cascade of dynamic details which the Impressionists so loved and which they were so skilled at painting. Marquet's Paris is almost devoid of detail.

In the Hermitage canvas it reveals itself with vertiginous speed, and the viewer's imagination penetrates into the depth of the painting instantly and joyfully. Perspective is constructed with a truly Cézannesque energy, but there is also something totally distinctive about it, an insistence peculiar and specific to Marquet: the artist's angle of vision is exceptionally broad. He is like a photographer using a wide-angle lens, but he applies his own laws, which are far from canonical. The space in the picture imperiously and swiftly "draws in" the viewer's gaze, which catches the main essence and no longer seeks to search out trifles. This effect is enhanced by the rhythmical alternation of shady and sunlit buildings on the embankment of the Ile-de-la-Cité, which also attract the eye into the depths of the picture, and the diagonal brushstrokes,

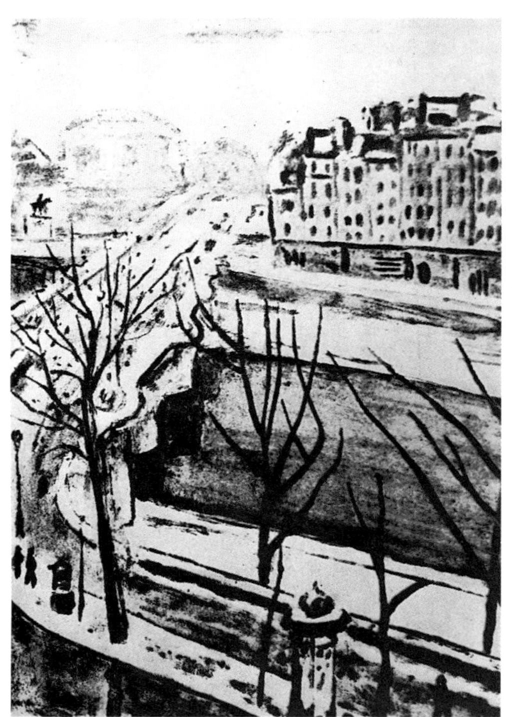

Albert Marquet.
The Pont Neuf.

60

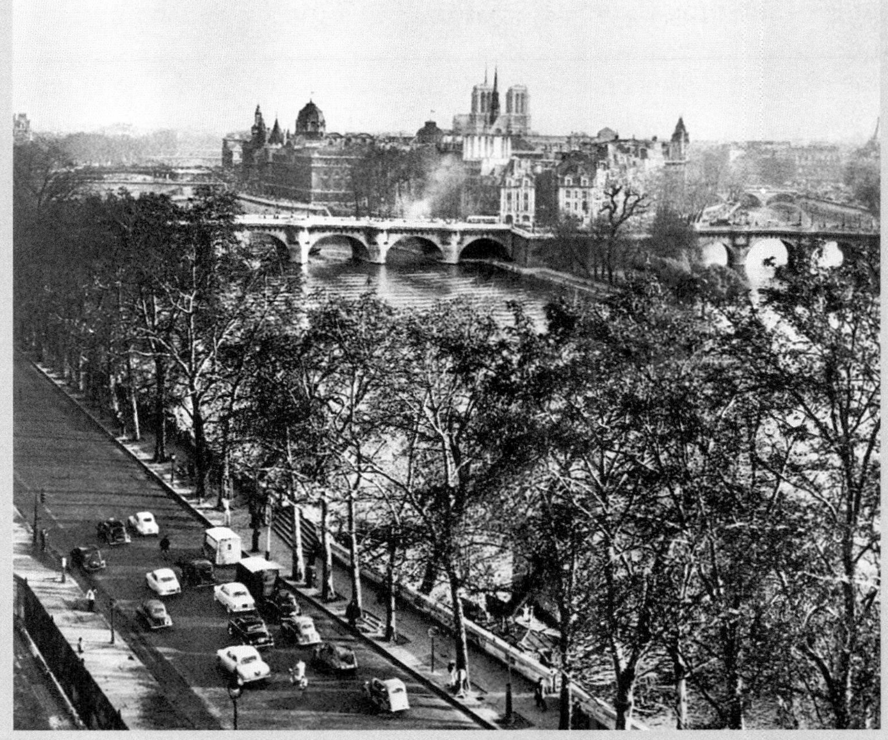

View of the Ile-de-la-Cité and the Pont-Neuf.

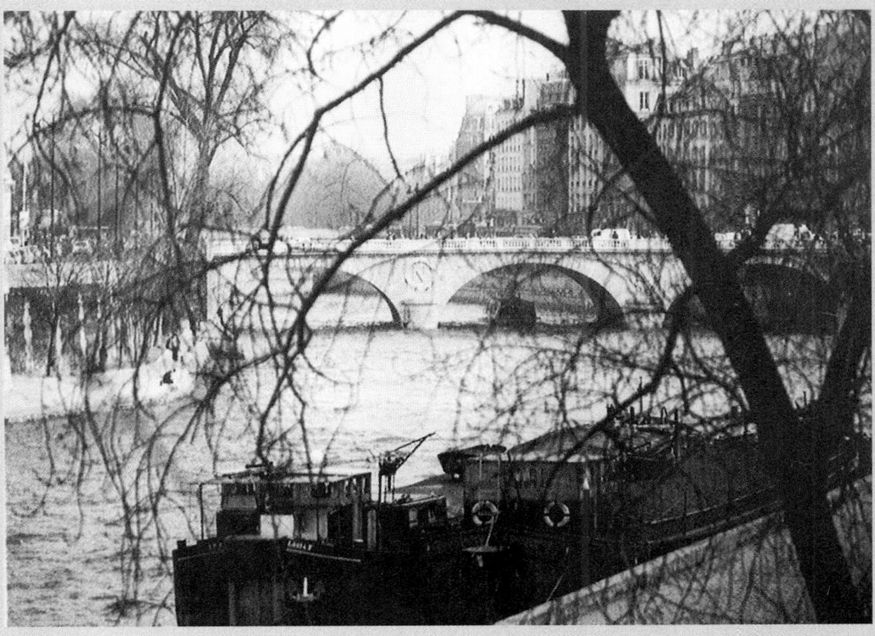

View of the Seine.

and indeed all the motion of the consistently "skewed" elements which dominate in the painting.

One has the impression, moreover, that Marquet was scrutinizing the city from a viewpoint that was not fixed: his gaze greedily reaches out to embrace the space. Following in the artist's footsteps, the viewer begins to feel himself master of the space created on the canvas.

Yes, that is the right word — Marquet created space and did not reproduce what he saw. He created his own world from the simplified, important, and exclusively significant elements, the determinants in the "formula of the city", from all that is vital for an understanding of its essential uniqueness. On the canvas he arranged those elements in a certain correspondence with real life, but — first and foremost — proceeding from his own artistic will. The correlation of patches of colour, the rhythm of volumes and lines in all its perspicacious and celebratory individuality — all this is heightened in the extreme in Marquet's paintings. He seeks that version of perfection about which Antoine de Saint-Exupéry wrote, the perfection that is achieved not when nothing more can be added, but when nothing more can be pared away.

Of course, we should not forget that Marquet had around him art that he would scarcely have been able to ignore even had he wished to. Picasso was already famous. His painting of the Blue Period with its shattering air of tragedy and savage system of forms strangely combining bold innovation and mediaeval tradition was an important part of the artistic milieu in which Marquet was living. Moreover, the genesis of his Parisian landscape coincided in time with the consolidation of Cubism. That means that the temptation to structuralize space, to radically simplify it and abandon the medium of air, was great. And it is hardly creditable that Marquet was completely free of all this. He simply preserved his individuality. Yet there are, to be sure, certain influences of the very latest innovations to be seen in his art. And indeed, are there not in this mutability of the artist's viewpoint, which seems to move in space, remote, "conjunctural", but nonetheless undeniable links with the tenets of Cubism? By the same token, the powerful simplicity of his volumes may possibly, like much in the art of the beginning of the century, have its root in the lessons provided by primitive culture, which so occupied minds at that time.

Paris in Winter. The Quai Bourbon (1907; Pushkin Museum of Fine Arts, Moscow) is a painting which conveys with astonishing precision the feeling of a frosty day. There are all the same lines of the embankments racing towards the horizon, only this time they go off into a cold fog and melt into it together with the dull, spectral houses. Here more than anywhere one can notice how the core of the colour scheme

QUAI BOURBON
1908
Oil on canvas. 92 x 73 cm.
Signed bottom left: *Marquet.*
Museum of Fine Arts, Bordeaux.

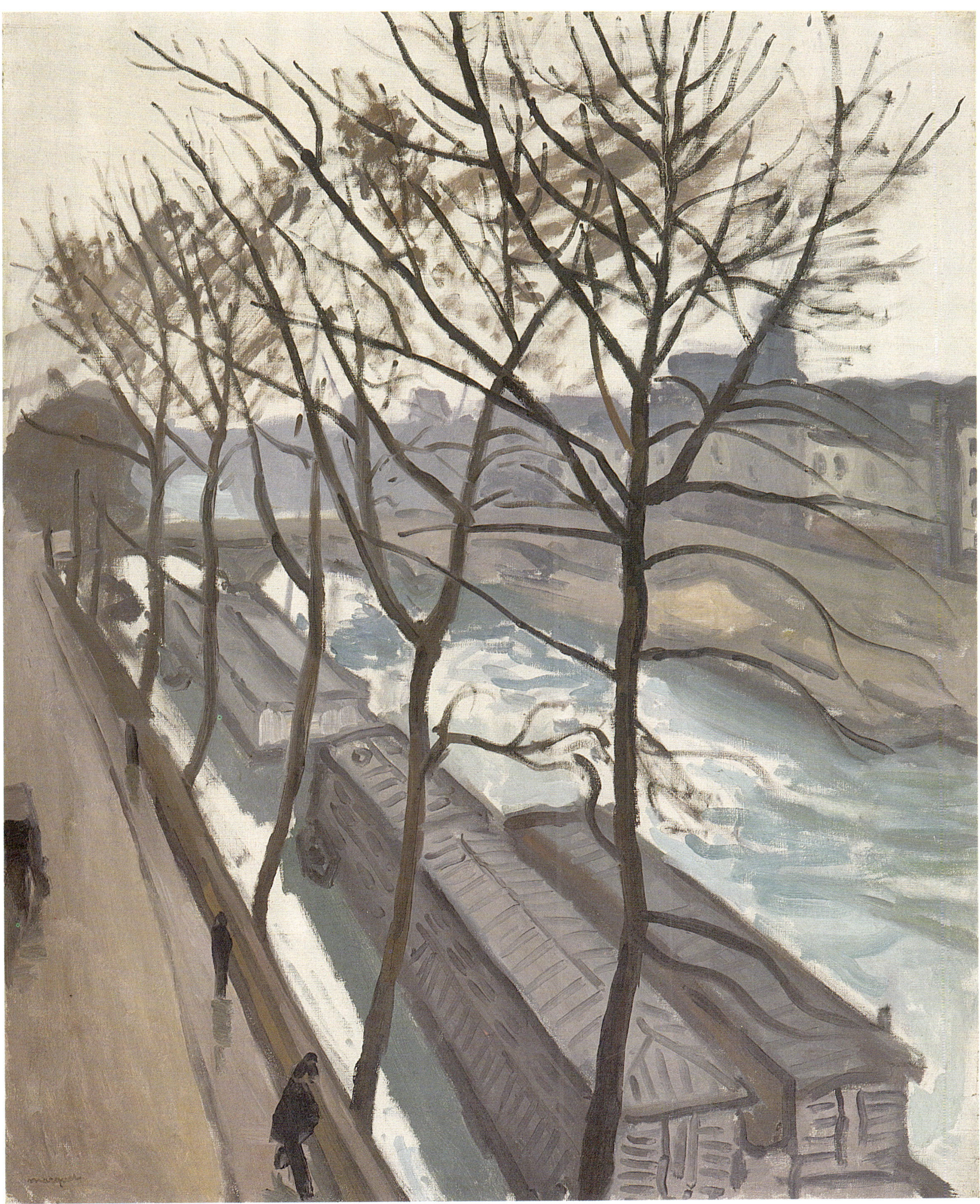

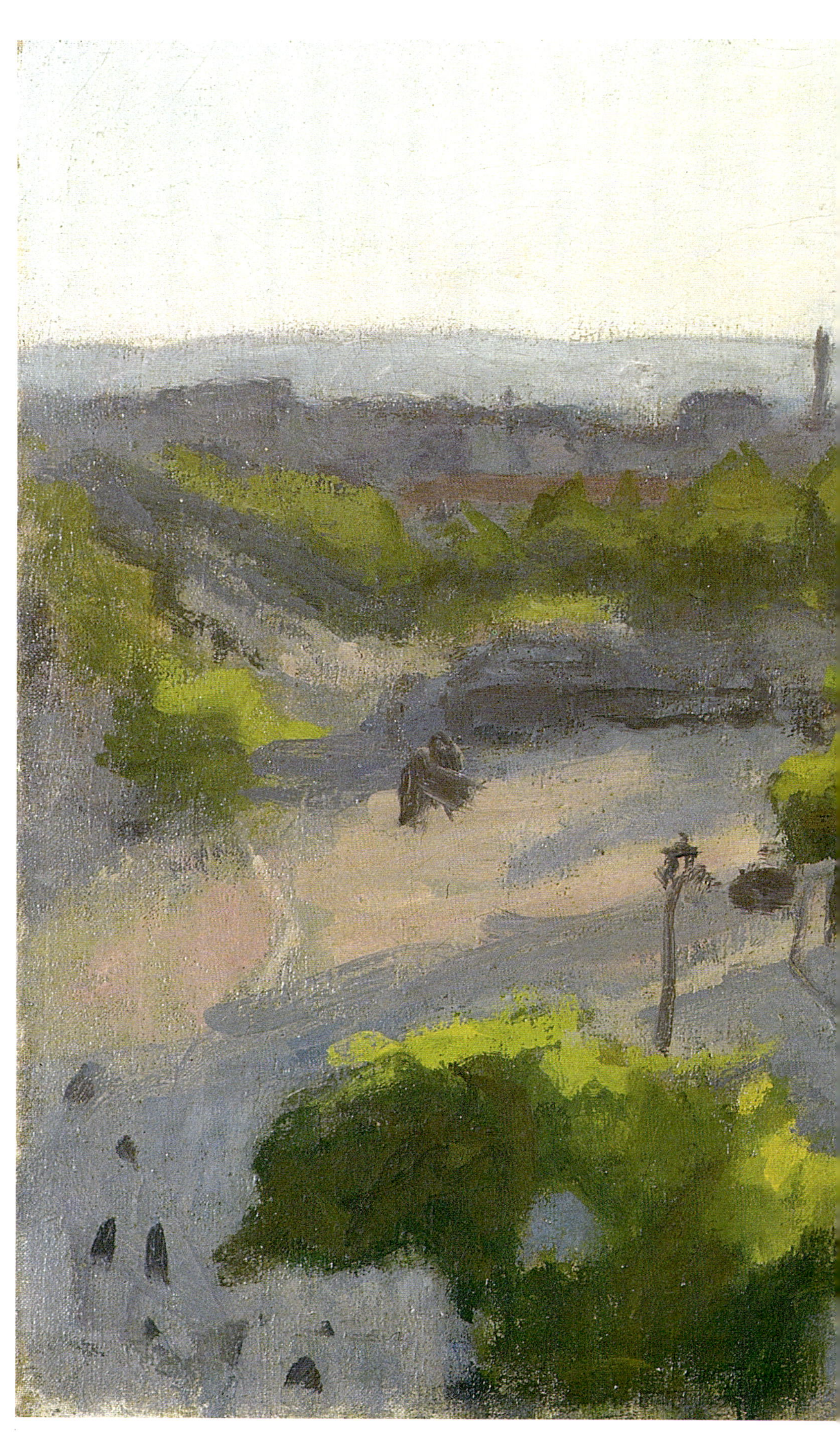

THE PORTE DE SAINT-CLOUD
1904
Oil on canvas. 50 x 61 cm.
Signed bottom right: *Marquet*.
Museum of Fine Arts, Bordeaux.

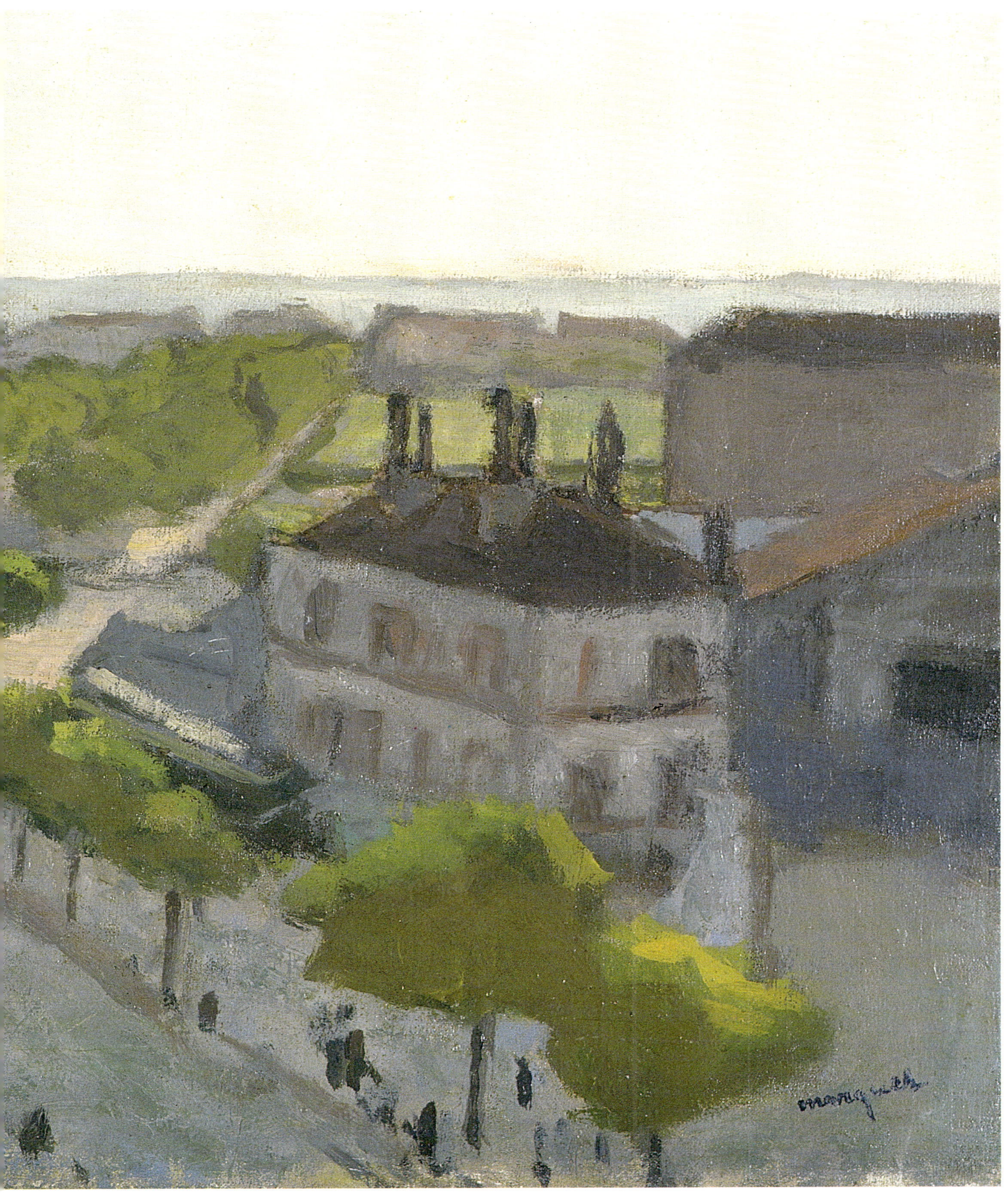

— the reddish brown walls of the Bateau-Lavoir-like buildings by the bank and the grey-lilac of the icy river — is synthesized with tonal and spatial structures, how pronounced is the spiral line of the smoke rising to the sky and how enhanced the gloomy angularity of the buildings.

Each object in one of Marquet's paintings inevitably undergoes a metamophosis; it is as if it becomes "more true to itself", sheds the accidental and incidental, revealing its persistent identity. ("All the random traits erase," Blok wrote, "you'll see then that the world is fair"). Those few details alone are retained which intensify the general impression: the shadows, unexpected on a foggy day, formed by the sun managing to penetrate the wintry gloom, the glistening of the sky on the tall roof of the house across the river on the Ile-de-la-Cité. The details accentuate the scale of the whole, becoming a sort of visual equivalent of musical overtones.

Paris is difficult to paint; its colours are at times totally elusive, like the smoky hue of the old buildings; among the finest shades of ash, graphite and pearl the colourful patches of carriages, posters or umbrellas flare up; the slightest change in the weather transforms the streets and squares. But Marquet slowly and painstakingly "deciphers" Paris, revealing through his persistence the simple within the complex, seeking the "universal features of the urban landscape". After all, almost no-one before him had painted the French capital in winter, while following the *Quai Bourbon* he created a whole gallery of hibernal Parisian landscapes. Perhaps winter makes especially noticeable the breadth or openness of the city, the slightly sad spaciousness of the embankments, the height of the sky, the eccentric rhythms of thin chimneys. Winter refined the artist's instinctive feel for colour, presenting him with an infinite variety of greys and umber-brown shades and enabling him to find unusual combinations of these, each time seeing the same city anew.

Marquet's series of Parisian winter landscapes evokes images of strolls along the cold, empty embankments of the Rive Gauche, the Ile-de-la-Cité and the Ile Saint-Louis, during which the unexpected appearance of the sun or a sudden gust of icy wind continually change the city's appearance; images of a calm succession of poetic, rather mournful evocations that are different yet at the same time inseparable. They seem to built up in layers one upon another, merging together like a number of days which memory joins into a single picture. And it is strange that in his Parisian landscapes Marquet — who might be perceived as anything other than a teller of tales — in this context assumes the role of a narrator, almost of a novelist. Perhaps this is because the succession of impressions he presents is like memories passing through our mind's eye. And most probably, because these landscapes

THE PORTE DE SAINT-CLOUD
Detail.
Museum of Fine Arts, Bordeaux.

were born of the national tradition and existed in French literature even earlier than in Marquet's painting. There are remarkable descriptions of Parisian landscapes in the works of Emile Zola and in the novel-memoirs of Anatole France — and also in books which had not then been written but are of exceptional importance for our contemporary perception of Paris: Hemingway's *Moveable Feast*, Remarque's *Arc de Triomphe*, Feuchtwanger's *Exile* and others.

Moreover, in Marquet's canvases, where people are usually only represented by a few rapid strokes, there is an ever-present invisible image of a man in love with the city, an idling dreamer. He it is who reveals to the viewer the secret and meaning of the beauty which he senses but has not entirely comprehended, a beauty which is not banal but individual to the point of painfulness. Marquet causes us to hear the "melody" of the city, in its original, simplest and most impressive tones.

Notre Dame de Paris in Winter (1908; Pushkin Museum of Fine Arts, Moscow) is possibly the finest Marquet in the Russian collections. The power and simplicity in the arrangement of masses and in the ascetic colour scheme are staggering even for this artist. The easy precision with which great volumes are placed on the canvas brings to mind Poussin, of whom Marquet was so fond. And at the same time it would not be unreasonable to suggest that the extreme restraint in colour, the solemn earthy shades coupled with the heavy and simplified geometry of the forms is once again evidence that Marquet's paintings contain echoes, albeit distant, of the early Cubist experiments. There is no need to speak of influence, but there is a certain common atmosphere in which all artists, even the most independent, exist and which penetrates as a weak reverberation into even the most self-contained artistic worlds.

Rainy Day in Paris (1910; Hermitage, St Petersburg) is a more lyrical work. It conjures up the warm glistening of the rain-washed pavement, the rusty black silhouettes of the carriages and the foggy grey gloom out of which the towers of the cathedral loom, seemingly formed from that same murkiness and suddenly turned to stone.

Such things oblige us to think again how Marquet's work, traditional in all its outward qualities, fits into the art scene of the 1910s with its endless experimentation and, most significantly, its striving to depict, as Picasso put it, not what the artist sees, but what he tells himself about what he has seen. In point of fact, however true to life (in the full sense of the expression) and figurative Marquet's landscapes might be, they are, nonetheless, depictions of something experienced and not reflections of something seen.

To speak of Marquet's traditional realism is to blindly observe

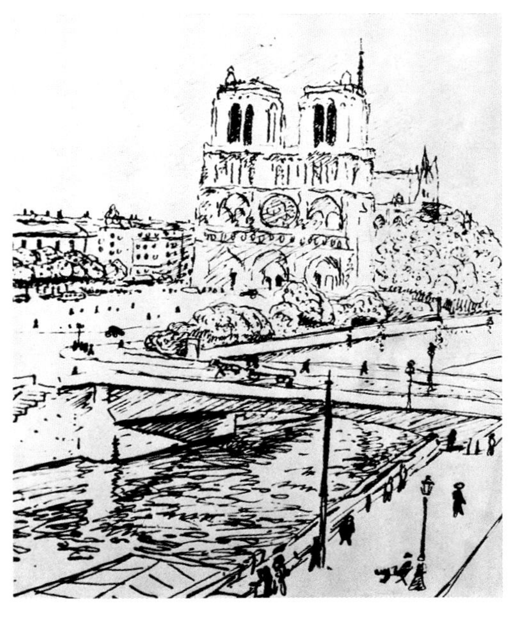

Albert Marquet.
Notre Dame.

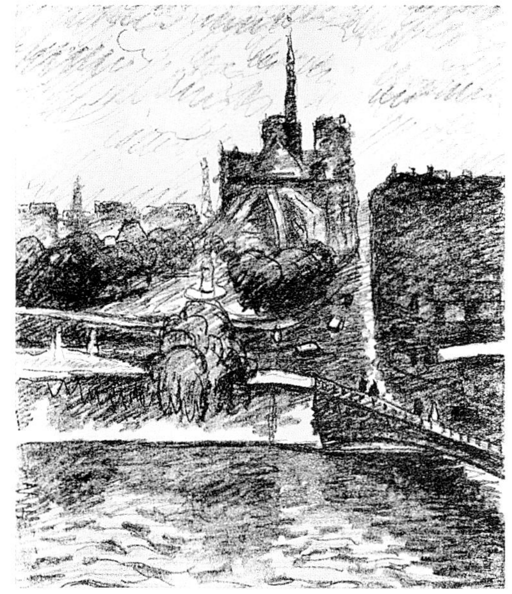

the conventional opposition: "objective - abstract". Marquet is above all absolutely free, to the extent that an artist who engages ever more frequently in quotation and self-quotation can be free. Yet, even so, his absolutely convincing, recognizable, uniquely individual Paris is also an autonomously existing artistic world, a self-embracing structure with a manner of organization no less valuable than Klee's "magic squares" or Picasso's violins.

This is all the more apparent because Marquet, perhaps for the first time in the history of the urban landscape, resolutely rejects any indication of time. This too is an example of artistic autonomy. The city is essentially presented as something atemporal, where time is conveyed only by the sum of artistic devices. It — time — is not in the motifs, but in the essence of the art, in the painter's individuality.

Yet in the complex system of Marquet's vision, the eternal values of classical art can also constantly be detected. Balance and harmony never disappear either from his perception or from the medium used to record that perception on canvas. Of course, it is not all that difficult to distinguish the carriages from the cars in his paintings, but the essence lies elsewhere. In Marquet's landscapes there is frequently no evidence of time at all: the sky, the trees, the old houses — things that have barely changed for the past two hundred years. Nonetheless, no-one looking at his pictures could ever imagine that they were created in some other century.

Marquet saw the world not only as an artist of the modern age, but also simply as a man of the twentieth century. He was accustomed to speed, to instantaneous changes of impressions, a painter striving to express this changing view on canvas. He saw the world as someone familiar with the metamorphoses of perception presented to art by the invention of the locomotive and the internal combustion engine. Yet at the same time he perceived reality as an artist who had not forgotten the eternal values of classical art. That is the origin not only of Marquet's customary sense of balance and harmony, but also the constant (very deeply concealed) state of hidden escapism: flight from easy complexity into a world of barely attainable simplicity. ("People need it more than anything, but the complicated is more understandable to them," Pasternak wrote about "unprecedented simplicity"). At an early age Marquet found his idiom and chose his main theme, which he then never changed. Usually this assertion is presented in an exclusively positive light. Indeed, an artist of his calibre hardly needs defending. It has already been stated that in terms of style he almost did not evolve at all. There is no doubt that this was a distinctive combination of staunch conservatism, loyalty to the classic conceptions and a certain degree of conscious isolationism. It was not only

69

the tragic life of the twentieth century that passed Marquet by: there were several artists who created masterpieces only indirectly reacting to contemporary currents — Cézanne yet again provides an example. Marquet also distanced himself almost entirely from changes in art; he did not enter into a dispute, nor a dialogue with them, nor indeed, apparently, have any sort of contact with them.

This "Marquet phenomenon" at a time of fervent mutual influences (Fauvism, the Parisian school, the emergence of abstract art, surrealism, and so on) can, of course, be regarded with delight or with regret, but it cannot be overlooked. A poet and hermit, he became, as it were, the guardian of enduring values in a changing world. Even so, changes, if you look at it that way, are also inherent to the twentieth century. And here we sense that peculiarity which makes Marquet's art both an exclusively valuable feature of our century and something in opposition to it.

For often it seems that Marquet was more sensitive to Space than to Time.

It was during his endless travels that a new vision, or at any rate new motifs, invaded his art while his discovery of the world continued. And the introduction of that new world into the structure of Marquet's calm, clear, concise artistic univer-secontinued also. This process was not affected either by age or by his marriage in 1923.

Marcelle Martinet, who became Marquet's wife and shared the rest of his life with him, was a writer. We are indebted to her for a romantic and accurate book about the artist's life, without which we would know nothing about this secretive man other than superficial events.

As time went on, the range of Marquet's travels expanded: Egypt, Spain, Romania and, in 1934, the Soviet Union. As well as Moscow and Leningrad, Marquet also visited the Ukraine and the Caucasus.

In 1931 Marquet moved to the Rue Dauphine which leads directly onto the Pont Neuf — in other words to the very centre of his beloved motifs. His fifth-storey windows afforded a panorama of the embankments and the Ile-de-la-Cité right as far as Notre Dame.

Once a French man of letters who had climbed to Honoré Daumier's studio on the Quai d'Anjou looked at the view of the Seine through the window and exclaimed: "What a Daumier!"

"What a Marquet!" you feel like constantly saying on the Parisian embankments.

From his windows on the Rue Dauphine the artist saw and painted what has now become the property of every observer endowed with any kind of refined vision. In his canvases Paris becomes grander and at the same time more poetic. One

1931
Oil on canvas. 65 x 50 cm.
Unsigned.
Museum of Fine Arts, Bordeaux.

70

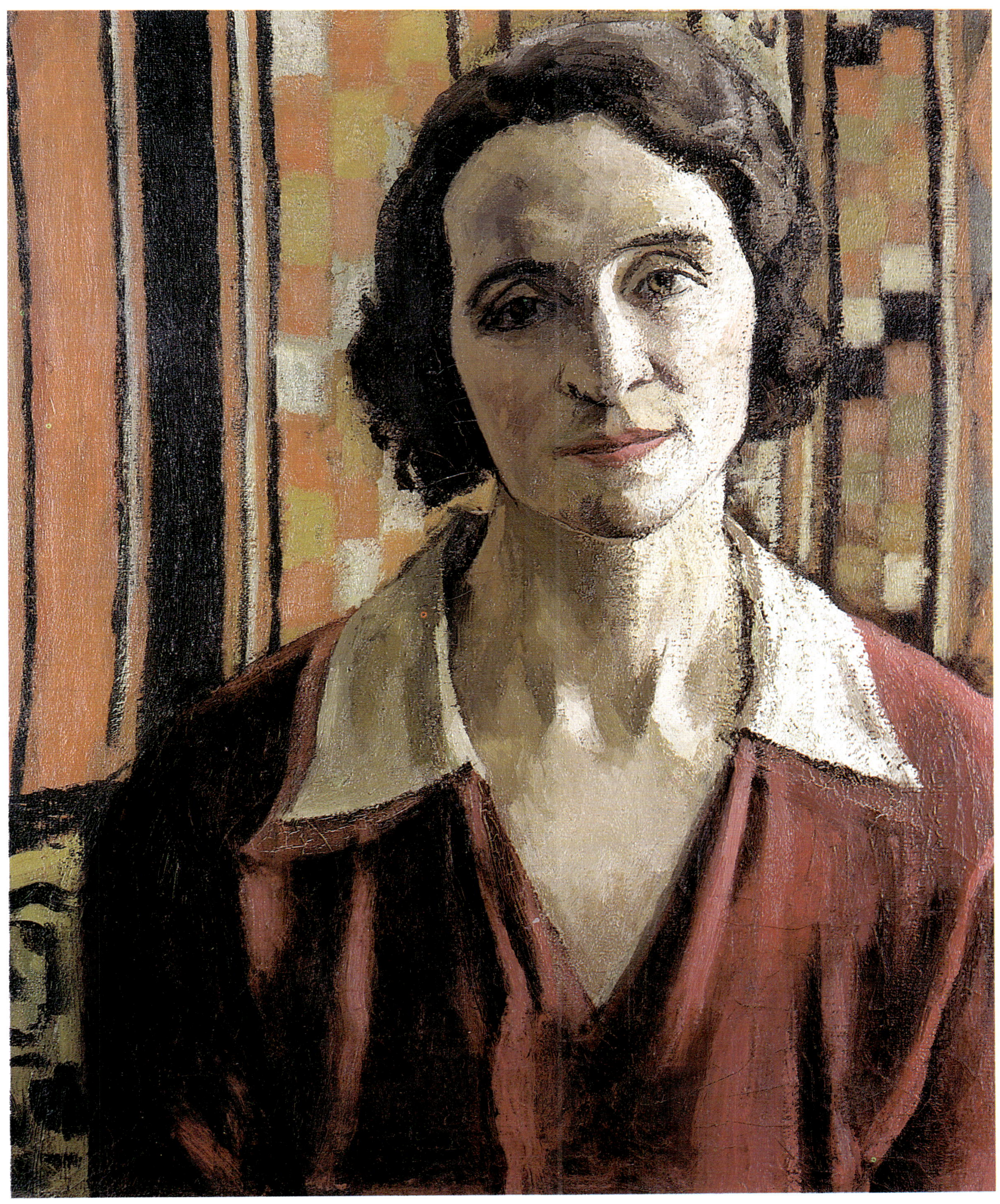

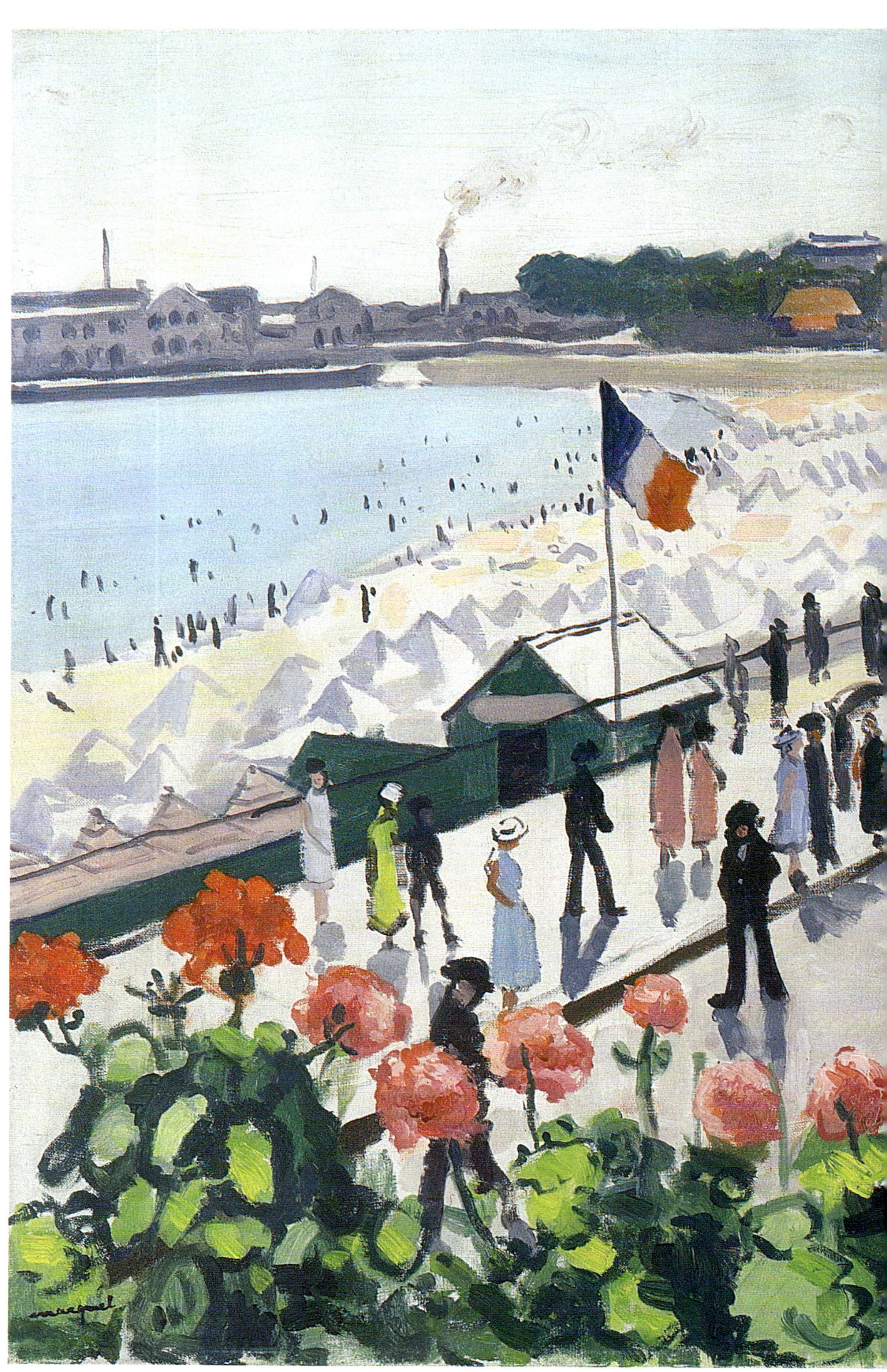

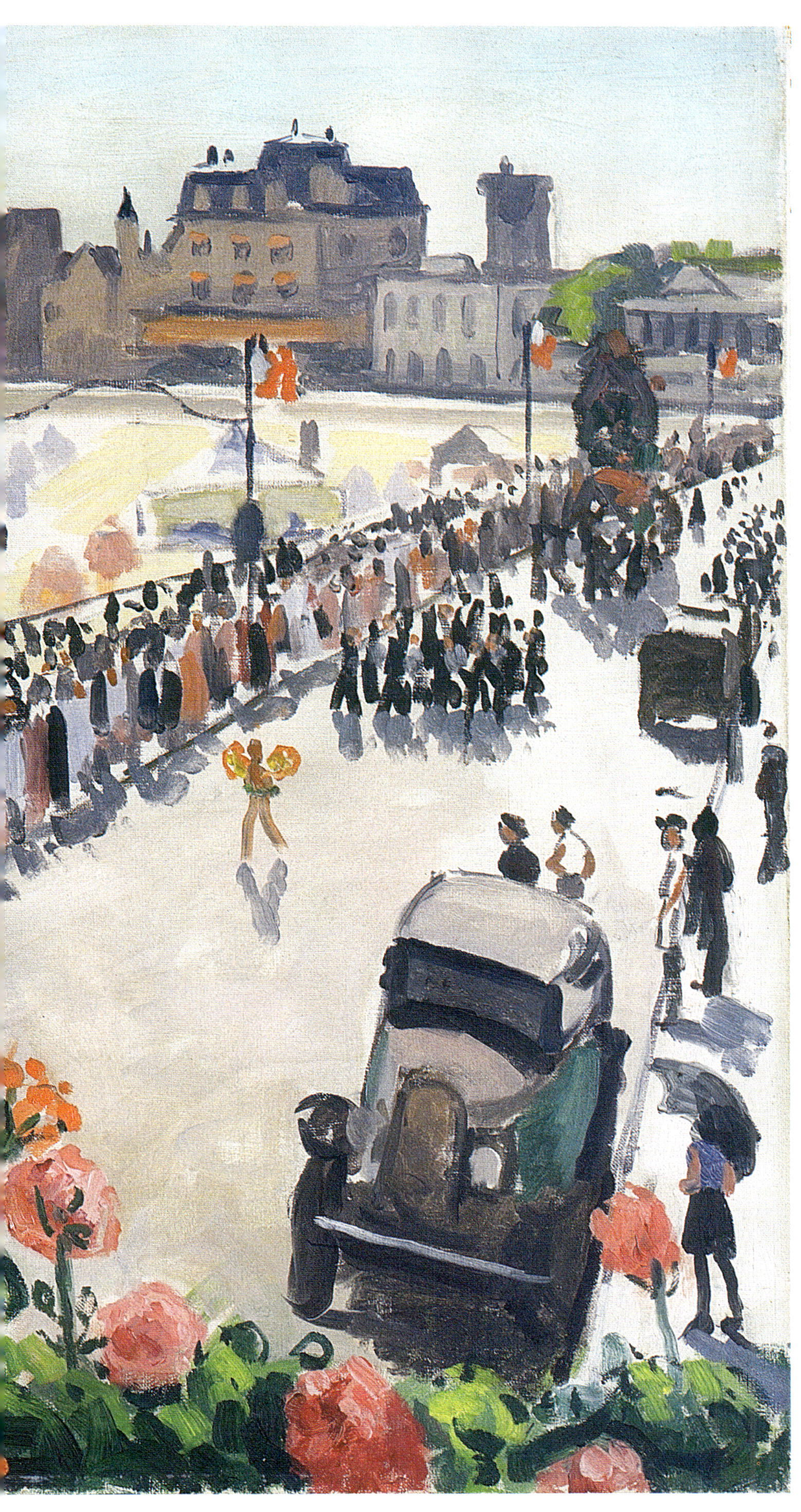

FESTIVAL AT THE SABLES D'OLONNE
1933
Oil on canvas. 65 x 81 cm.
Signed bottom left: _Marquet_.
Museum of Fine Arts, Bordeaux.

can suggest that, subconsciously perhaps, Marquet felt a growing alienation from the art that existed around him. The greatest masters of the twentieth century — Picasso, Matisse, Moore, Magritte, Dali — all lived in a completely different artistic space to Marquet. Their hands and imaginations were creating a tremendous experiment, constructing a new reality. Marquet was known, liked and respected; the doors of the galleries were open to him; his works sold readily. The little that is known about Marquet's life gives no grounds to suggest that the artist was saddened by his remoteness from what was being done by his famous peers. He was intolerant only towards himself, uninterested in honours, indeed he positively avoided and rejected them.

Nevertheless, from an objective viewpoint Marquet found himself playing a completely exceptional role — the only well-known artist of his time to have maintained his devotion to the figurative landscape. At the same time he remained wholly modern.

There is probably only one explanation for this: the trend established in his youth towards a maximum of simplicity, towards an exceptional concentration of colour and form, which attained such heights of tension that they took on a new force no longer linked to the environment of objects.

This great charge of "artistic energy" endows Marquet's paintings with surprising, reconciliatory significance. The world of objects is harmoniously combined with the striving inherent in contemporary art to express oneself in the language of visual formulae and interplays of colour.

In essence any art of note becomes such first and foremost because of its richness of content. We are not, of course, talking here about subject-matter, but about that boundless, mysterious individuality which can find expression equally in an abstract shape and in a verisimilar representation; about thought cast into a system of forms and colours. Marquet was me of who possess the striking ability to create a unique world of his own. And his was not a world of the imagination: in his paintings there was a recognizable reality without which he could not paint. The imagination lay only in the construction, the method of depiction. There too Marquet was an absolutely unique figure: there were no other artists in Europe of such significance who painted only from nature. A similar tendency did exist in the United States, but the work of American artists was constructed on principles diametrically opposed to Marquet's: on the poetic aspect of the illusory precision that was so important for a culture conscious of its own genesis.

The problem also lay in the fact that the public could hardly have appreciated the true degree of his independence. He had imitators who were nothing but salon artists. The main thing

FESTIVAL AT THE SABLES D'OLONNE
Detail.
Museum of Fine Arts, Bordeaux.

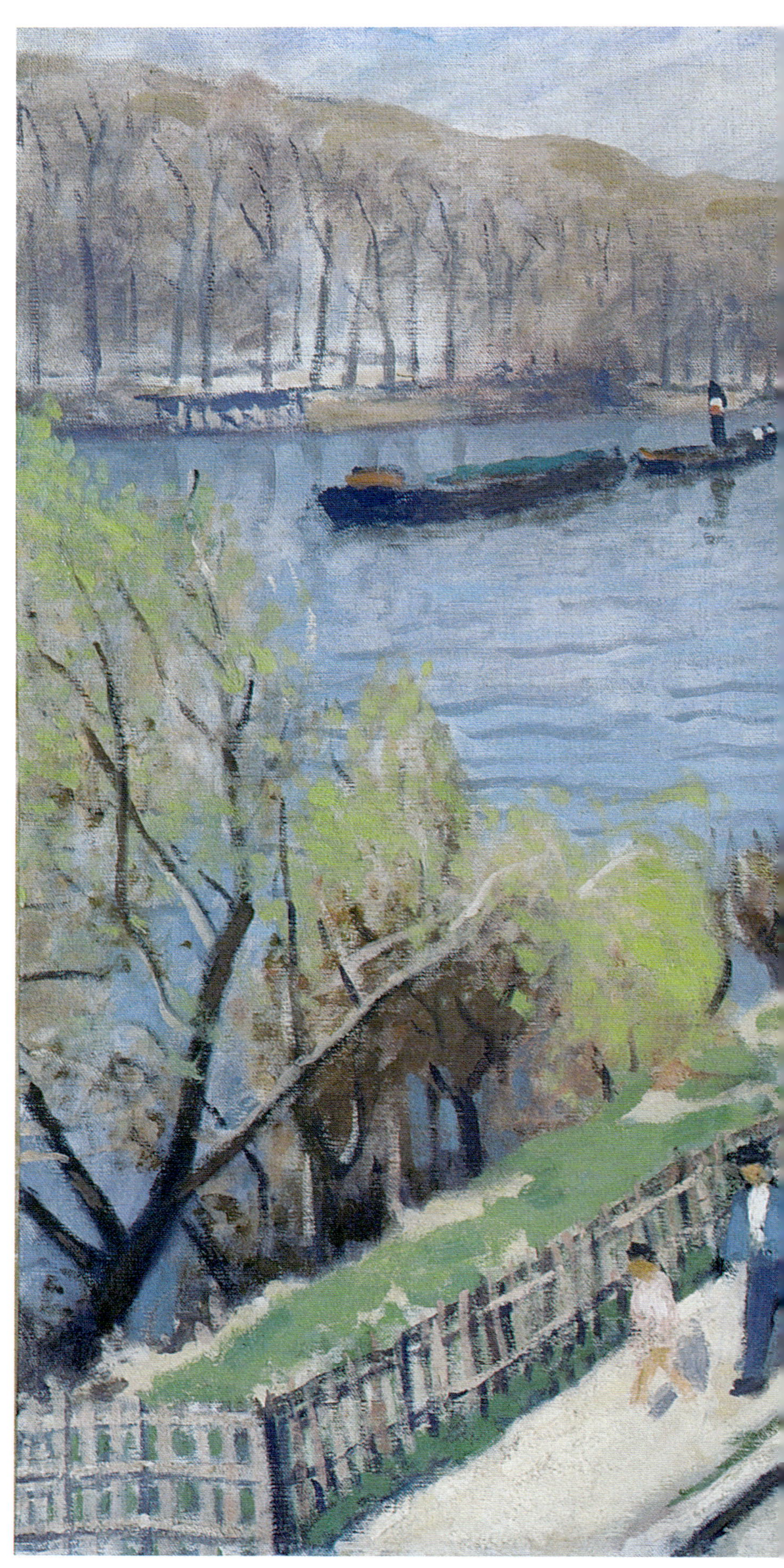

ROAD AT LA FRETTE
1945
Oil on canvas. 65 x 81 cm.
Signed bottom right: *Marquet*.
Museum of Fine Arts, Bordeaux.

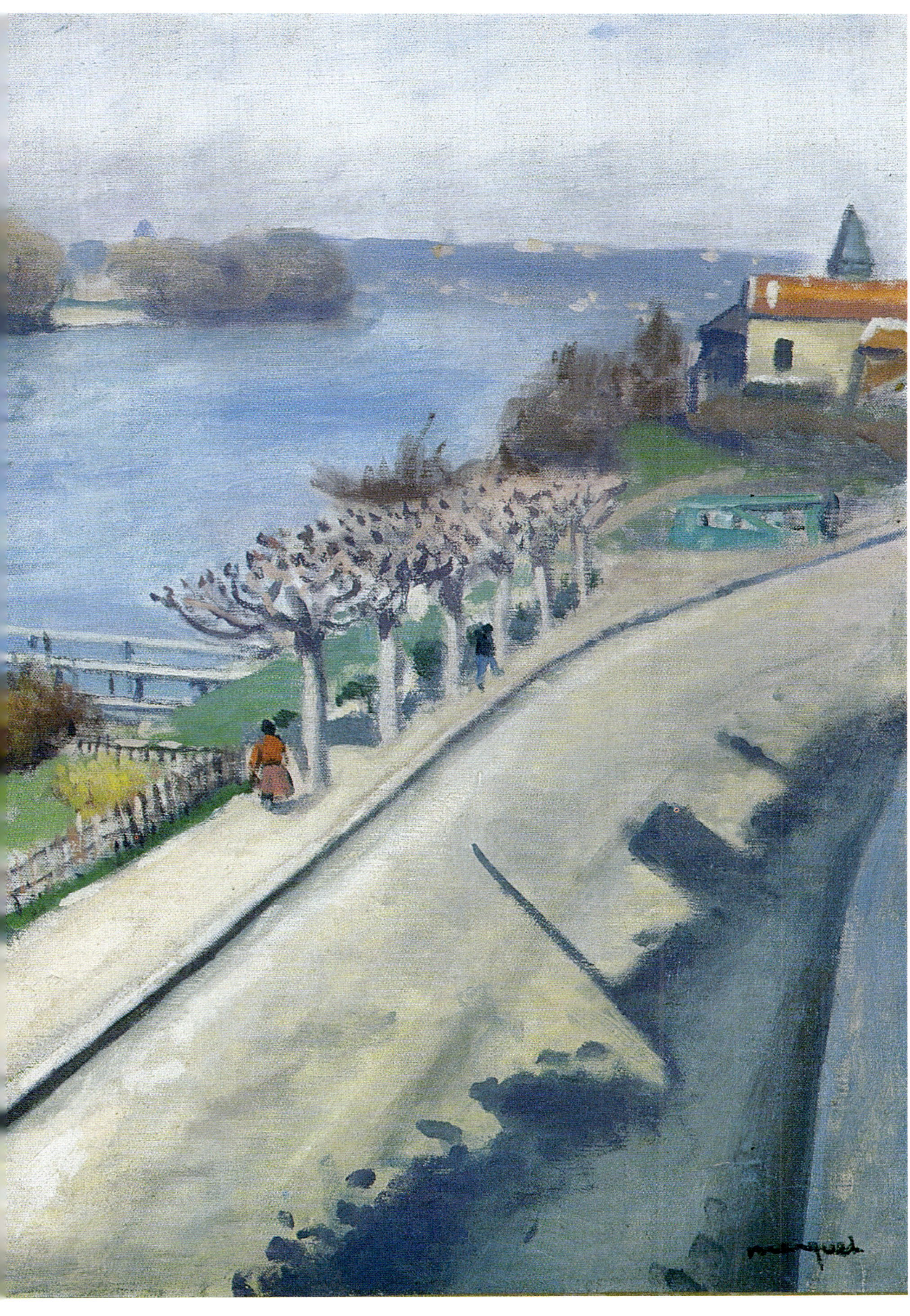

the average viewer saw in Marquet's works was not the stern nobility of his manner of painting, but simply the familiar beauty of Paris. But Marquet, to his own good fortune, was a man profoundly indifferent to both praise and abuse. There is nothing to suggest that he took his professional fate to heart. And perhaps there was no need.

Marquet possessed one more quality which was rare in the art of the modern period and which links him with a purely French tradition: he knew how to weave irony into his paintings, expressing it not in amusing scenes but in a sly, secretive play of lines — something which connects him with Callot, Watteau, Daumier and Guys. In his paintings the faces are indistinguishable, the people barely delineated. He more often depicts not a figure, but its motion, or even just a hint of that. And an astonishing "visual jollity" suddenly fills the canvas in the same way as the cinema screen "smiles" when the Little Tramp of whom Marquet was so fond appears on it.

For all his subtle individuality, for all his ability to see and express the world in a way profoundly his own, Marquet also remains a guardian of tradition, Both in his lifetime and with historical hindsight.

This is all the more apparent since the motifs in his works resolutely resisted change. He painted the city as a reality created by man, as a living organism breathing in unison. At times it is hard to make out its features, obscured by rain or fog, but Marquet's very manner of painting, bound forever to Paris, makes the viewer recognize the city. In the same way St Petersburg can be sensed in the very breath of Dostoyevsky's prose.

In the 1930s Marquet often painted the Pont Neuf. The view changed with the light and the time of the year. It can be remote and formal, it can be intimate like a long-lived-in room. The city as Marquet presents it seems alive: the bridge is thrown across the Seine with the naturalness of an extended arm, the movement of the carriages is like the circulation of the blood. Shapes softly, yet energetically flow into one another. The landscape undoubtedly possesses a striking visual "musculature".

Even so, Marquet sometimes tried his hand at effects that were unusual for him. In 1937, for example, he painted nocturnal Paris in *The Pont Neuf by Night* (Museum of Modern Art, Paris) — an astonishing carnival of lights strewn about the spectral urban darkness: streetlamps, lighted windows, speeding car headlights and reflections trembling on the water and the black asphalt. The darkness and the night sky are brilliantly painted; the gloom vibrates with erratic flashes, a vague emanation of light, the unextinguished urban glow.

In the late 1930s Marquet often visited La Frette, a little place outside Paris not far from Argenteuil of Impressionist fame.

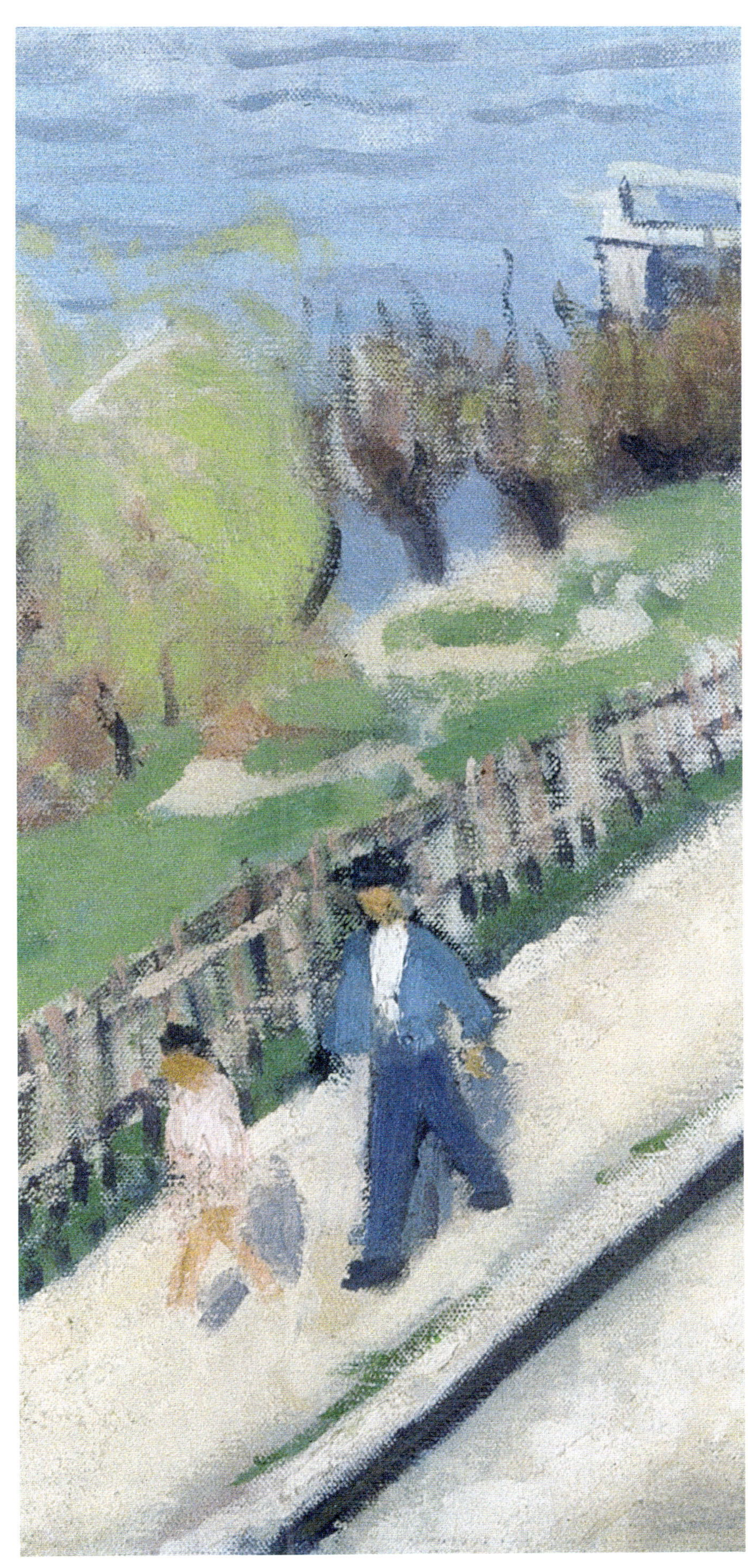

ROAD AT LA FRETTE
Detail.
Museum of Fine Arts, Bordeaux.

Later the artist bought a house there in which he stayed for months at a time. His wanderlust was a strong as ever. Only the war could force him to give up travelling.

He moved to Djenan-Sidi-Said in Algiers, where he stayed until the end of the war. Marquet was no warrior but his sense of decency and principle naturally made him a wholehearted anti-Fascist.

In Algeria he was involuntarily obliged to stay for a long period among landscapes that he had painted several times before, but under very different circumstances. Then the artist had been a visitor, now he was far away and cut off from the ashen

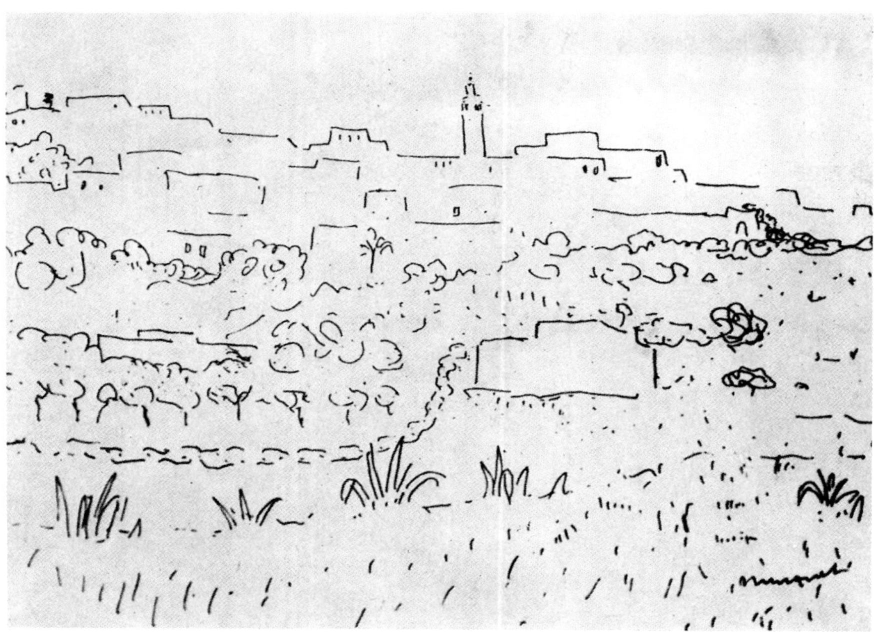

half-tones of Paris and his beloved studio on the Rue Dauphine. He never had either the ability or the desire to paint what was not in front of his eyes, and so the war years were for Marquet the African sun beating down and the sea which it seemed to have melted. And beyond the sea one can only guess at the France he had left behind.

The most characteristic and telling image of that time is a canvas which was painted in his studio in Djenan-Sidi-Said: the door open onto a balcony shaded by a striped awning, the three-legged easel, thin, even somehow helpless, and beyond it the distant sea (*Easel and Striped Awning. The Balcony in Algiers*. 1945; Marcelle Marquet collection). This simple study from nature seems to be permeated with his homesickness, although there is always a danger of reading too much into a work with hindsight.

But Marquet really did feel a constant nostalgia. After all, he was cut off not only from his home, but from his favourite Parisian motifs, the mainstay of his work.

Remote from those urban impressions, Marquet was obliged to paint many landscapes in the most traditional meaning of

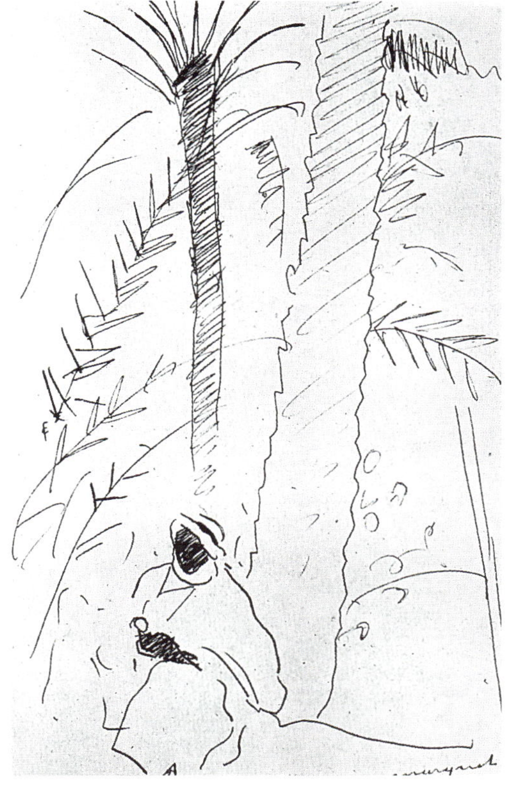

the word. He painted nature almost untouched by civilization. Yet, while in speaking of Marquet's urban landscapes we noted that people are barely denoted, in these far-from-urban landscapes, depictions of completely "wild" corners of nature, we nevertheless sense the presence of people. Houses, boats, gardens, the cranes and jetties of the port, carriages or distant lighthouses — not to mention plain, simple human figures — do not allow the beholder to forget that Marquet is painting *la terre des hommes*, "the inhabited Earth".

The artist's involuntary isolation caused him to look ever more attentively at what was around him. He painted his studio many times, but even in this small, poor room it is not difficult to sense the energetic movement of the view so characteristic of the artist and his strict, calm rhythms. For him the room in Algiers was a part of the universe where he could demonstrate the wonderful logic of spatial relations, light and objects. The interior was not a new field for Marquet. For all his complete and undoubted devotion to the landscape, Marquet would turn his hand to any other motifs, consistently avoiding only one thing: the composed picture. He always painted from nature, often simply from an impression, from a hasty jotting, but never ever invented. From his early days — we might recall the Hermitage's *Milliners* of 1901 — he frequently painted figures in interiors. At times these paintings are in the nature of portraits, but they never feature events, something which is true of all the artist's work.

He painted everything he saw around him: a window open onto the garden shaded by shutters; the garden of his house, small, but luxurious in the southern way. He drew and worked

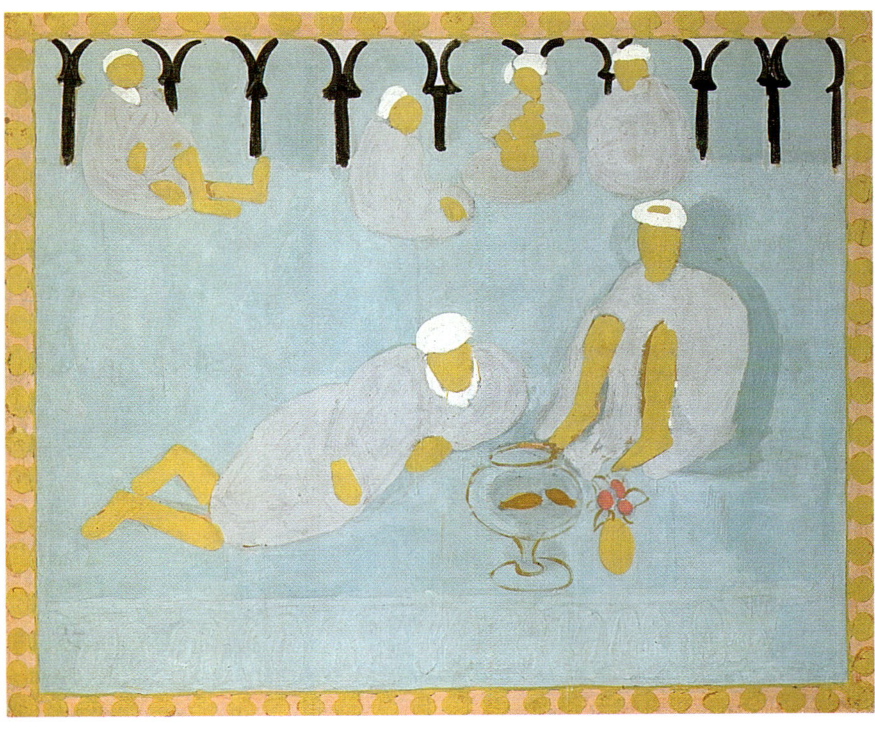

Henri Matisse.
Arab Coffehouse.
1912-1913.

in watercolour. He spent his time actively, although the gnaw-
ing worry of the war years and increasing health problems
constantly interfered with Marquet's inherent calm, steady
optimism. In 1945, as soon as it became possible, Marquet
returned to Paris and the Rue Dauphine. He was fortunate
to find his studio intact, even the tiles in the bathroom which
he had painted himself had survived and the view from the
window was still the same.

Marquet kept out of political disputes. His life seems to
have passed at some remove from social strife. But the war,
involvement in the Resistance, the general enthusiasm and
the euphoria of liberation — the whole experience introduced
into Marquet's reclusive life a naive, lofty kind of animation
typical of French liberal-minded intellectuals.

In his memoirs Ilya Ehrenburg recorded something Marquet
had told him in 1946: "Over the course of the war I came to
understand a lot. The Communists are right... It's terrible that
many people haven't understood anything and want to turn
everything back..." Madame Marquet recollected the artist
saying that he now knew "what must be said 'no' to." Marquet
had acquired a new perception of the place of art, or at any
rate of the artist personally, in the social struggle. Together
with Picasso and Matisse he became actively involved in
organizing an exhibition of anti-Fascist artists.

But, as before, Marquet shuned any form of official activity
and refused point blank to stand for membership of the Insti-
tut de France, although he would certainly have been elected.
He also refused a second time (the first time had been in
1914) to accept membership of the Légion d'Honneur, this
time in the rank of Commander.

Neither age nor illness could make Marquet cease working.
He again applied himself to his long-loved motifs with the
delight of first discovery and in 1946 he painted an autumnal
landscape at La Frette. Again the pale Seine flows to the horizon, again the lumbering barge puffs smoke in the distance
and the washed-out reflections of the sparse trees stir on the
water. In this canvas, perhaps painted in a single session, one
can feel with especial intensity something that was always
characteristic of Marquet, but now became particularly noticeable — his artistry. In other words, that degree of mastery
where skill, experience and complete knowledge of all the
secrets of art endow each brushstroke with the appearance
of free, unconstrained improvisation. Marquet had always
been among those artists who were able to conceal the doubts
and searchings which led to a work with confident brushwork
and an energetic line. But now, in his declining years, every
stroke is absolutely free. It preserves the motion of the artist's
hand, leaving a visible record of the actual process of working,
not only giving the viewer a knowledge of the artist's technical

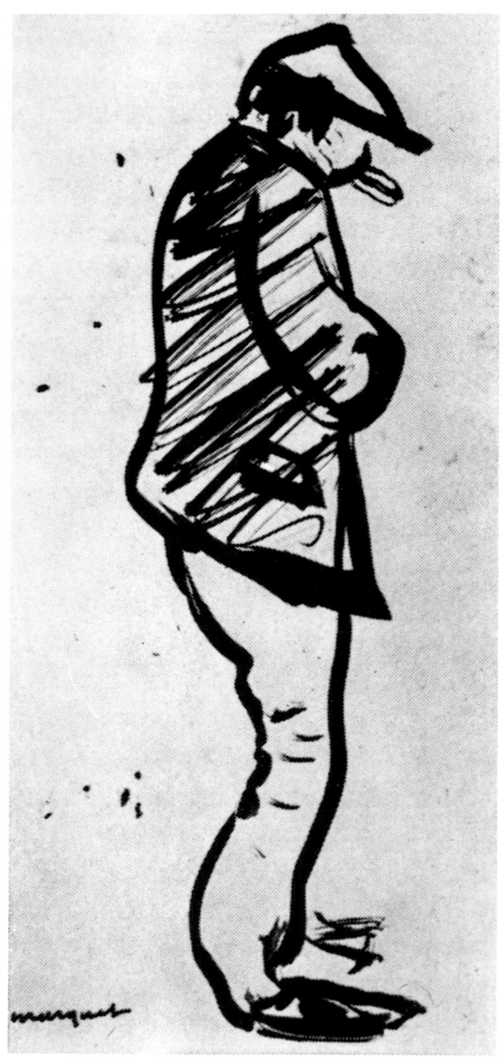

secrets, but also introducing him to the emotional atmosphere of creativity.

Marquet spent his last two years in his house at La Frette. Only when his health took a final turn for the worse did he return to Paris. He underwent a major operation, but sadly it was of little help. He continued painting to within days of the end, as long he could still manage to hold a brush.

Paris still generously revealed its beauty to Marquet, although by now the city was simply the view from his studio windows — the artist could no longer walk. The last painting, *The Quai de Conti in the Snow* (Museum of Fine Arts, Bordeaux) was created early in 1947: the old building with arcades on the corner of the Rue Dauphine and the Quai de Conti, the asphalt wet with melting snow, patches of snow remaining on the pavements, ledges and roofs of the cars, trees wreathed in mist and the Seine hidden in an opalescent fog. Little has changed on the embankment since that time. The building with the arcades is just as gloomy, blackened with the dirt of ages; the wrought-iron streetlamps are still there. And the perception of these places imbued in us by Marquet's painting has also endured: a sense of mournful spaciousness, the swiftly-moving perspectives of the embankment, a noble harmony in shades of grey.

Albert Marquet died on 14 June 1947.

Marquet's road in life may seem to have been a difficult one, since in period when European culture was marked by painful — at times obscure and morbid — searchings, bitter disappointments, a fashion for heaping abuse on others' efforts, and the appearance of new artistic systems with which it was hard for a follower of Poussin and Cézanne to come to terms, he chose the role of consistent guardian of tradition. Yet it could be that the difficulty is all in our own imagination.

Marquet said: "I cannot create more or differently." For some people remaining true to themselves is easy, the only possible course, for others it is a hard lot to be borne. What Marquet's knightly loyalty to his beliefs cost him is something no-one will ever know.

He did not attempt to preserve devices from the past which had long since lost their right to exist. He lacked many of the characteristics which might seem typical of an artist of the modern age: scepticism, and interest in the daunting secrets of the subconscious, abrupt changes of style, nihilism. He did not make life more complex, neither did he reduce it to a paradigm. Marquet grasped the simplicity, value and glorious significance of existence in the original sense. Possibly an integrity of this kind also led to the loss of certain things. But if Marquet's peers also strove after the same goals that he was seeking in the world he saw around him, then they went about it by far more devious and subtle routes.

Albert Marquet.
A Smoker.

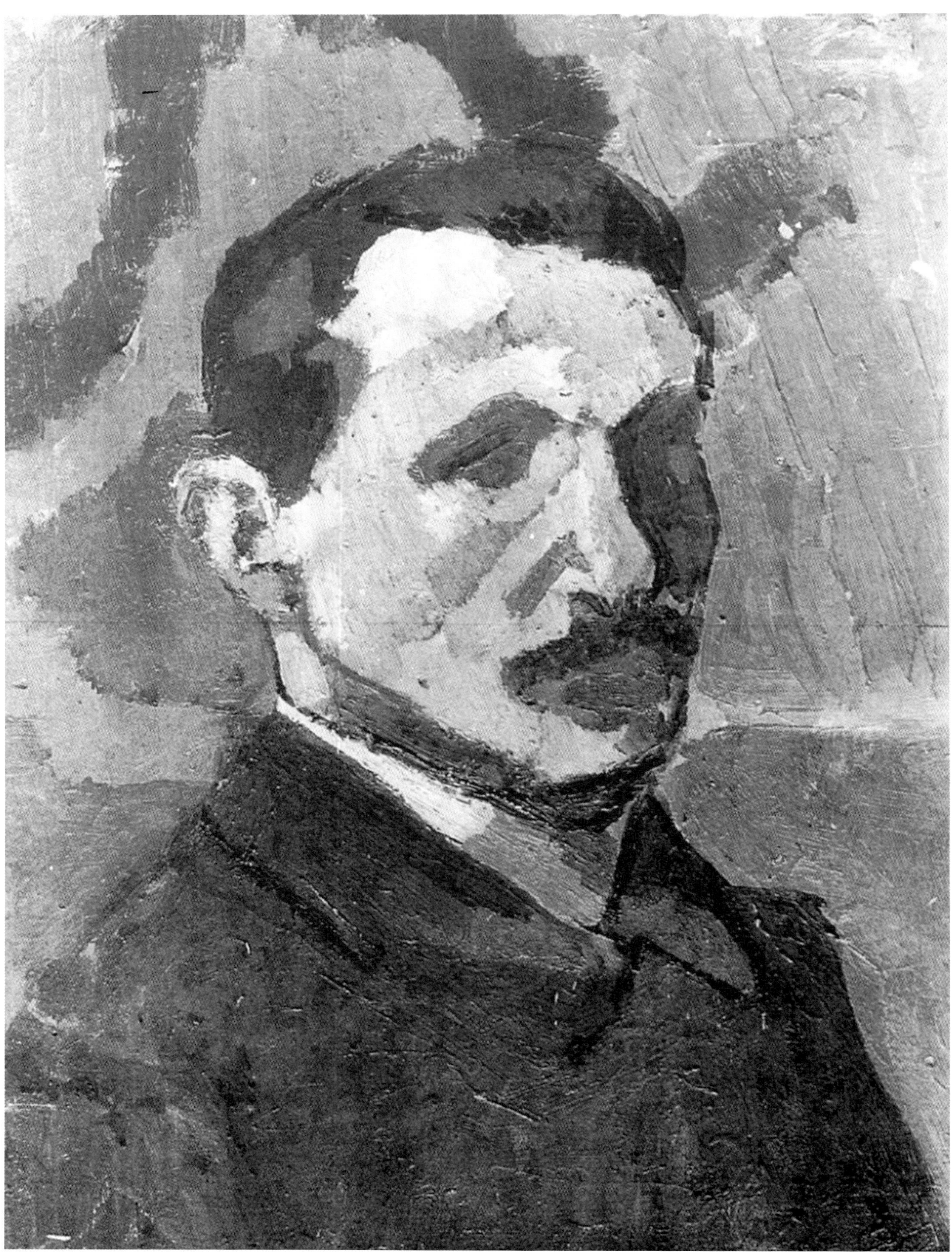

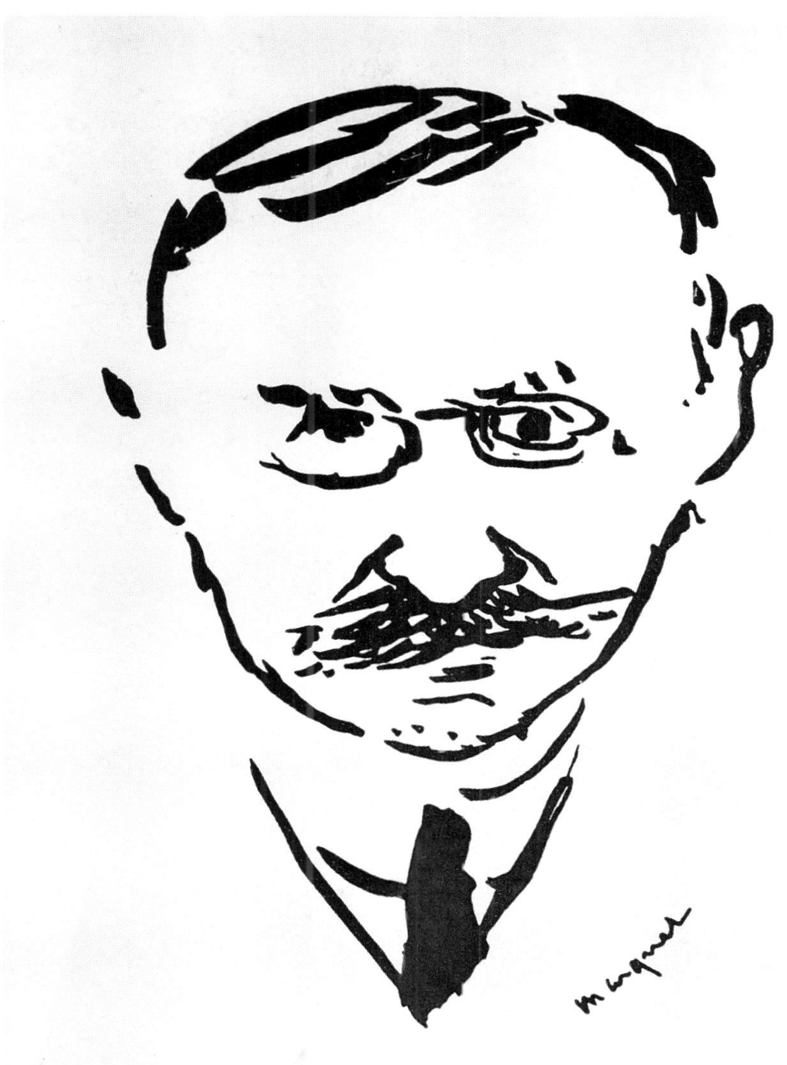

Marquet's links with the artistic experiments of the age remained deeply private and emerged only in the course of a complex dialogue, at times almost a polemic. Yet, on the other hand, Marquet was never alienated from his age.

Albert Marquet's unique "self" emerges not from his conflict with his era, but from his ability to both heed the age and to absorb its ambitions into his own painting, and, most significantly, from his demonstration that retaining one's inner stability and immutability of execution in an all-destroying tidal wave of changes is also a positive action, one of which only a strong artistic temperament is capable.

Marquet preserved his freedom.

The paradox of Marquet lies in his belonging more to the past and to the future than to the present. His art awaits a dispassion which has possibly not yet claimed it. But it also teaches people to appreciate precious pauses and thus to strive after that inspired peacefulness that was always so important for the artist himself.

Mikhail GUERMAN

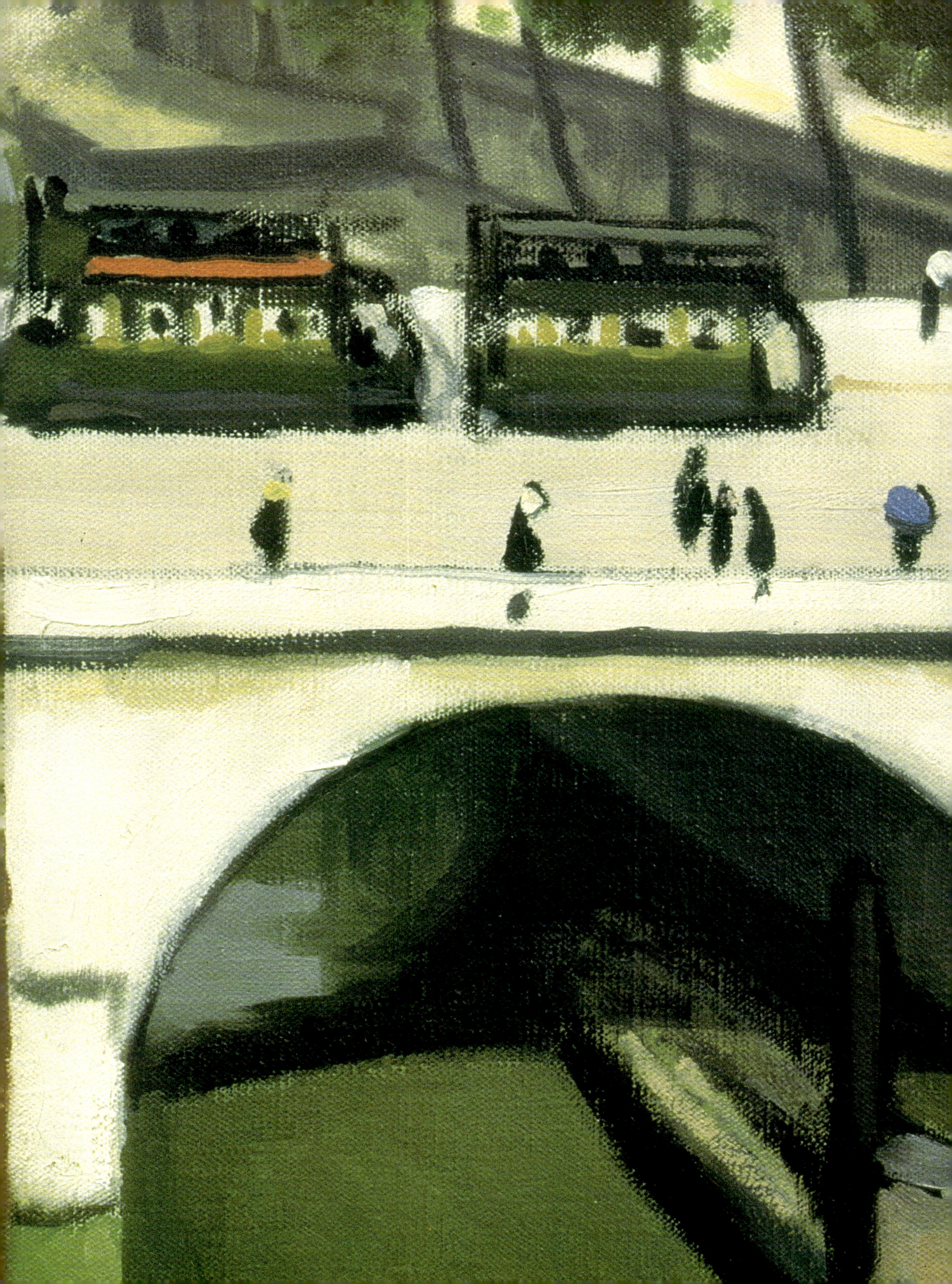

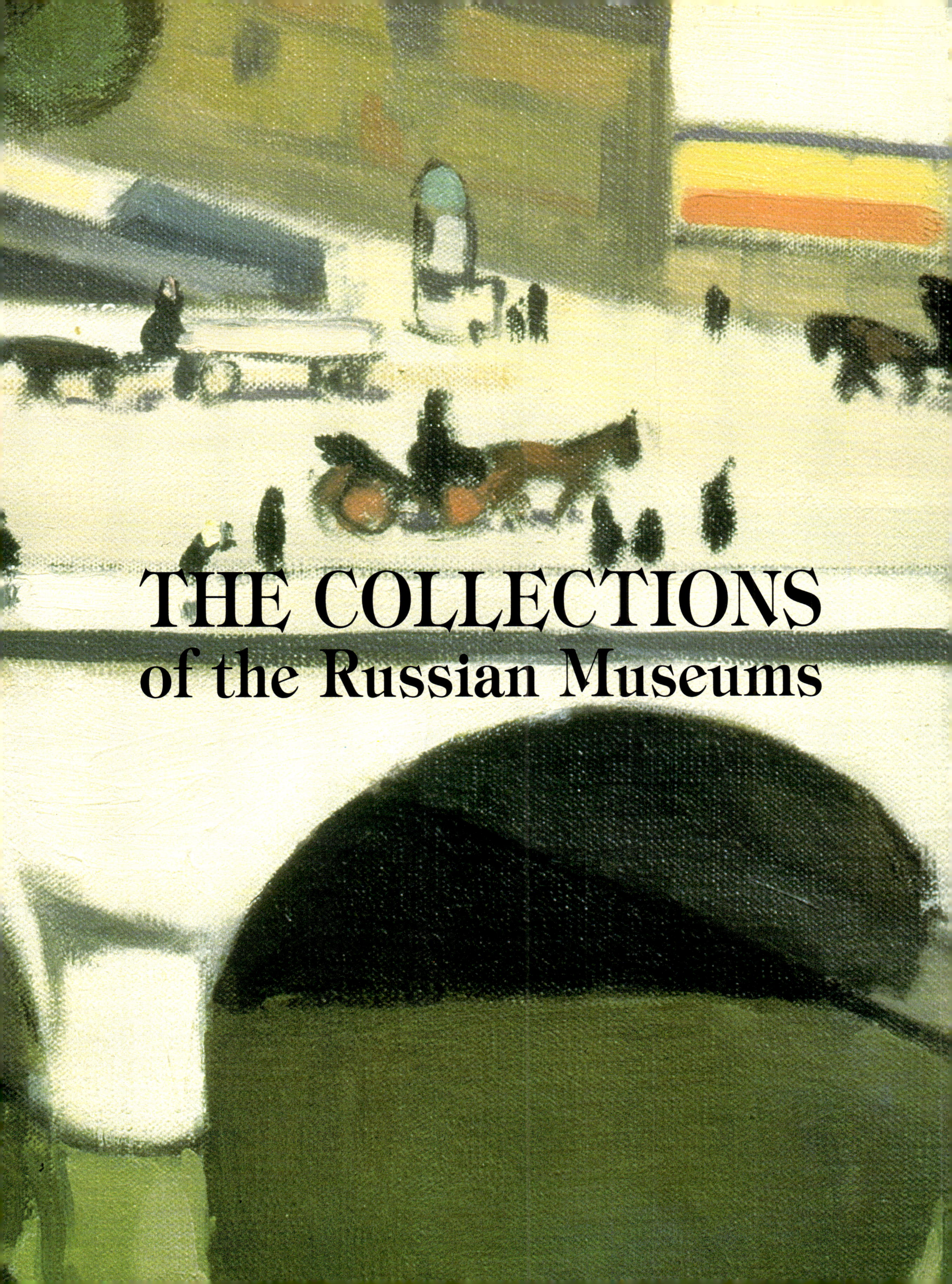

THE COLLECTIONS
of the Russian Museums

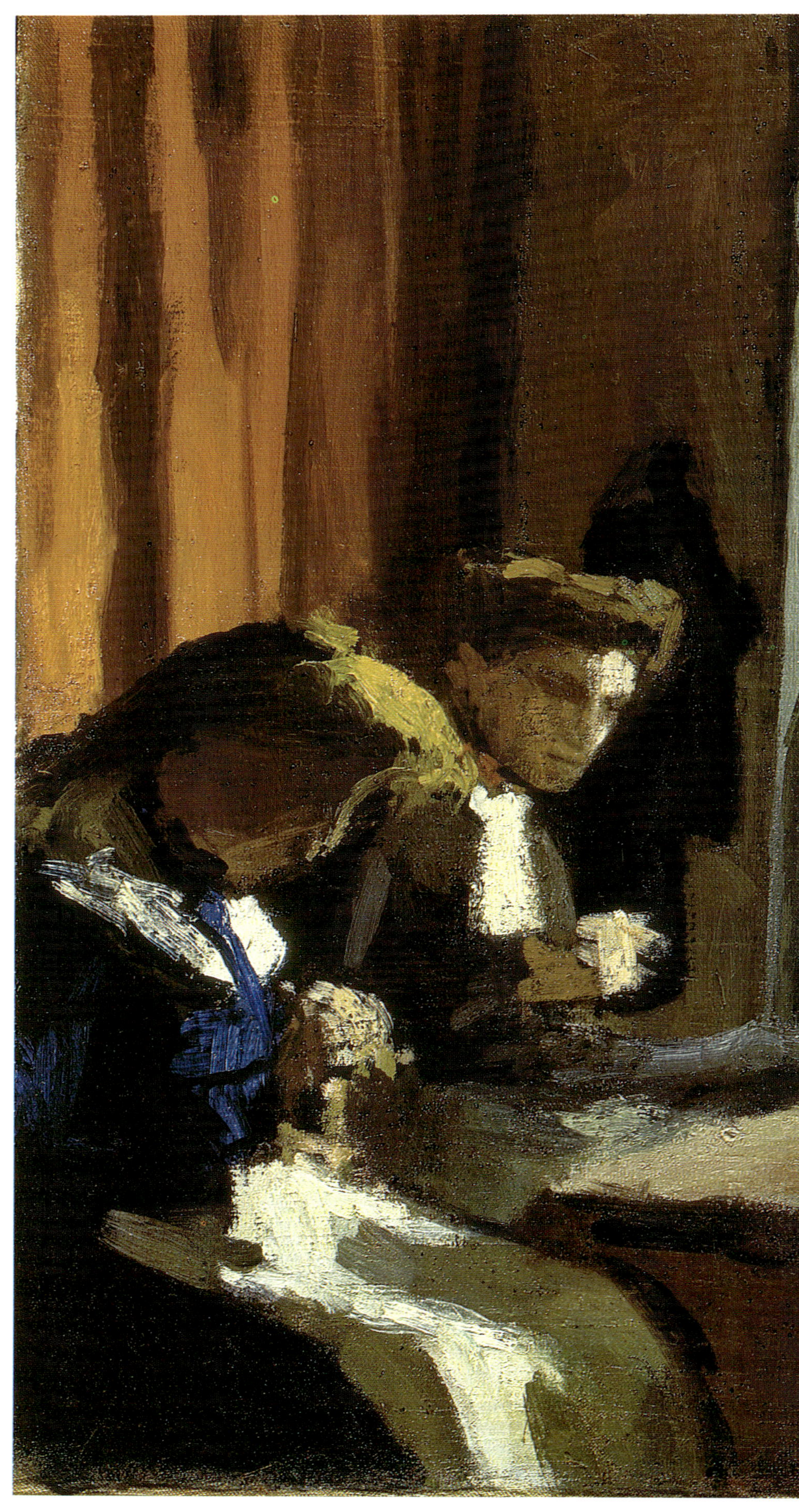

MILLINERS
1901
Oil on canvas. 50.5 x 61 cm.
Signed bottom right: *Marquet*.
Provenance: Galerie Eugène Drouet, Paris;
Sergei Shchukin collection, Moscow;
1918, Second Museum of Modern
Western Painting, Moscow;
1923, Museum of Modern Western Art,
Moscow;
from 1948, The Hermitage, St Petersburg.
Inventory No. 9030.

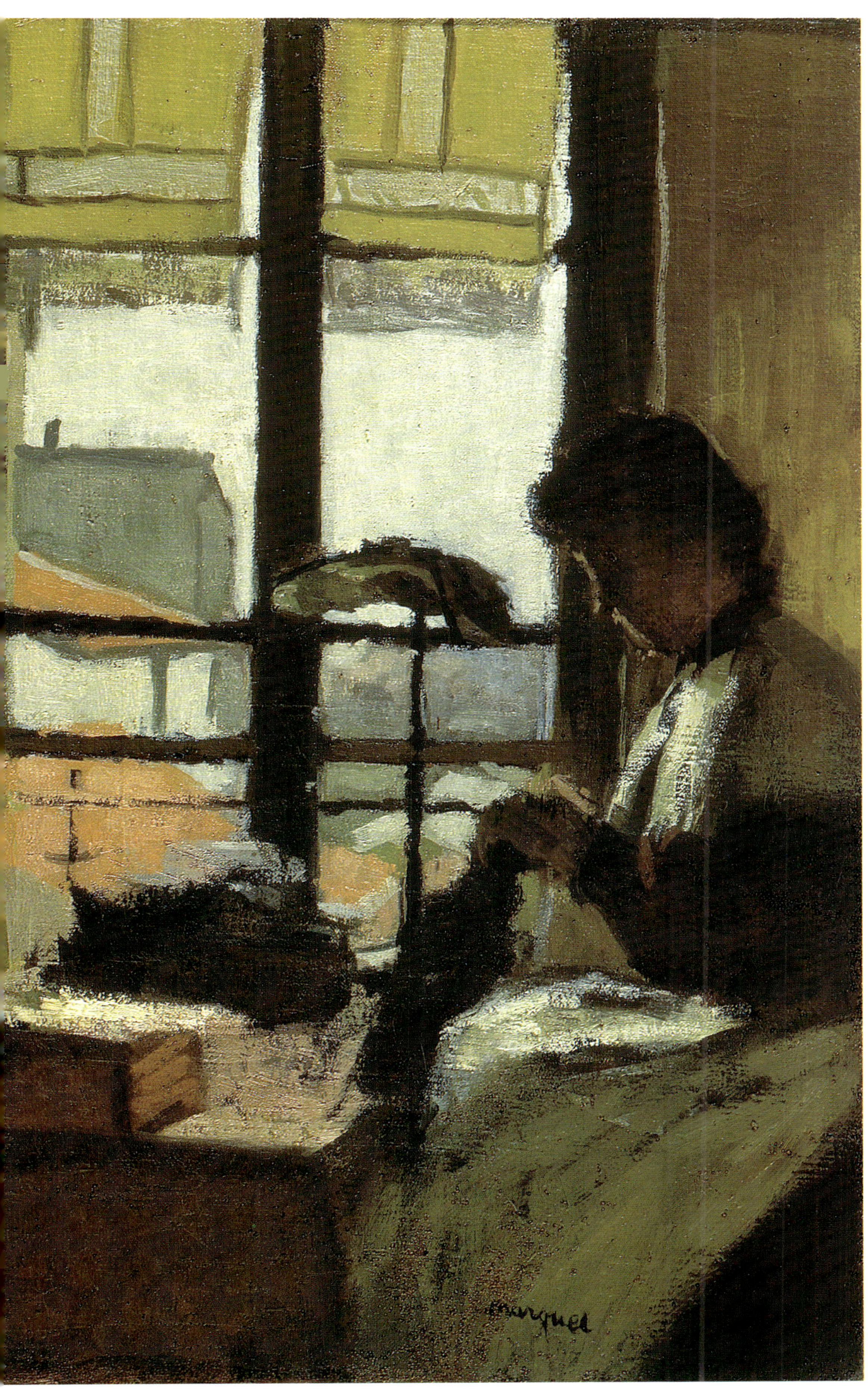

MILLINERS
Detail.
The Hermitage, St Petersburg.

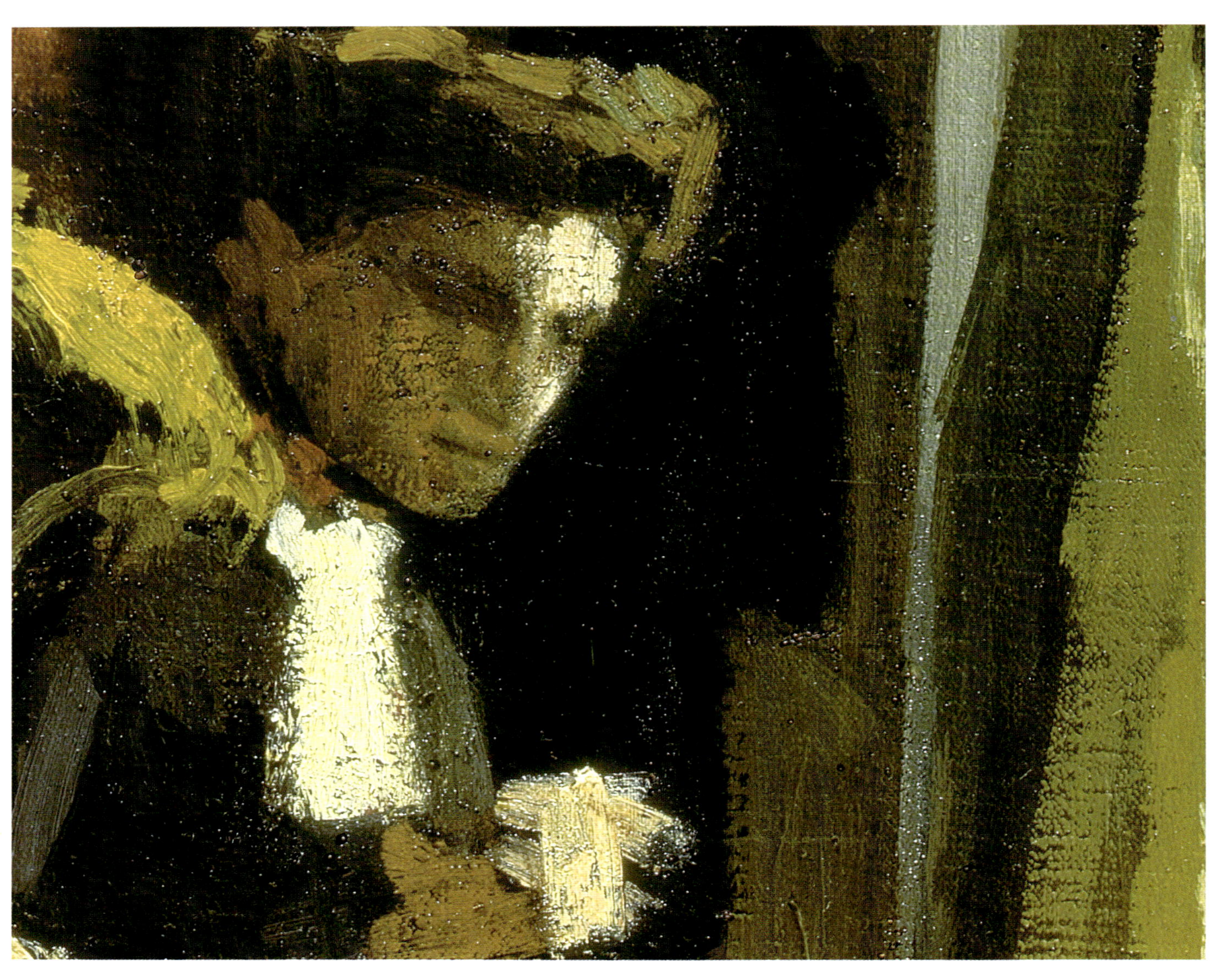

MILLINERS
Detail.
The Hermitage, St Petersburg.

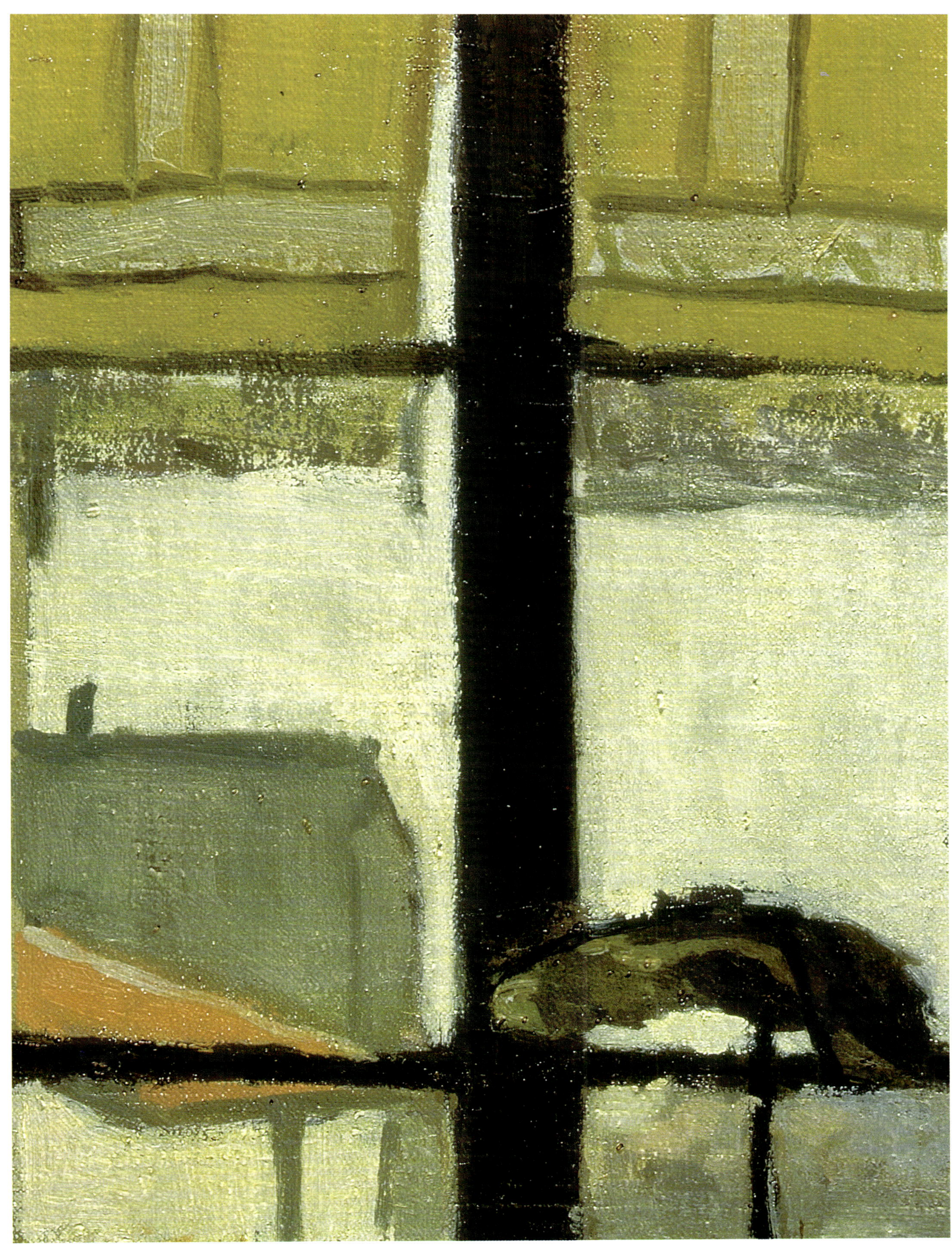

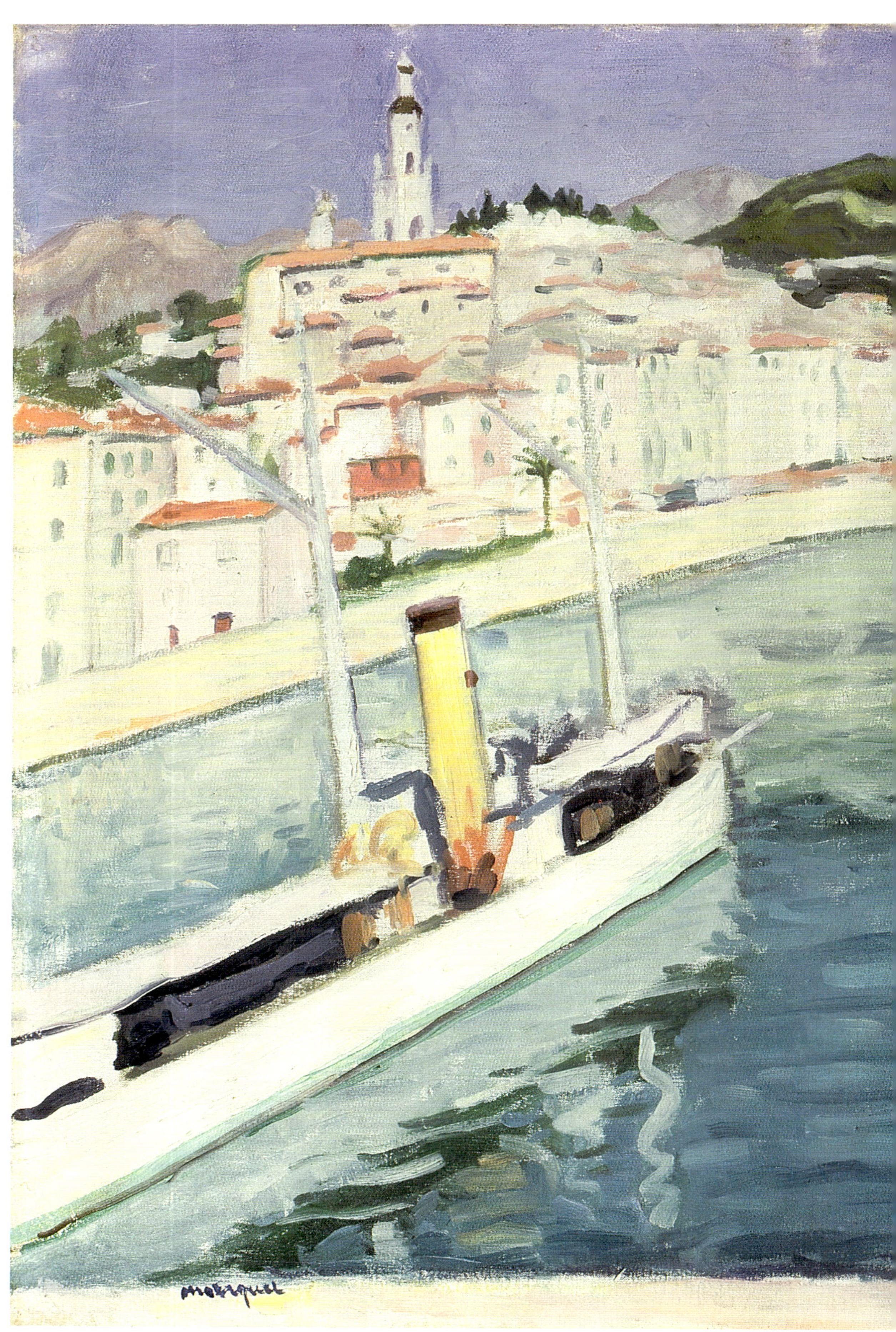

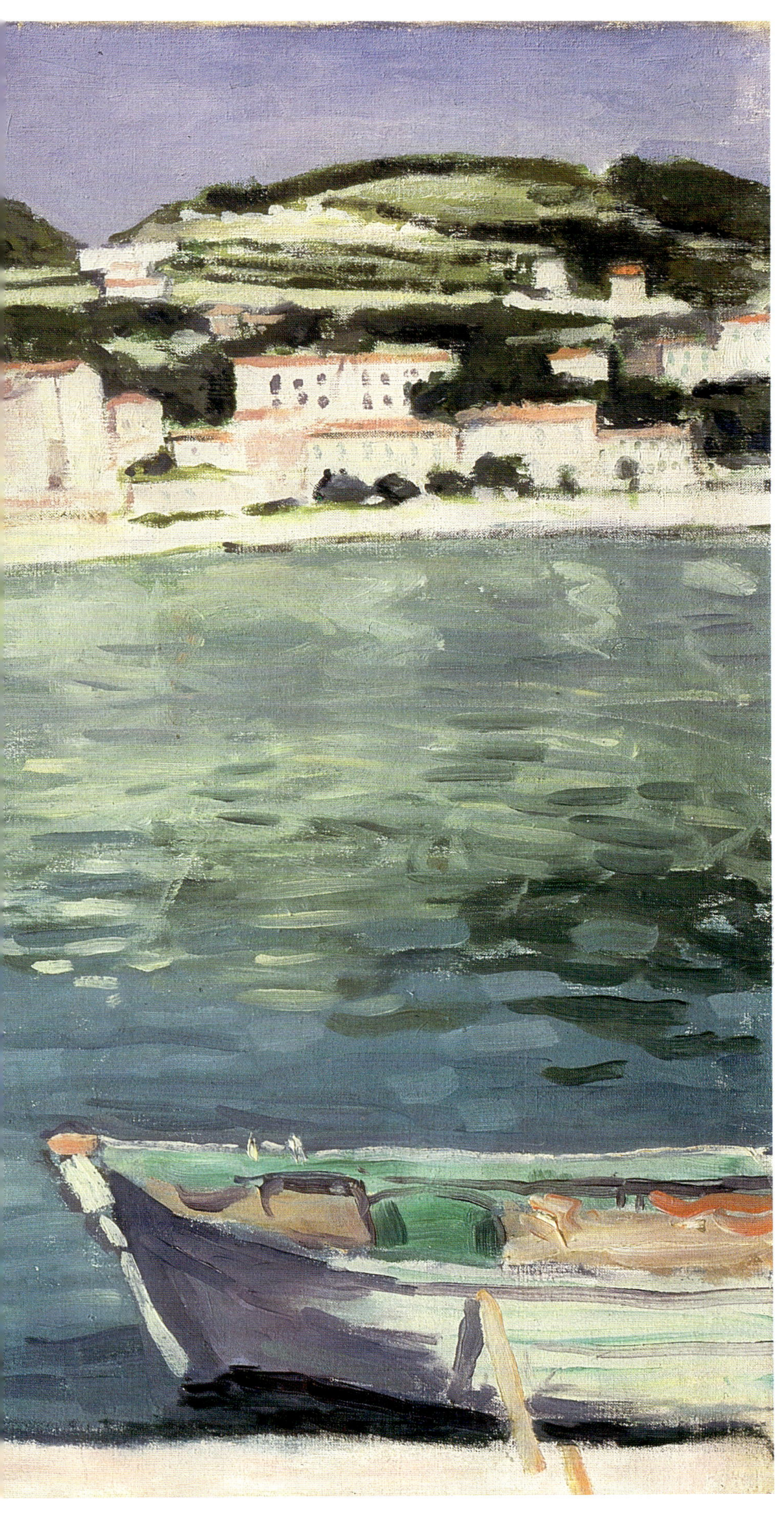

MENTON HARBOUR
1905
Oil on canvas. 65 x 81.5 cm.
Signed bottom left: *Marquet*.
Provenance:
Hans Haasen collection, Petrograd;
from 1921, The Hermitage, St Petersburg.
Inventory No. 4906.

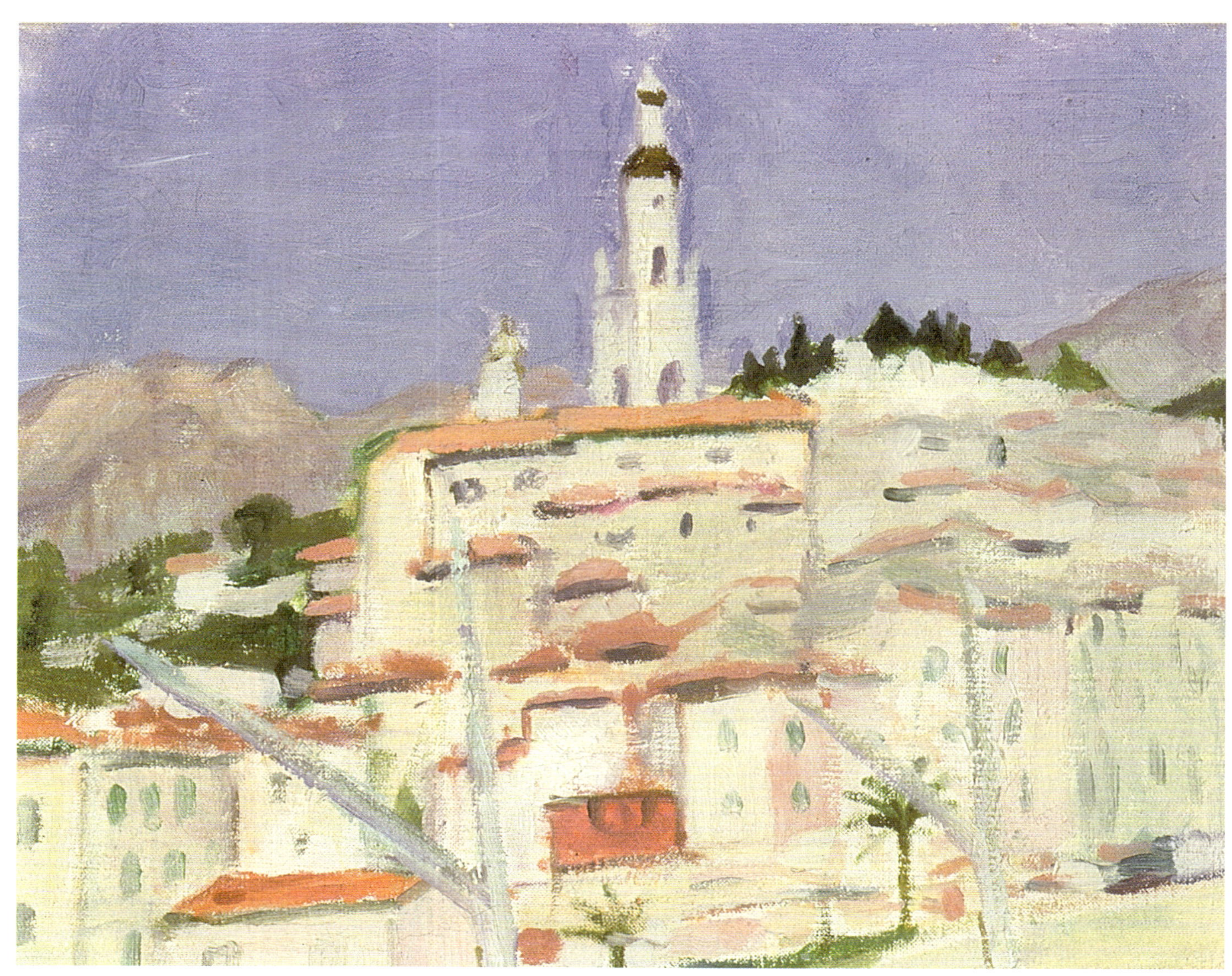

MENTON HARBOUR
Detail.
The Hermitage, St Petersburg.

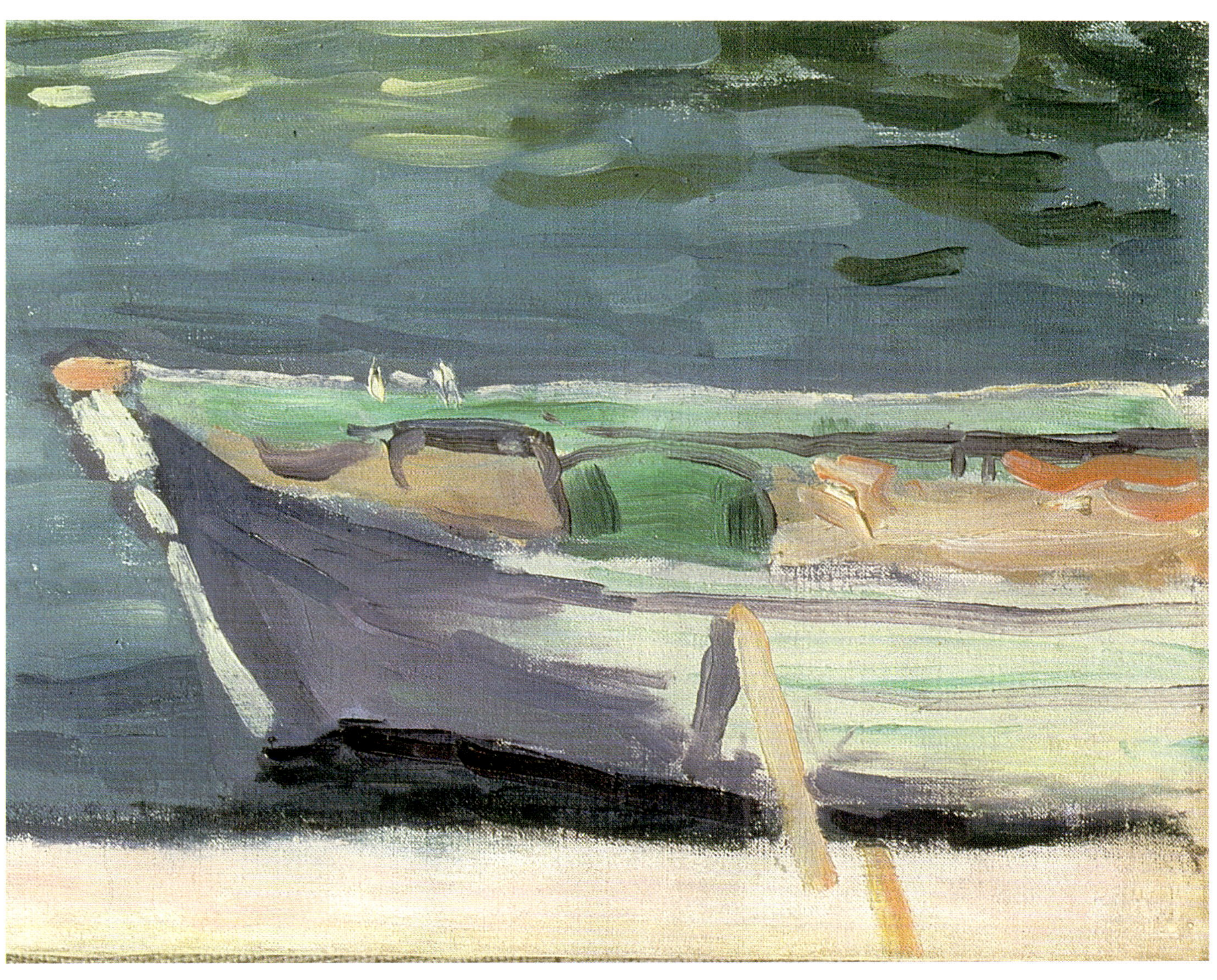

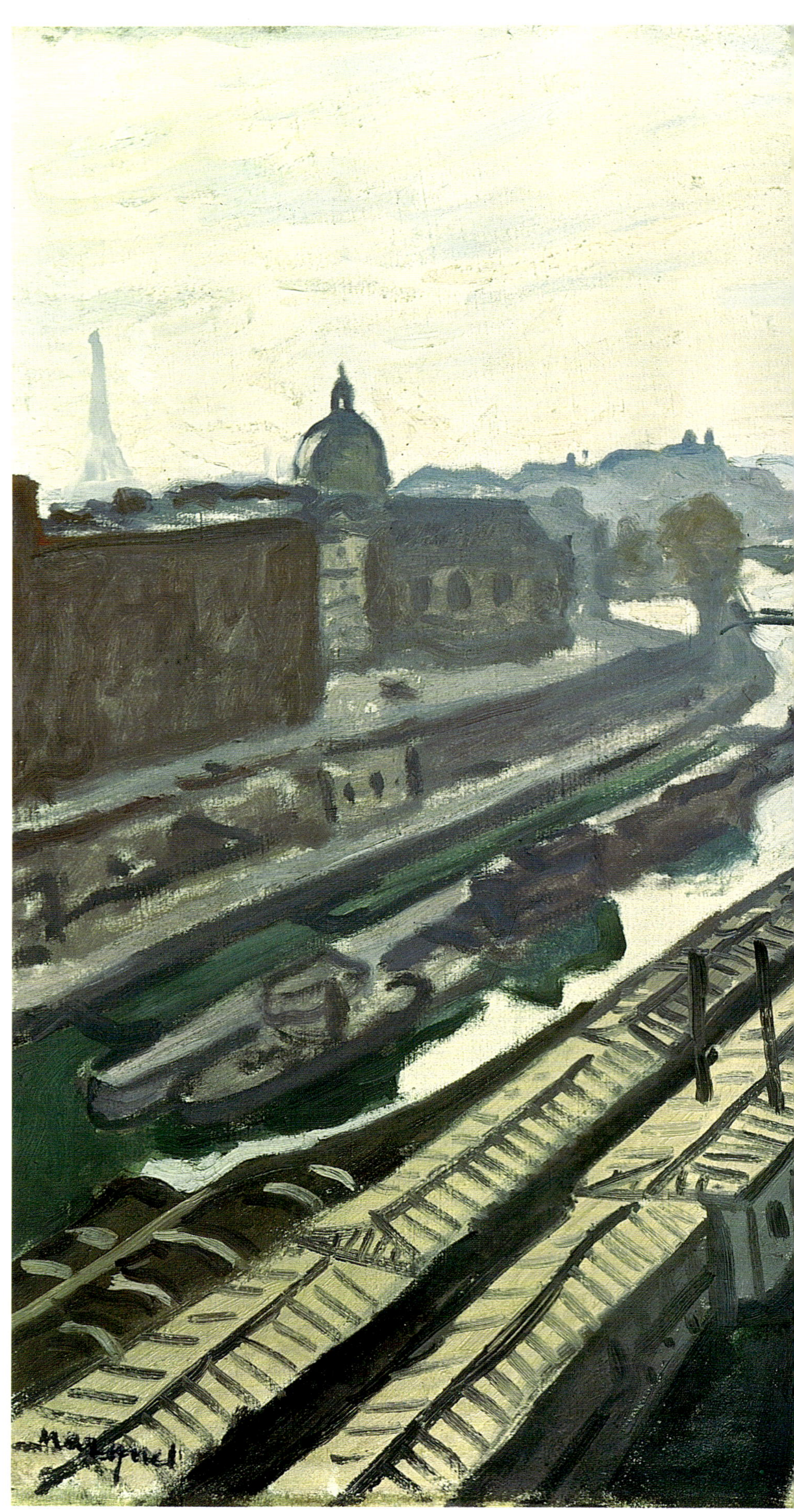

VIEW OF THE SEINE
AND THE MONUMENT TO HENRI IV
Ca. 1906
Oil on canvas. 65.5 x 81 cm.
Signed bottom left: *Marquet.*
Provenance: Galerie Eugène Drouet, Paris;
1908, Ivan Morozov collection, Moscow;
1918, Second Museum of Modern
Western Painting, Moscow;
1923, Museum of Modern Western Art,
Moscow;
from 1948, The Hermitage, St Petersburg.
Inventory No. 9151.

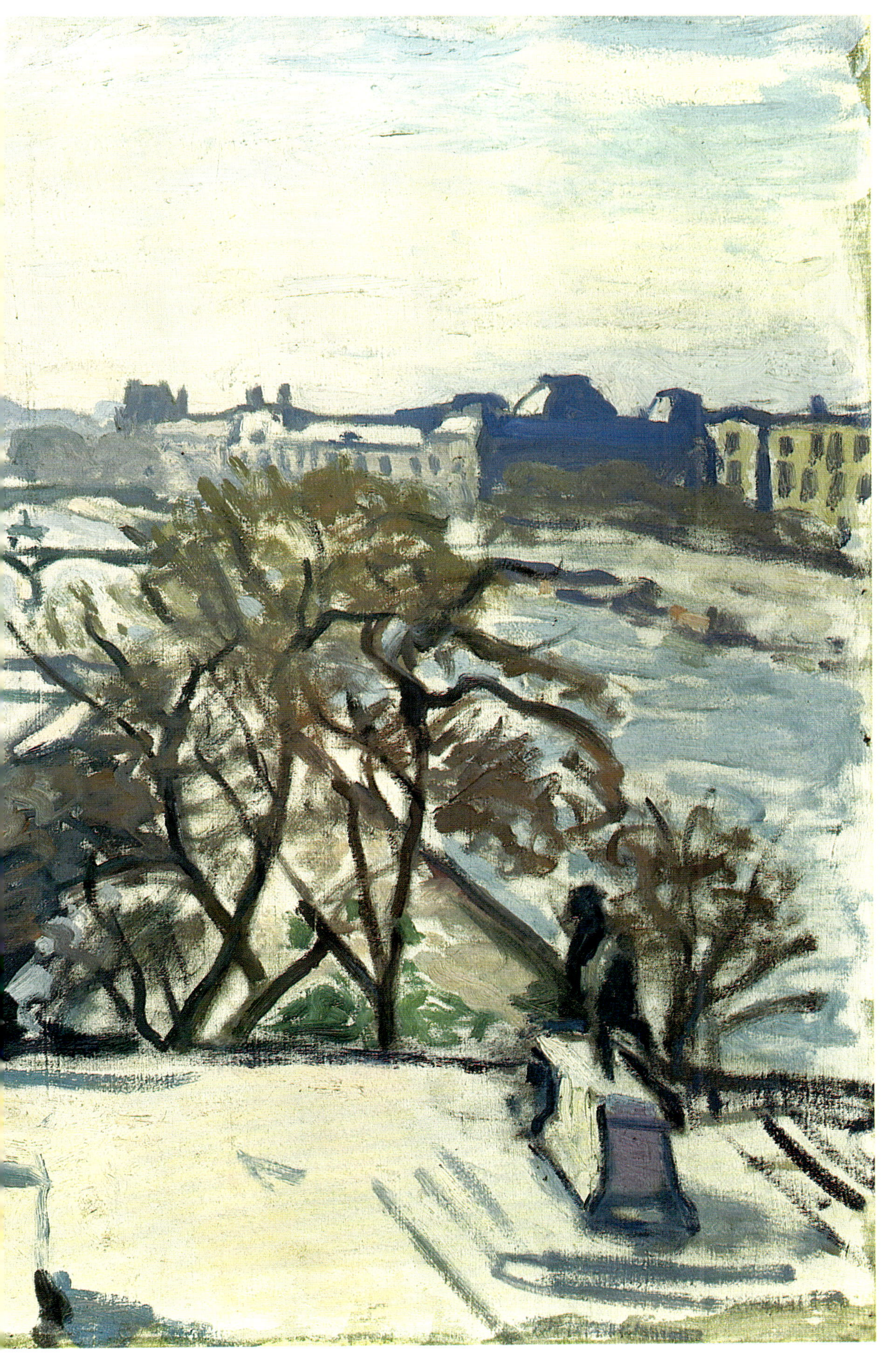

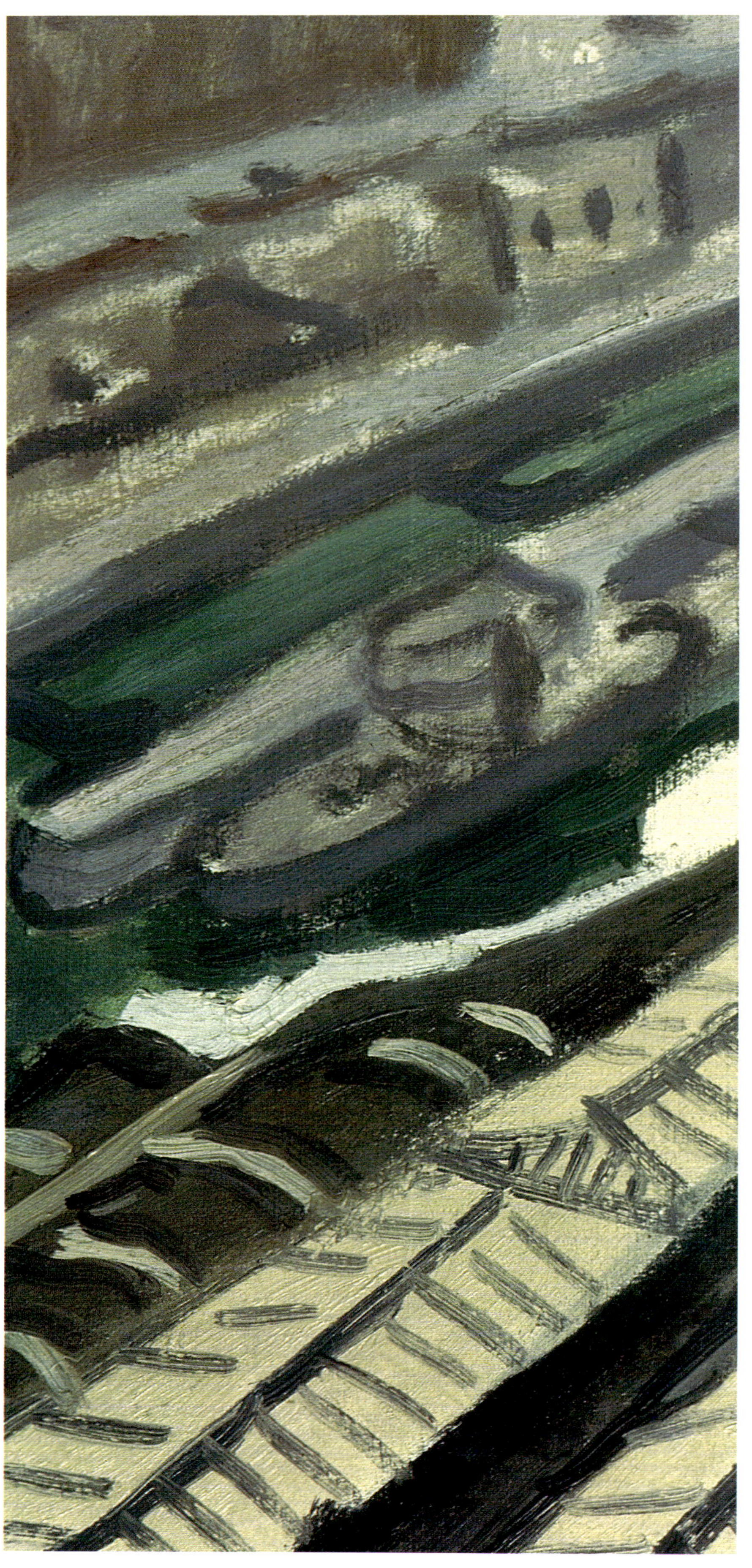

*VIEW OF THE SEINE
AND THE MONUMENT TO HENRI IV*
Detail.
The Hermitage, St Petersburg.

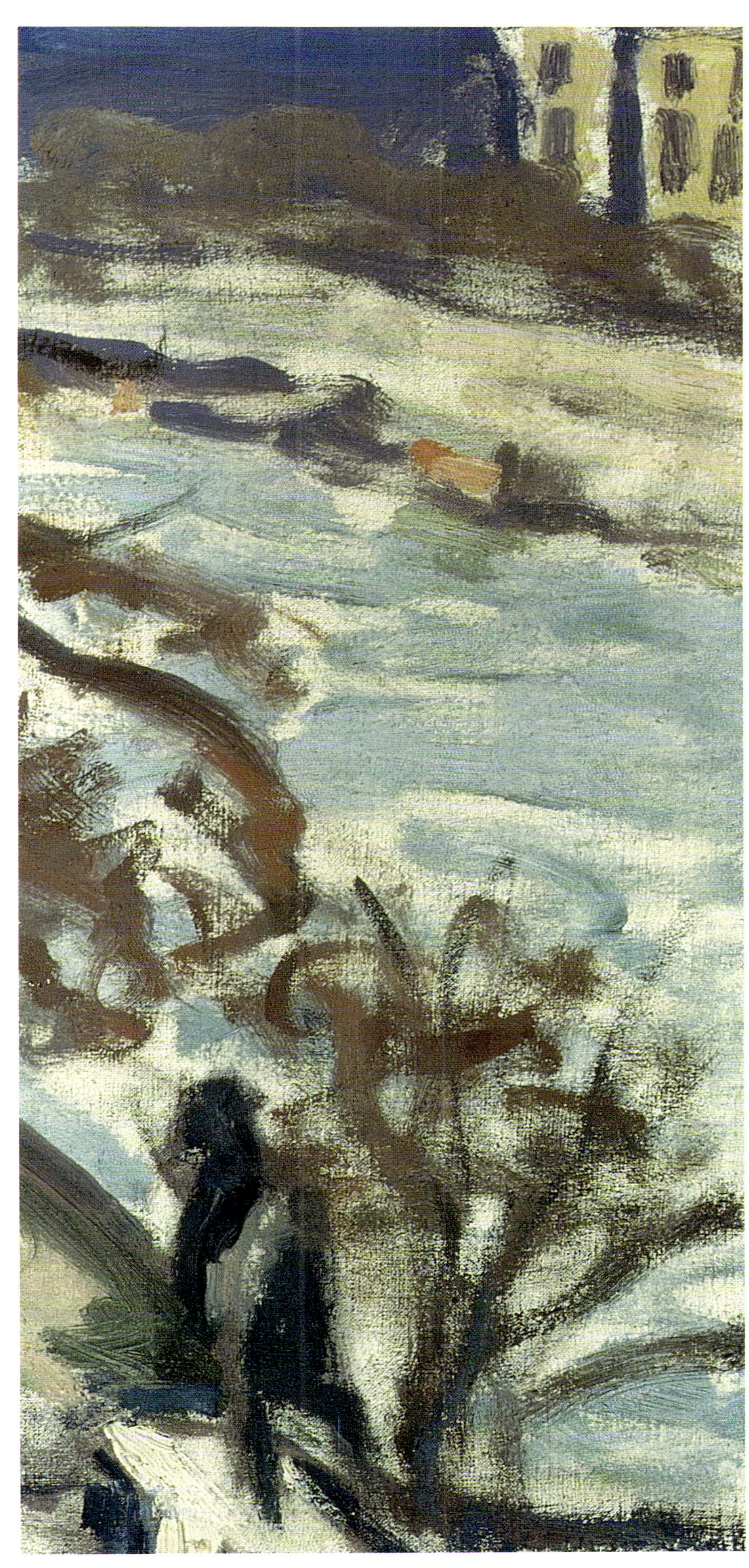

VIEW OF THE SEINE
AND THE MONUMENT TO HENRI IV
Detail.
The Hermitage, St Petersburg.

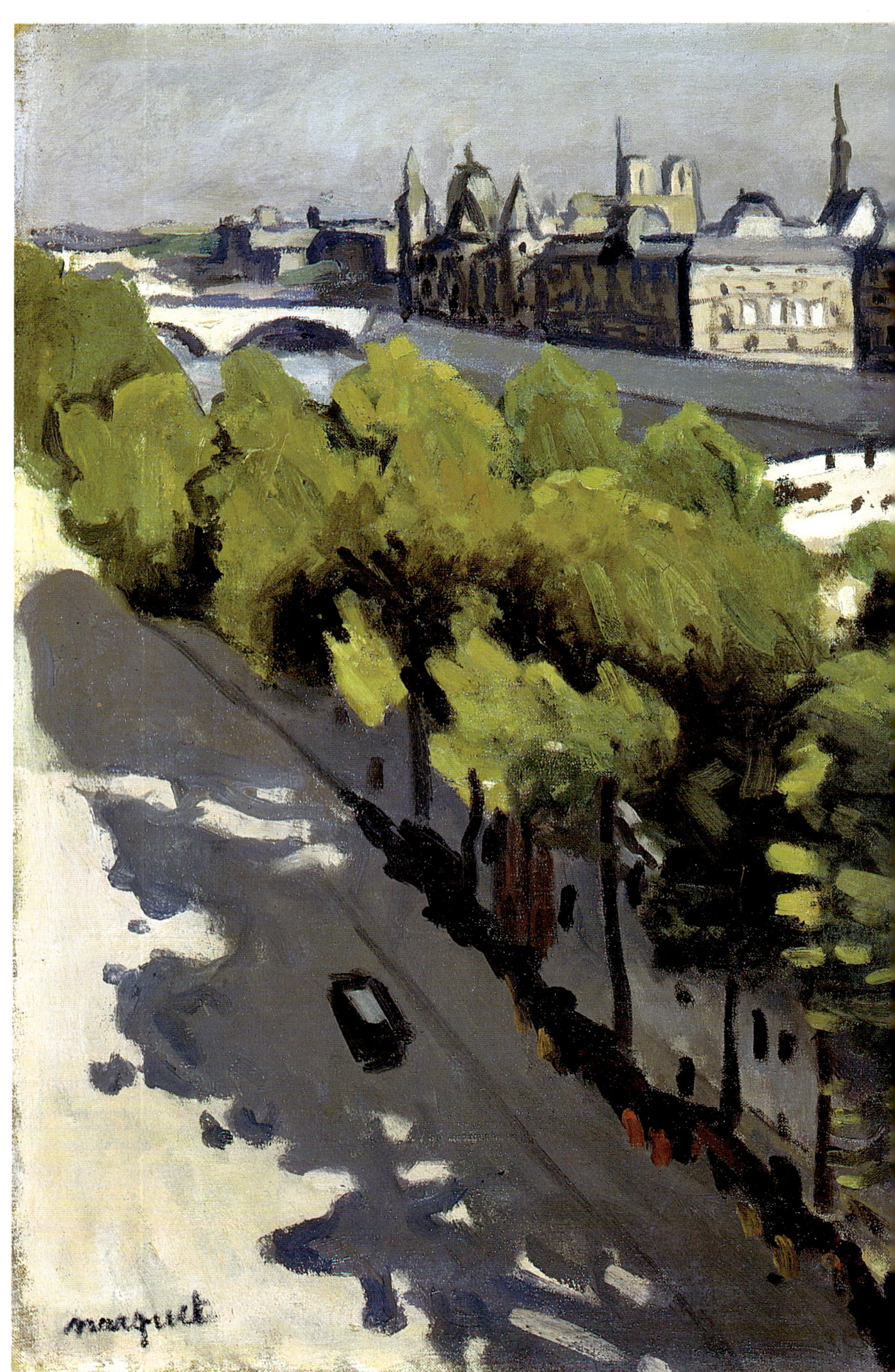

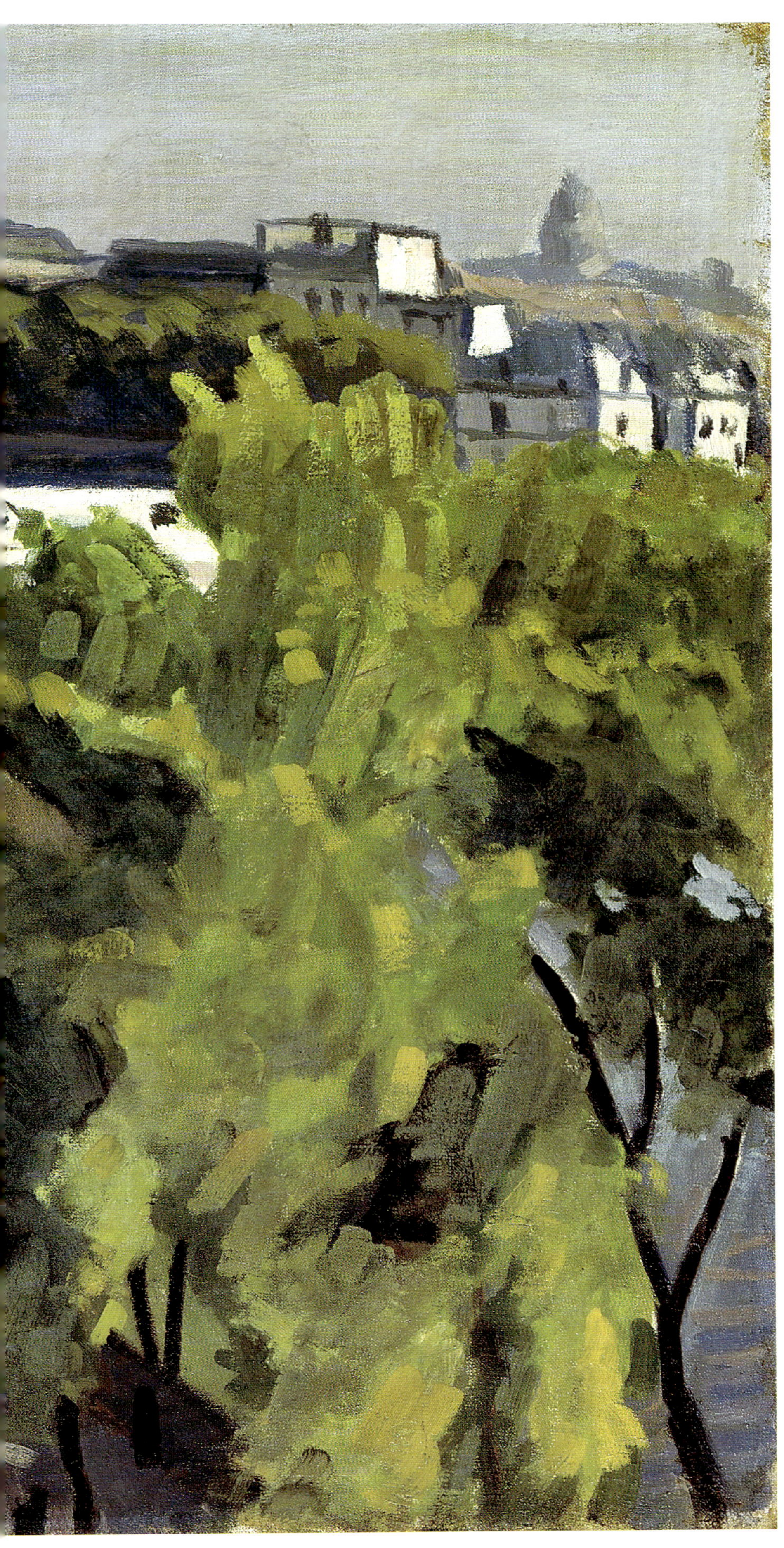

*THE QUAI DU LOUVRE
AND THE PONT NEUF*
1906
Oil on canvas. 60 x 73 cm.
Signed bottom left: *Marquet*.
Provenance: Galerie M. Blot, Paris;
1907, Ivan Morozov collection, Moscow;
1918, Second Museum of Modern
Western Painting, Moscow;
1923, Museum of Modern Western Art,
Moscow;
from 1948, The Hermitage, St Petersburg.
Inventory No. 6525.

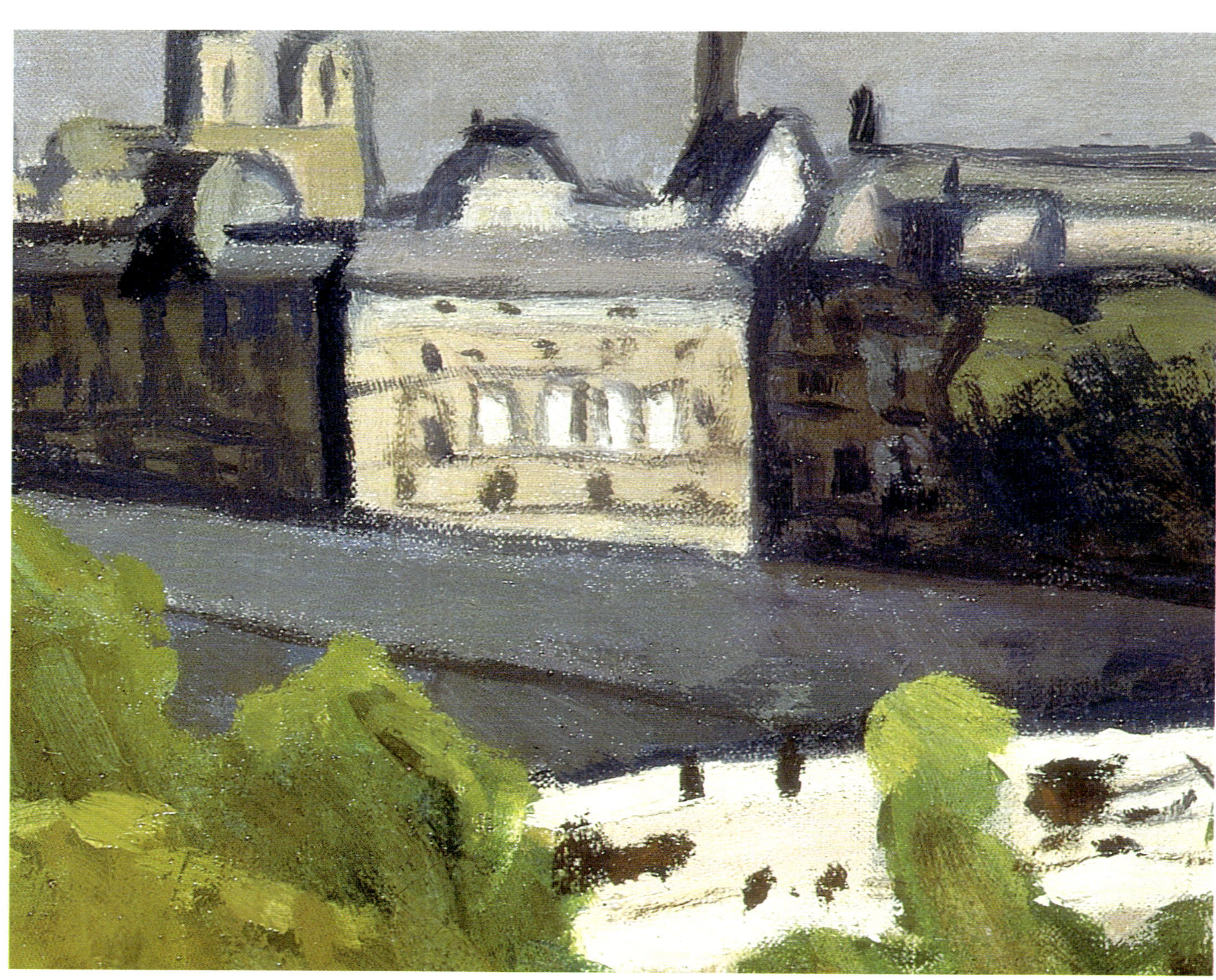

THE QUAI DU LOUVRE
AND THE PONT NEUF
Detail.
The Hermitage, St Petersburg.

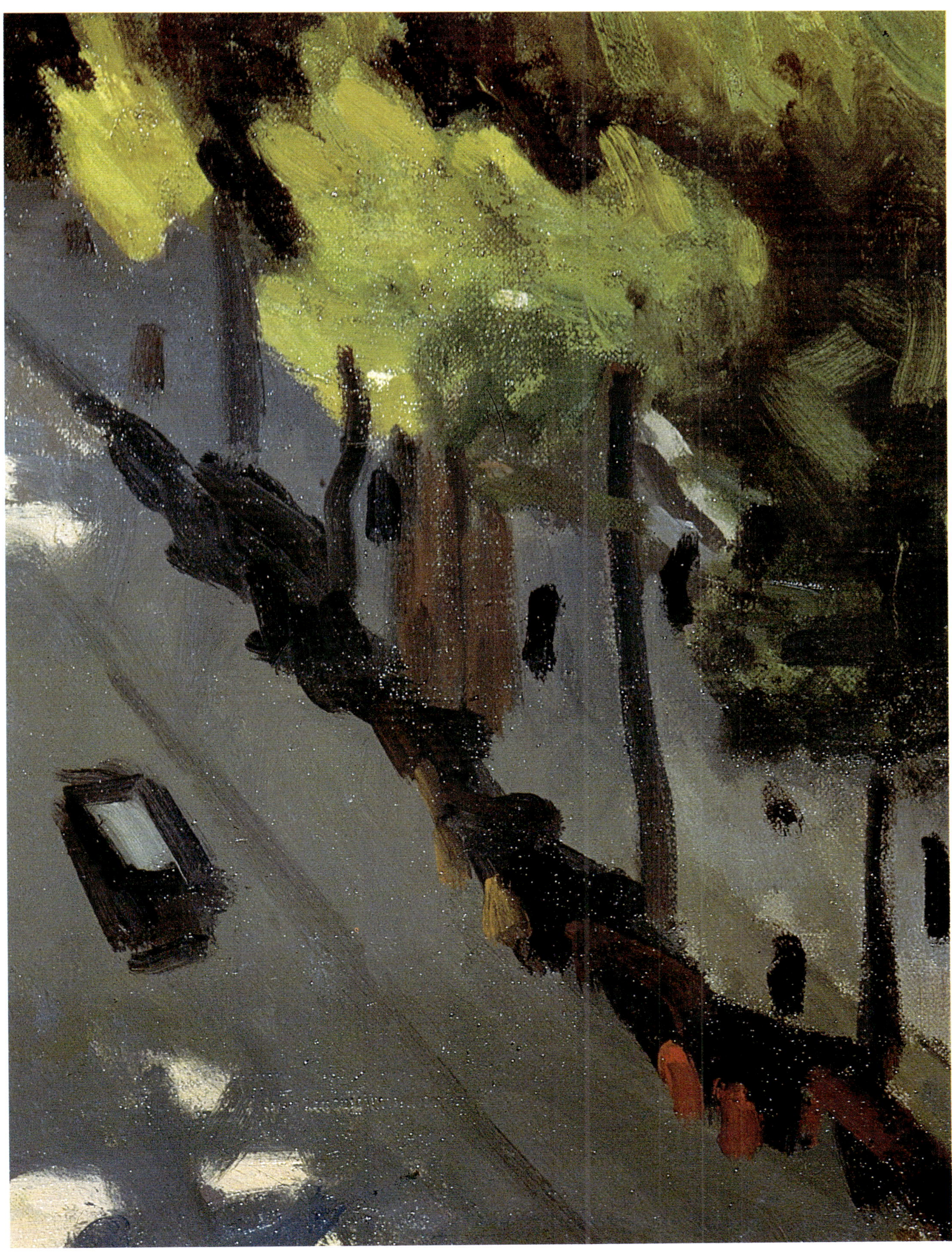

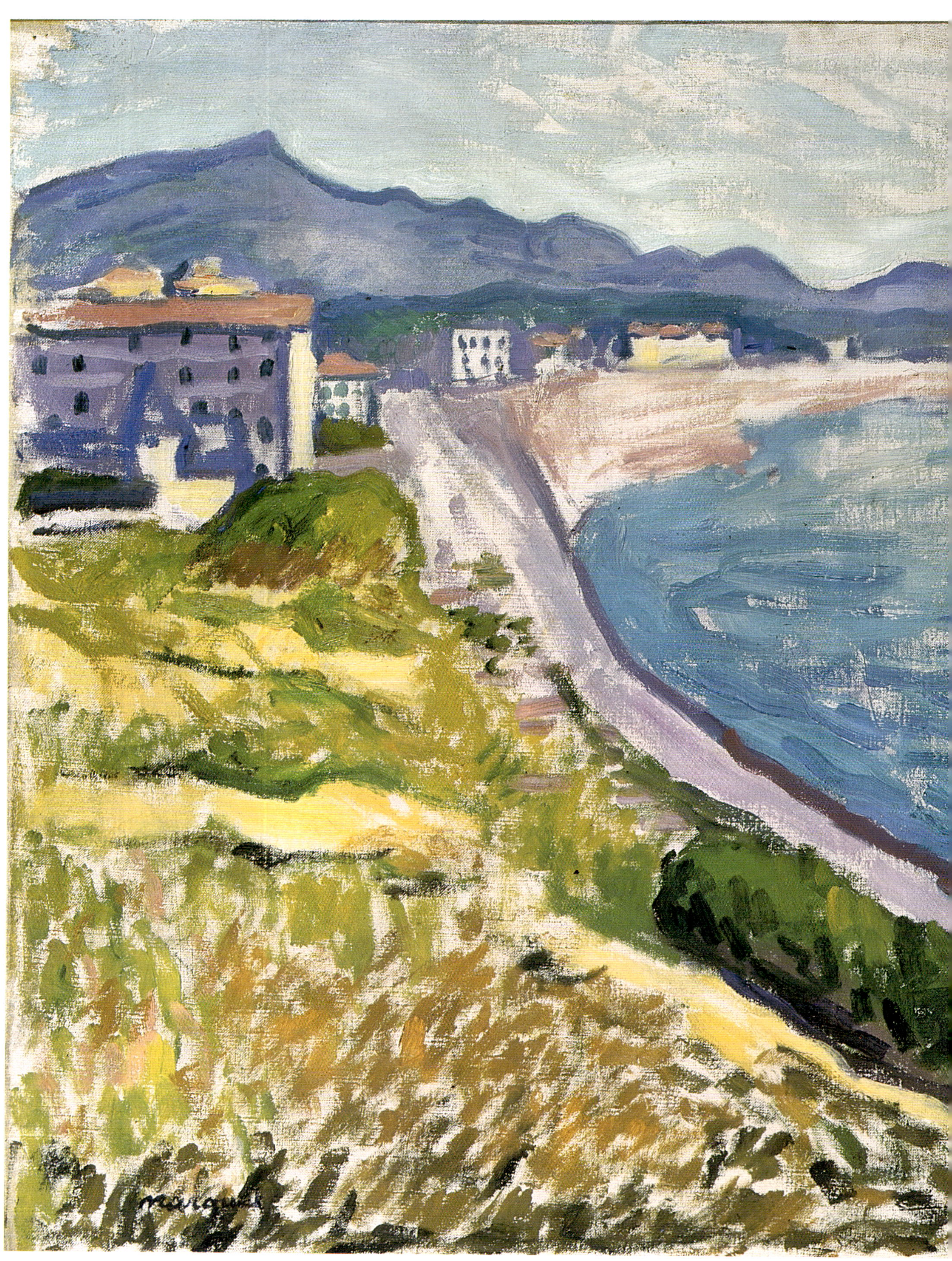

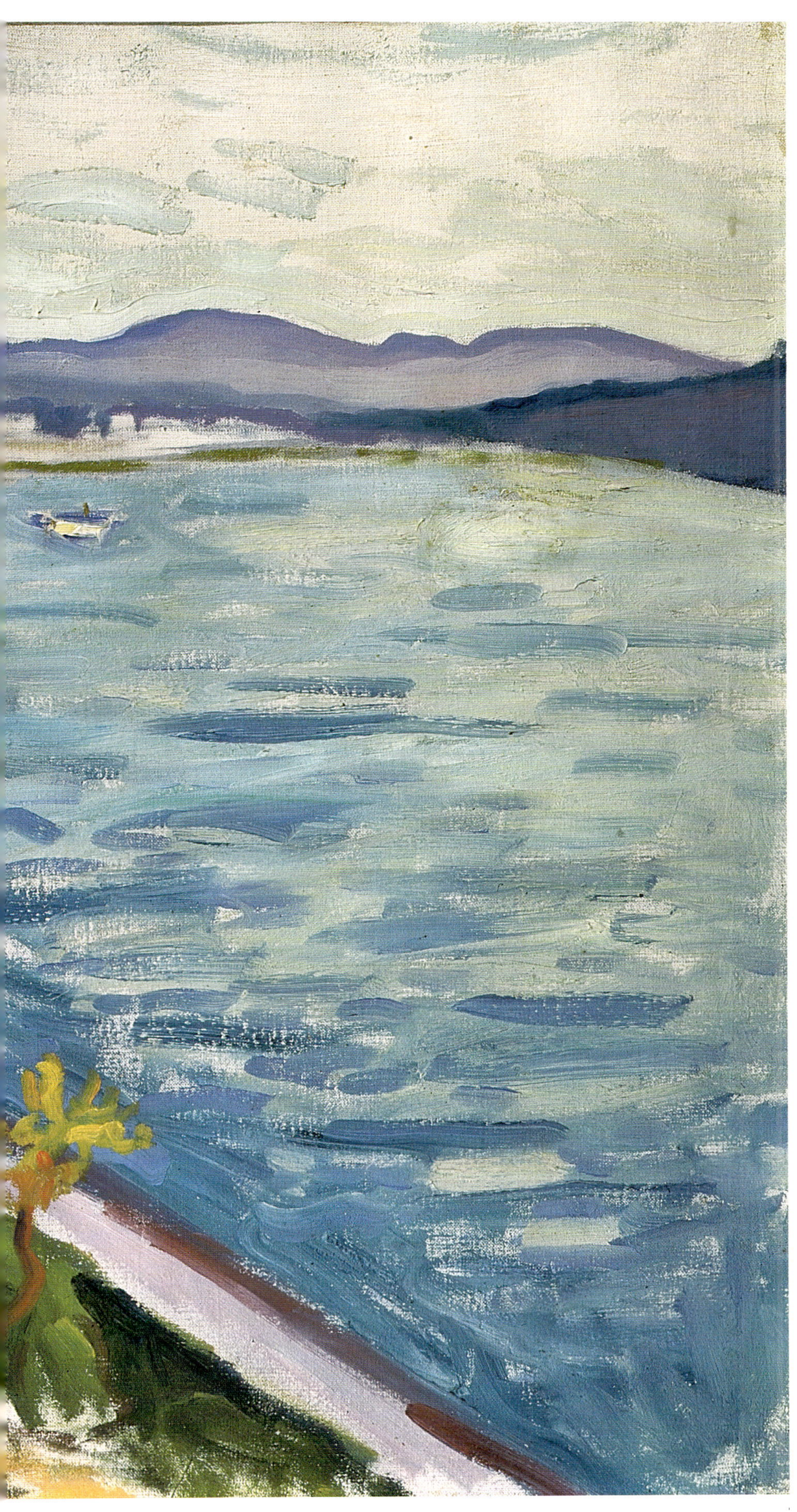

SAINT-JEAN-DE-LUZ
1907
Oil on canvas. 60 x 81 cm.
Signed bottom left: *Marquet*.
Provenance: Galerie Eugène Drouet, Paris;
1913, Sergei Shchukin collection, Moscow;
1918, First Museum of Modern
Western Painting, Moscow;
1923, Museum of Modern Western Art,
Moscow;
from 1934, The Hermitage, St Petersburg.
Inventory No. 7226.

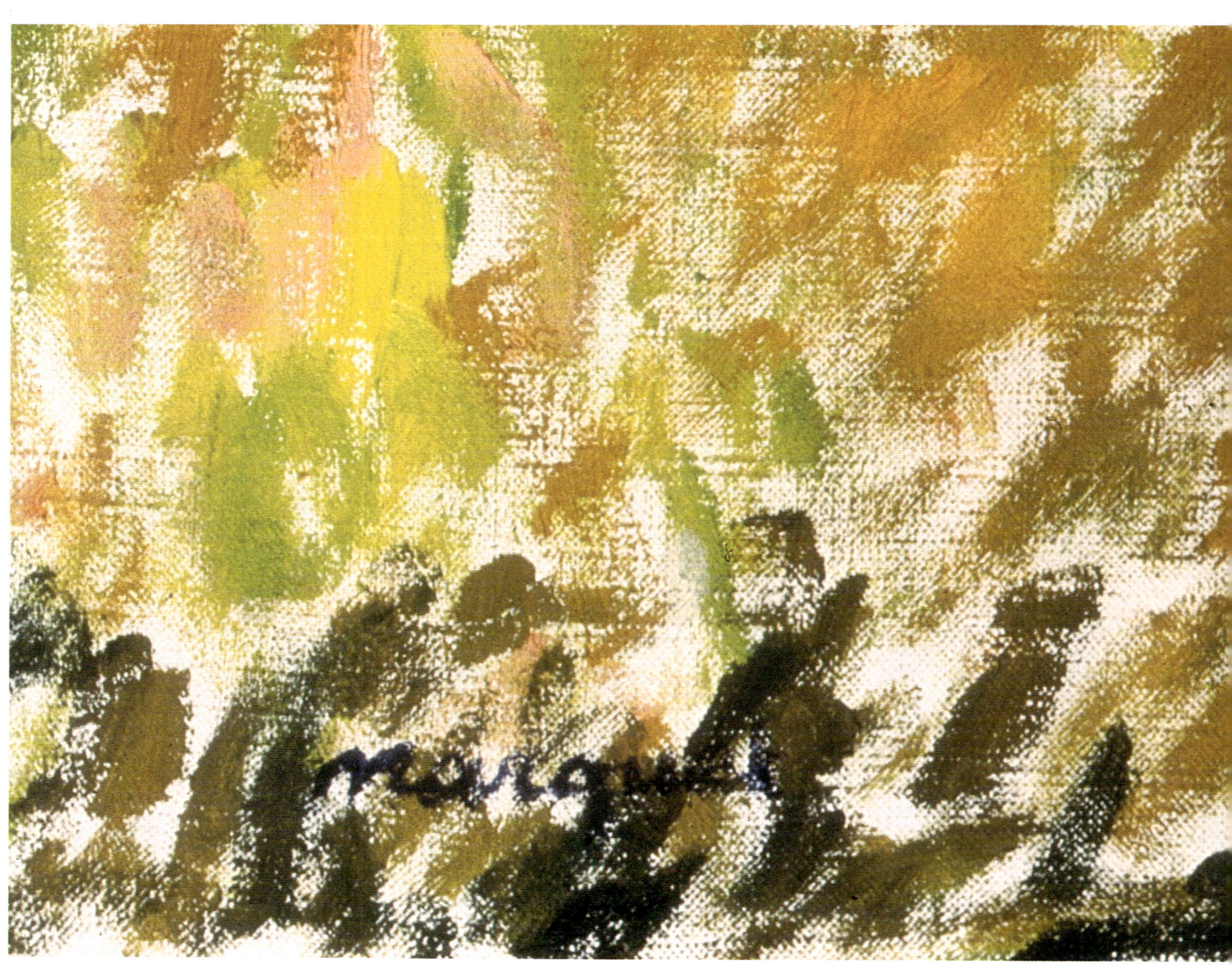

SAINT-JEAN-DE-LUZ
Detail.
The Hermitage, St Petersburg.

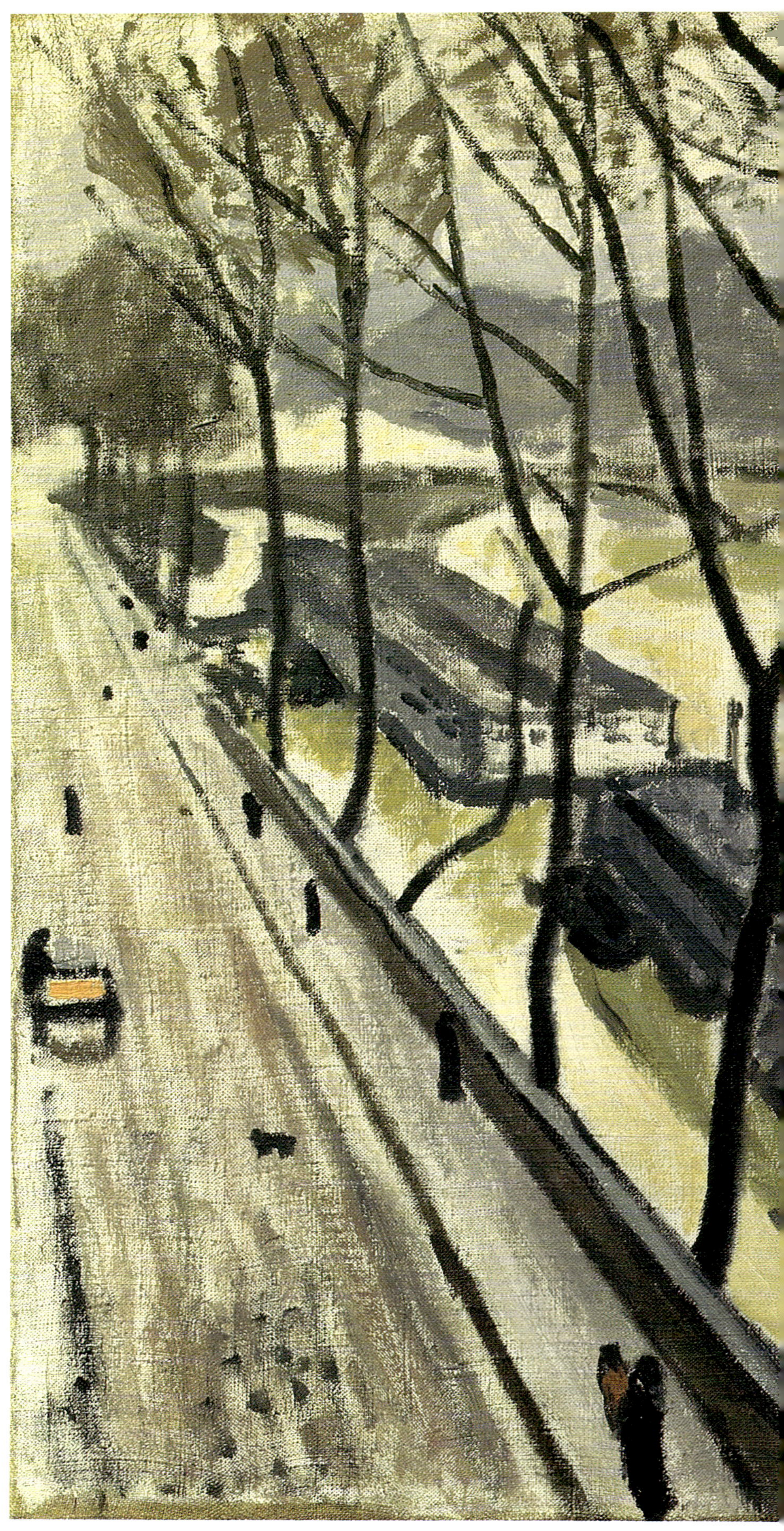

PARIS IN WINTER
THE QUAI BOURBON
1907
Oil on canvas. 65 x 81 cm.
Provenance: Galerie Eugène Drouet, Paris;
1913, Ivan Morozov collection, Moscow;
1918, Museum of Modern Western Art,
Moscow;
from 1948, The Pushkin Museum
of Fine Arts, Moscow.
Inventory No. 3390.

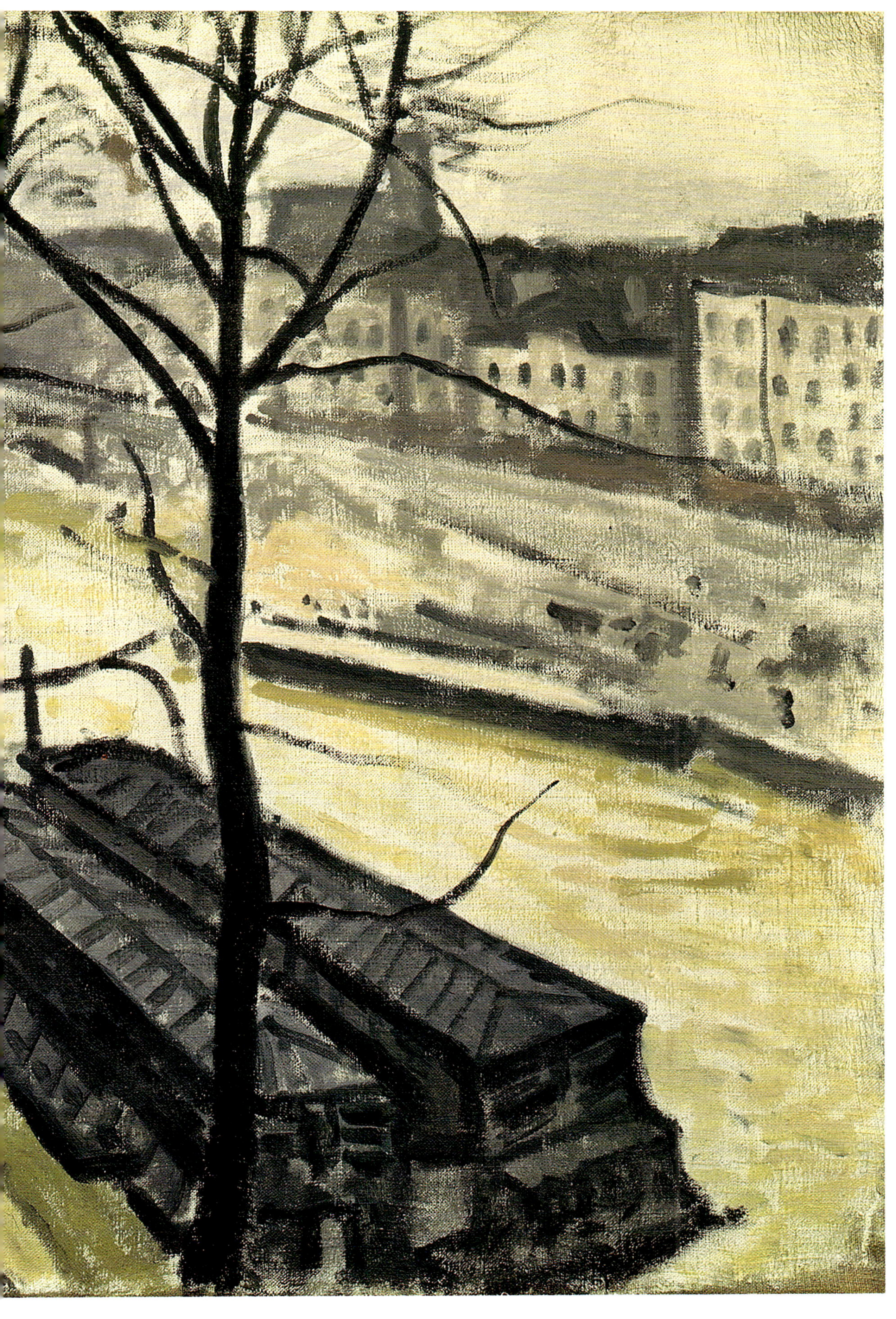

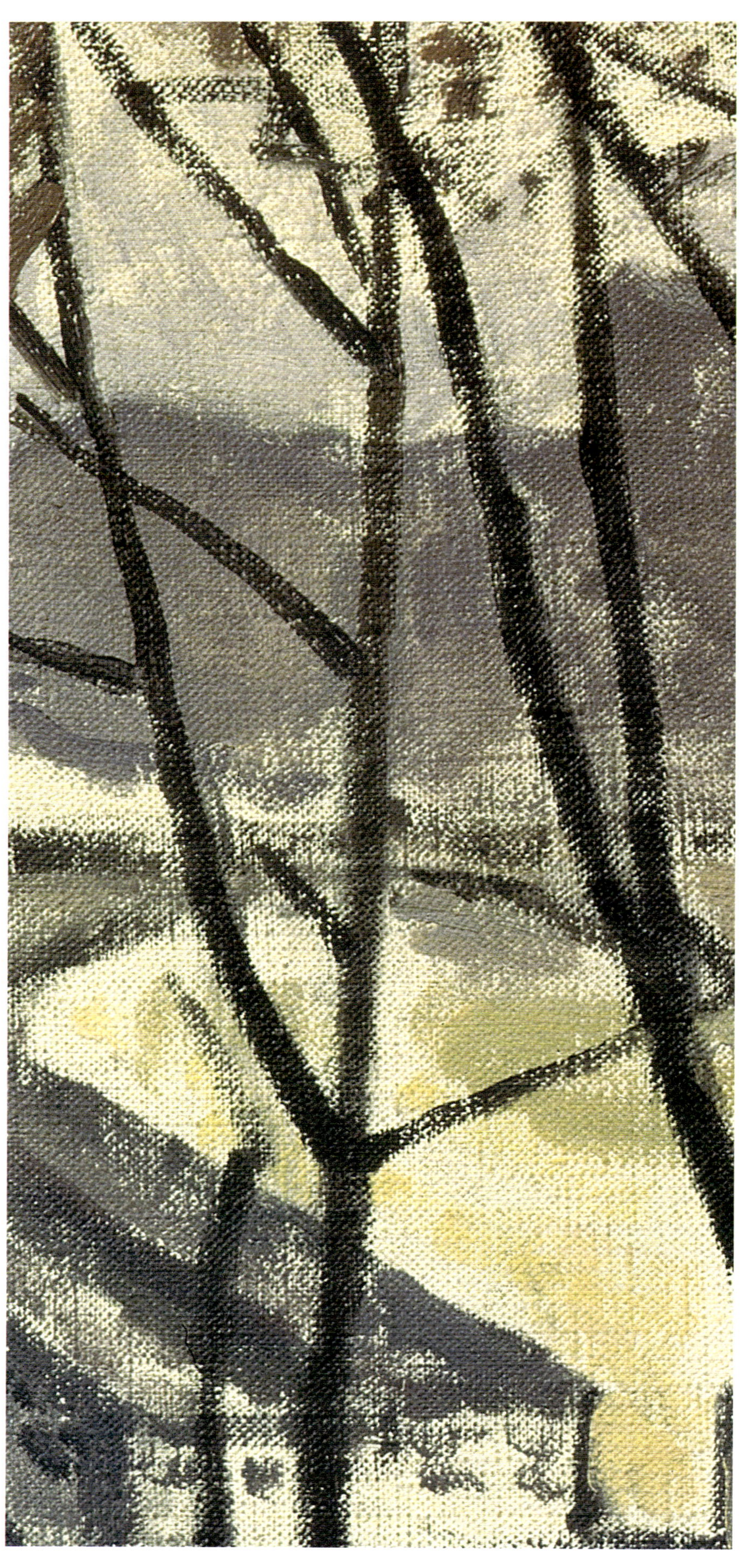

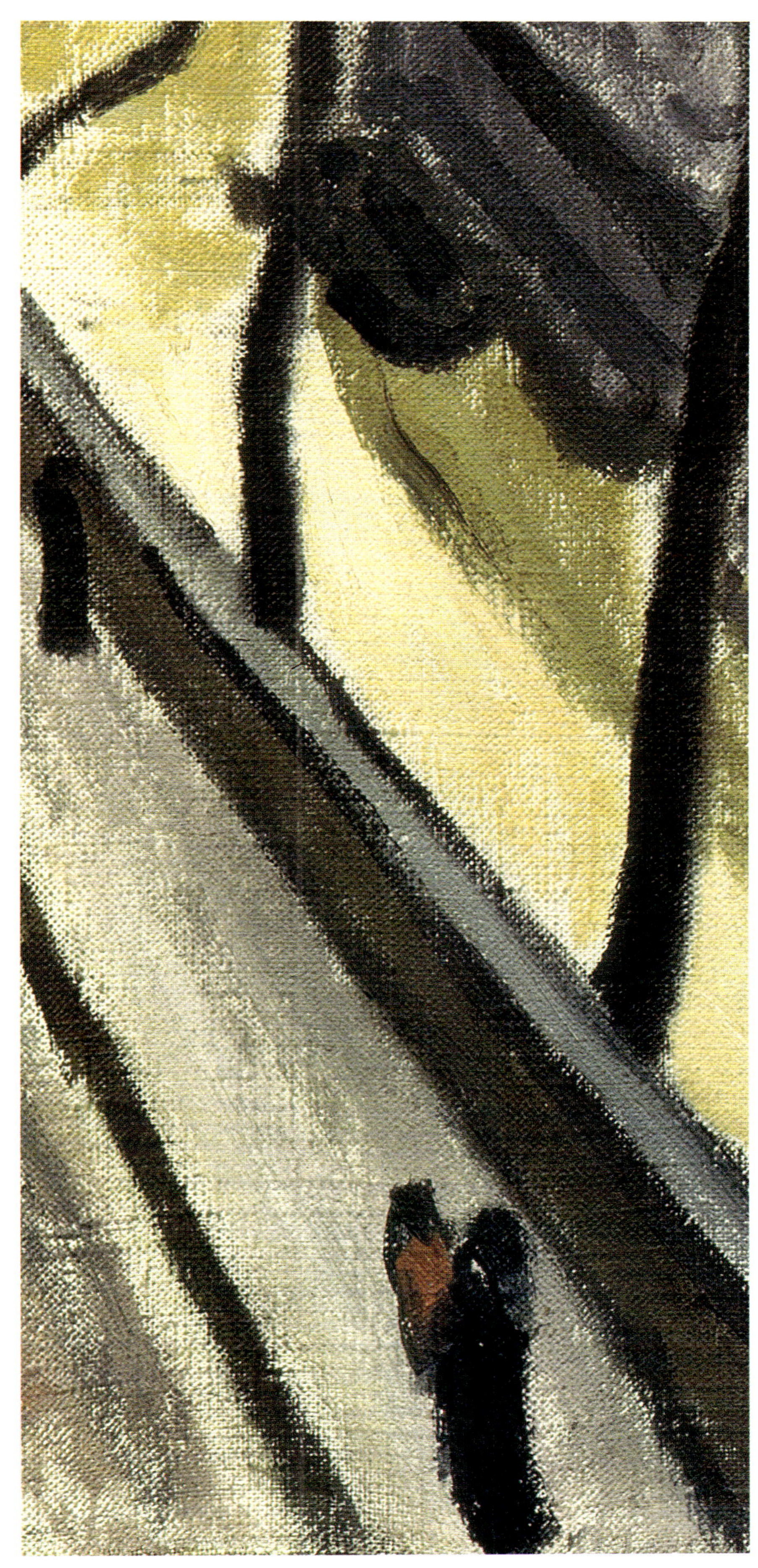

PARIS IN WINTER
THE QUAI BOURBON
Detail.
The Pushkin Museum of Fine Arts, Moscow.

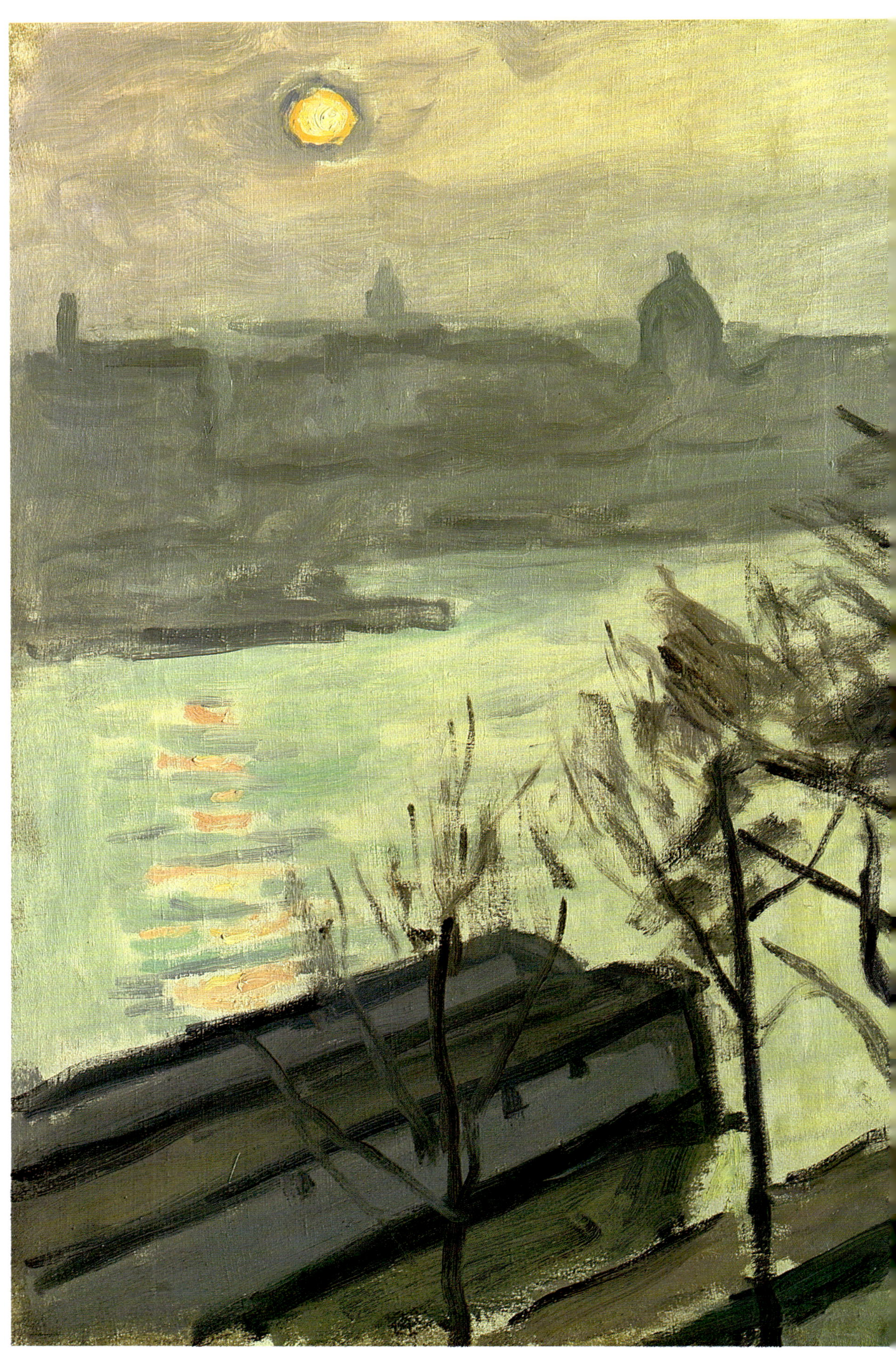

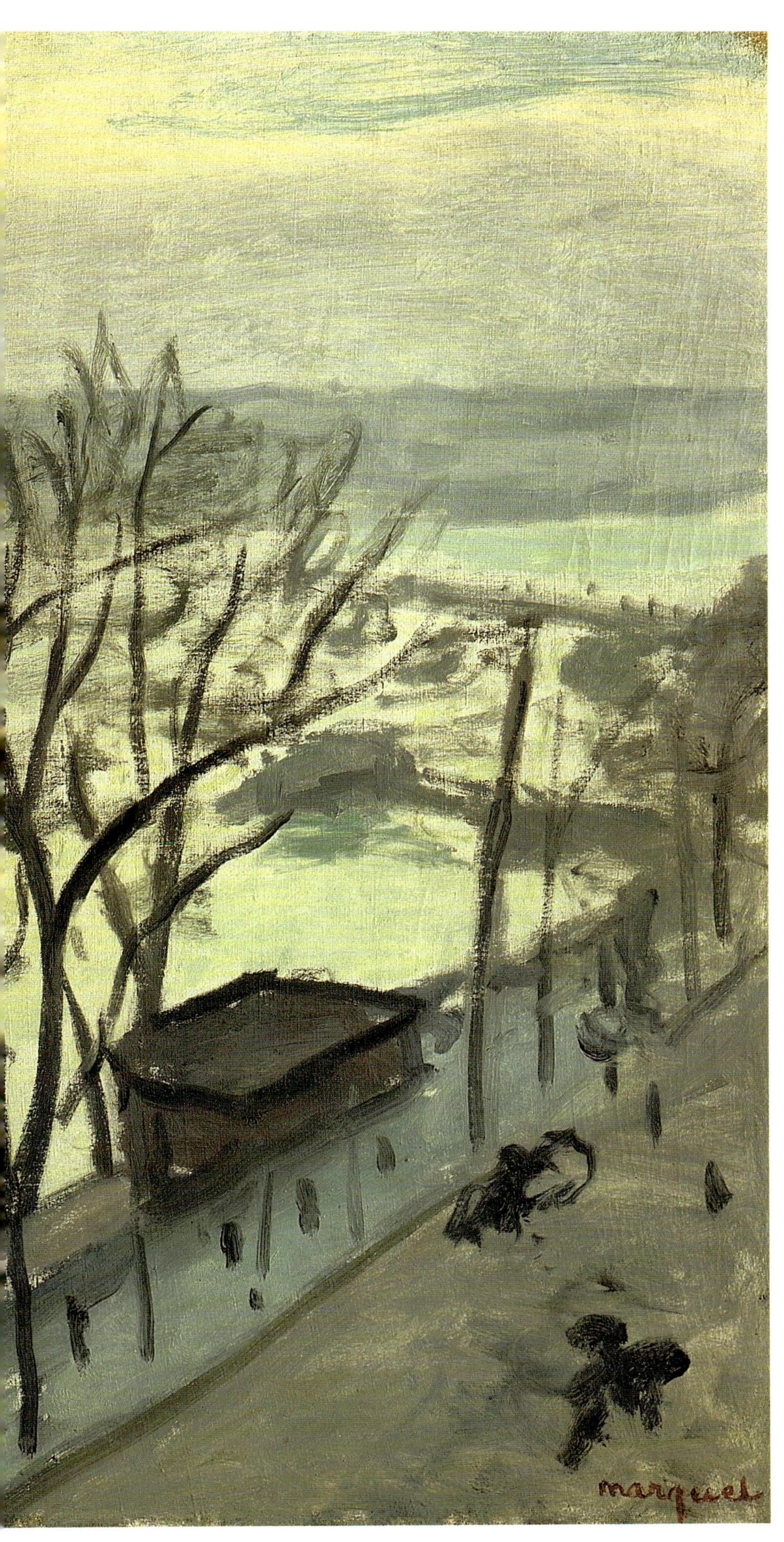

SUNNY DAY IN PARIS
THE QUAI DU LOUVRE
_Ca._ 1907
Oil on canvas. 65 x 82 cm.
Signed bottom right: _Marquet_.
Provenance: Galerie Eugène Drouet, Paris;
1913, Ivan Morozov collection, Moscow;
1918, Museum of Modern Western Art,
Moscow;
from 1948, The Pushkin Museum
of Fine Arts, Moscow.
Inventory No. 3391.

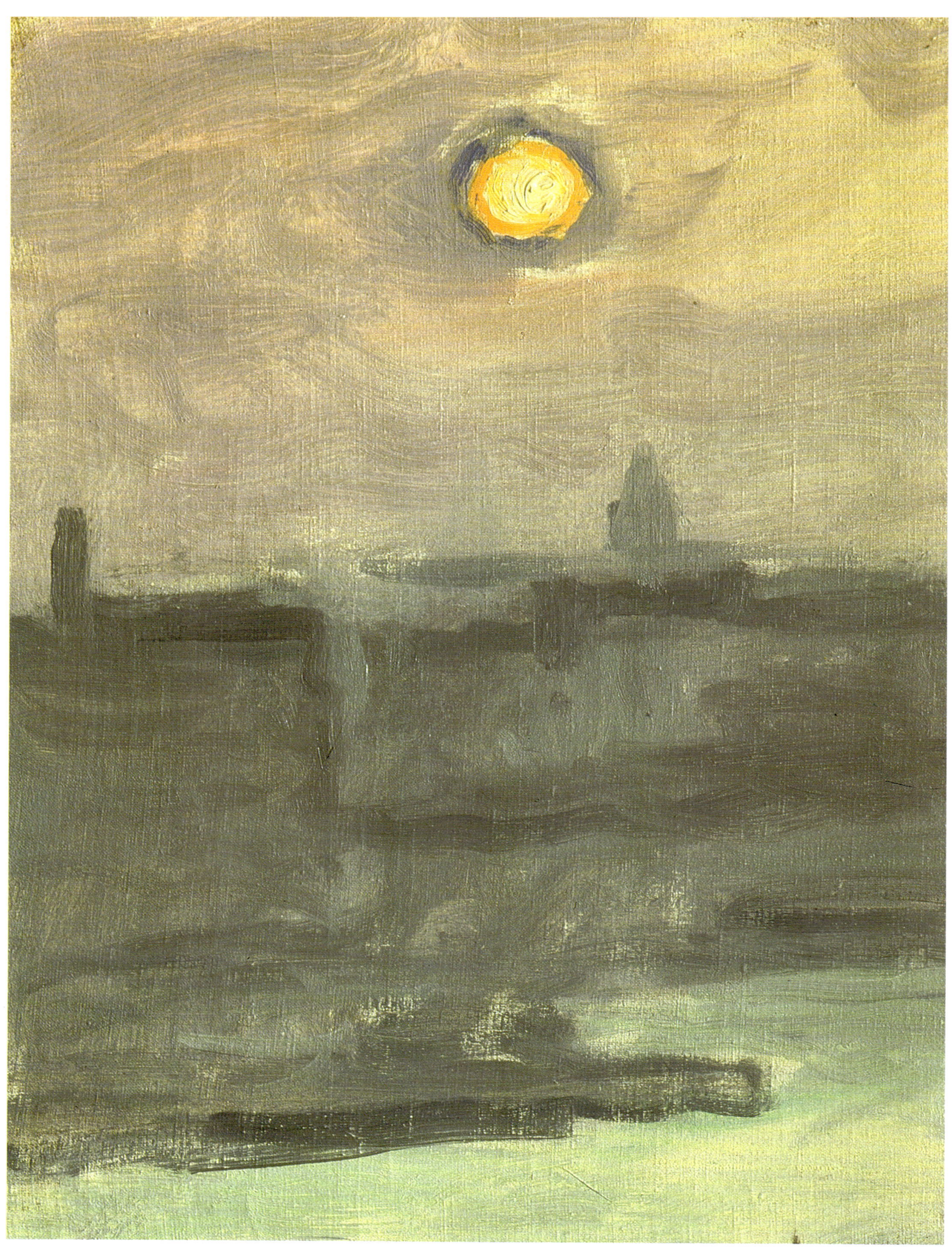

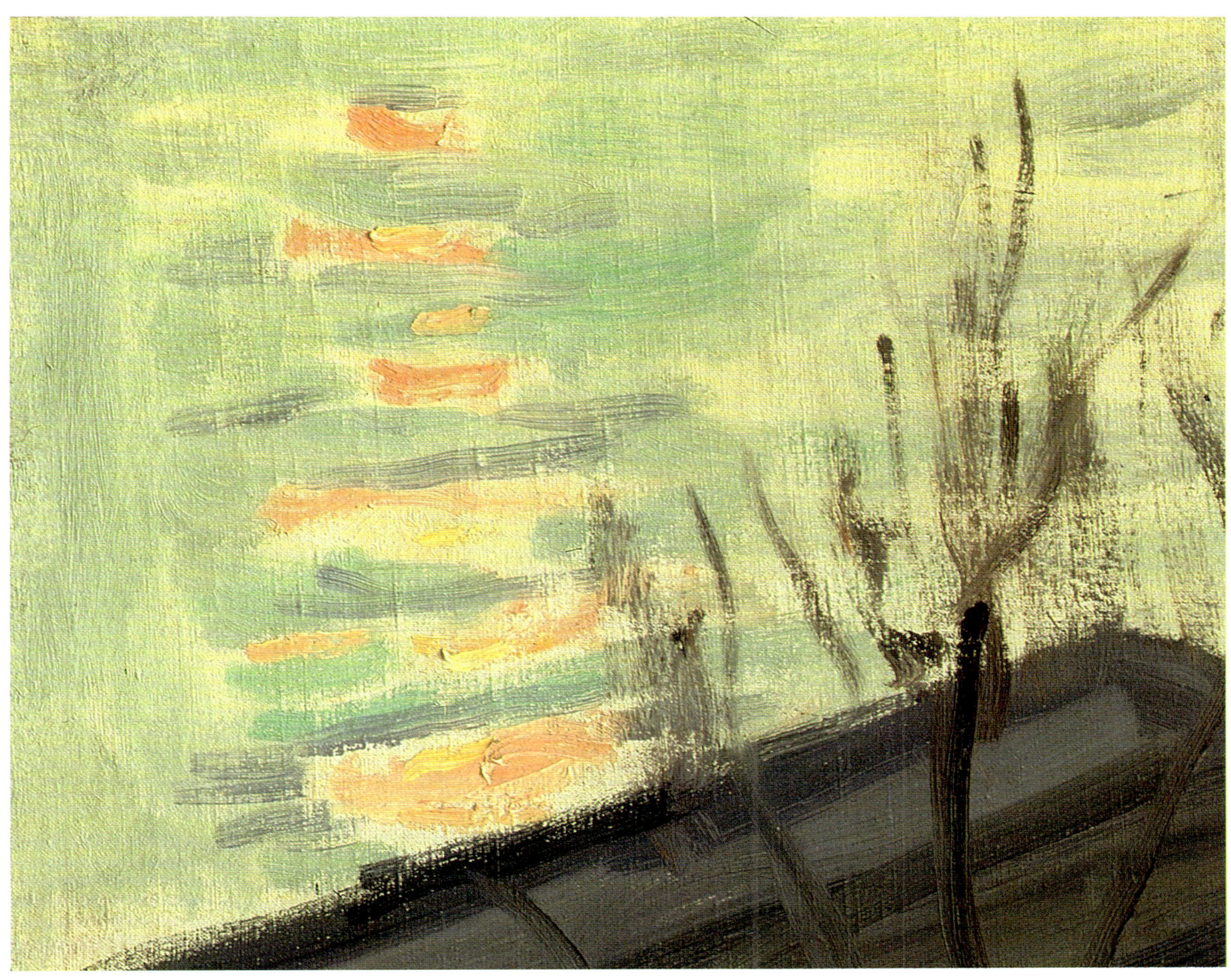

SUNNY DAY IN PARIS
THE QUAI DU LOUVRE
Detail.
The Pushkin Museum of Fine Arts, Moscow.

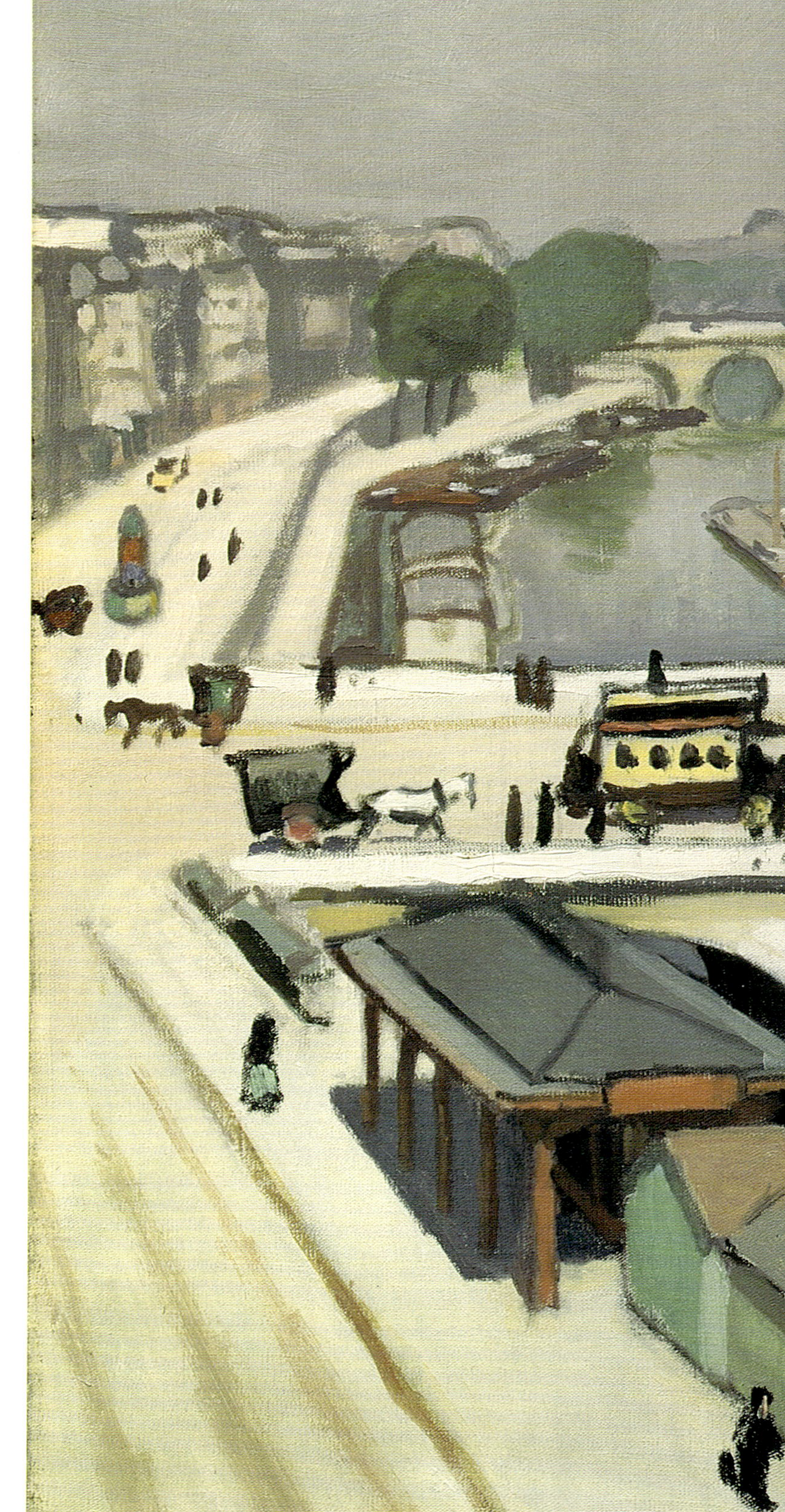

THE PONT SAINT-MICHEL IN PARIS
THE QUAI DES AUGUSTINS
1908
Oil on canvas. 65 x 81 cm.
Signed bottom right: *Marquet*.
Provenance: Galerie Eugène Drouet, Paris;
Sergei Shchukin collection, Moscow;
1918, Museum of Modern Western Art,
Moscow;
from 1948, The Pushkin Museum
of Fine Arts, Moscow.
Inventory No. 3289.

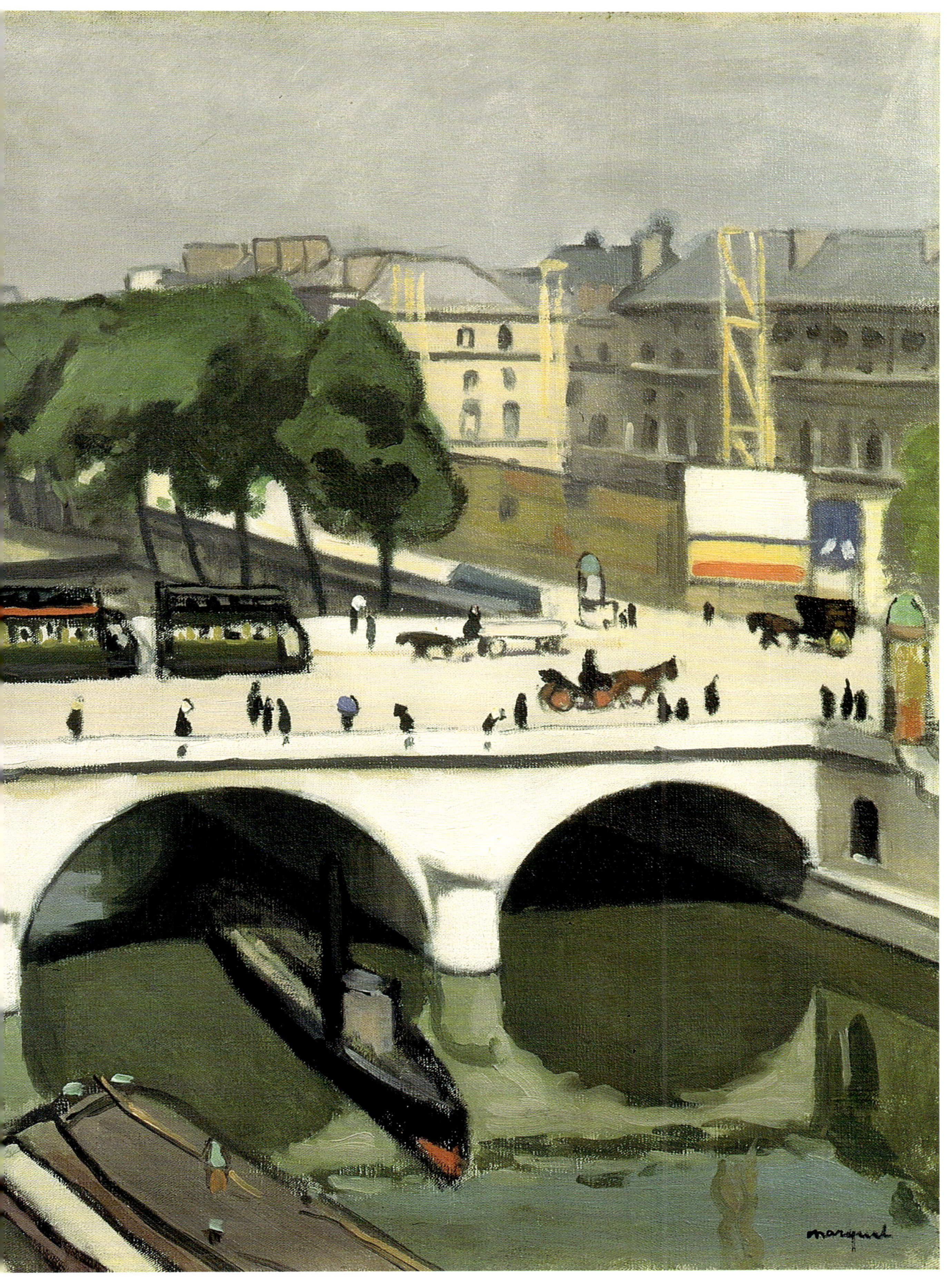

THE PONT SAINT-MICHEL IN PARIS
THE QUAI DES AUGUSTINS
Detail.
The Pushkin Museum of Fine Arts, Moscow.

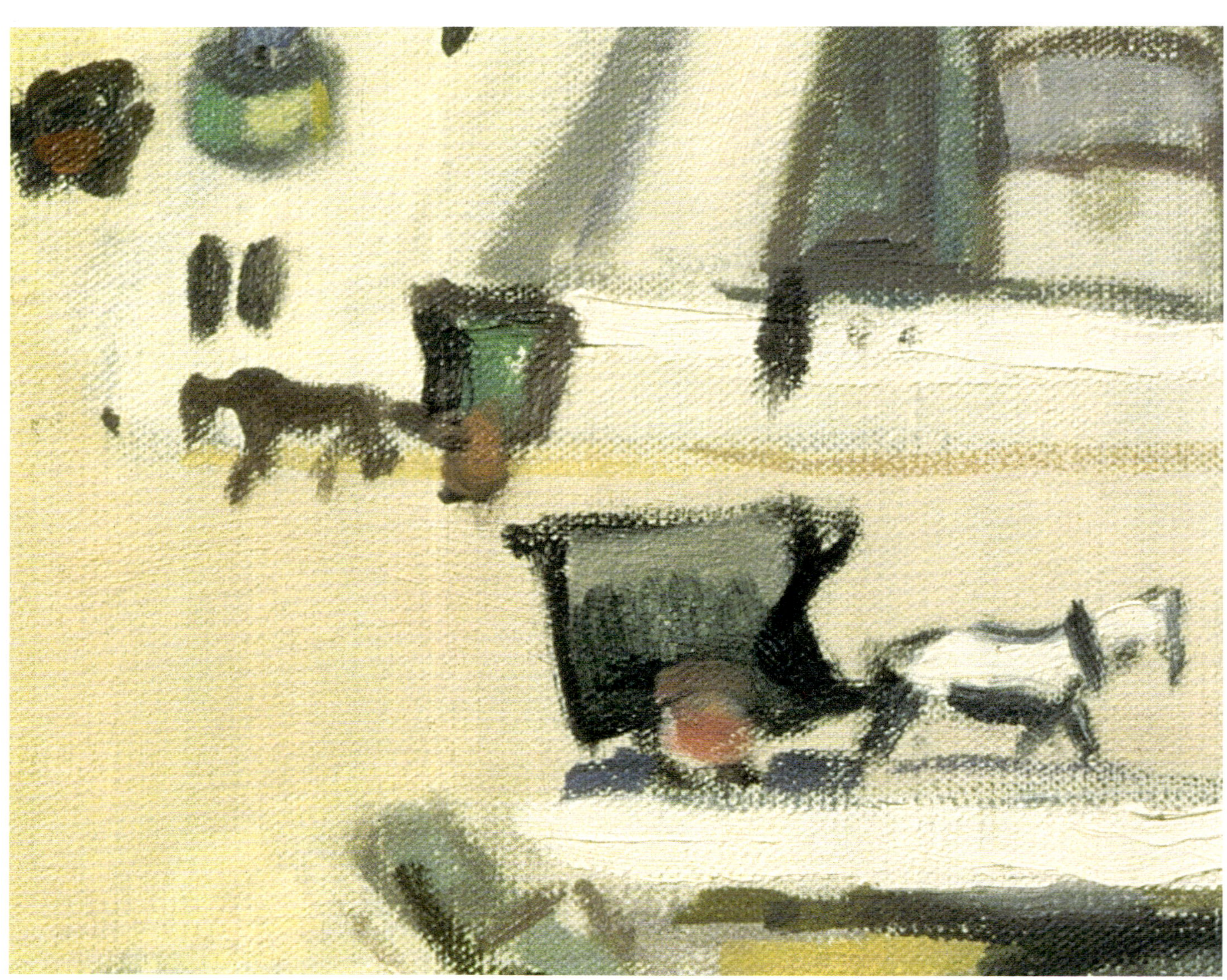

THE PONT SAINT-MICHEL IN PARIS
THE QUAI DES AUGUSTINS
Detail.
The Pushkin Museum of Fine Arts, Moscow.

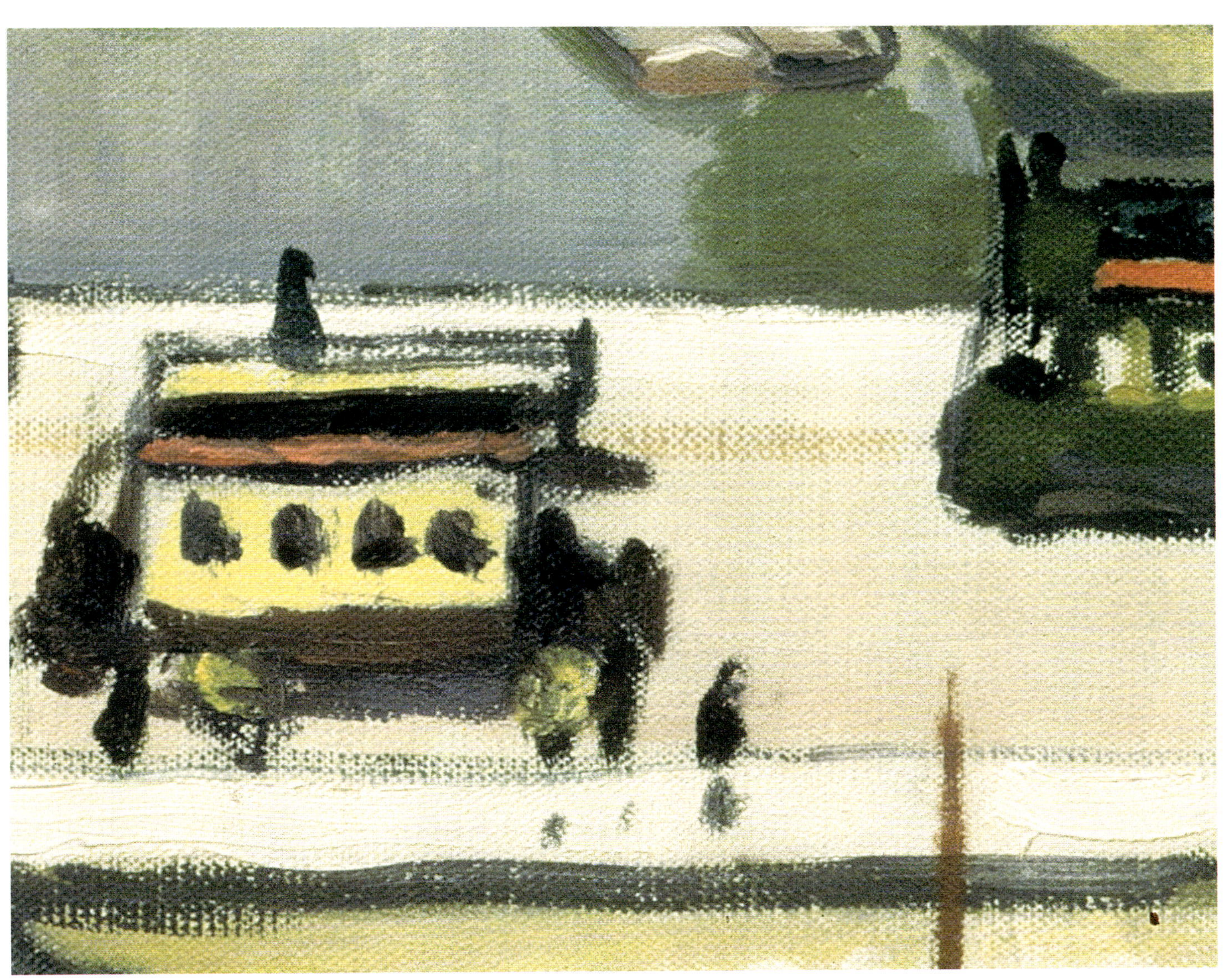

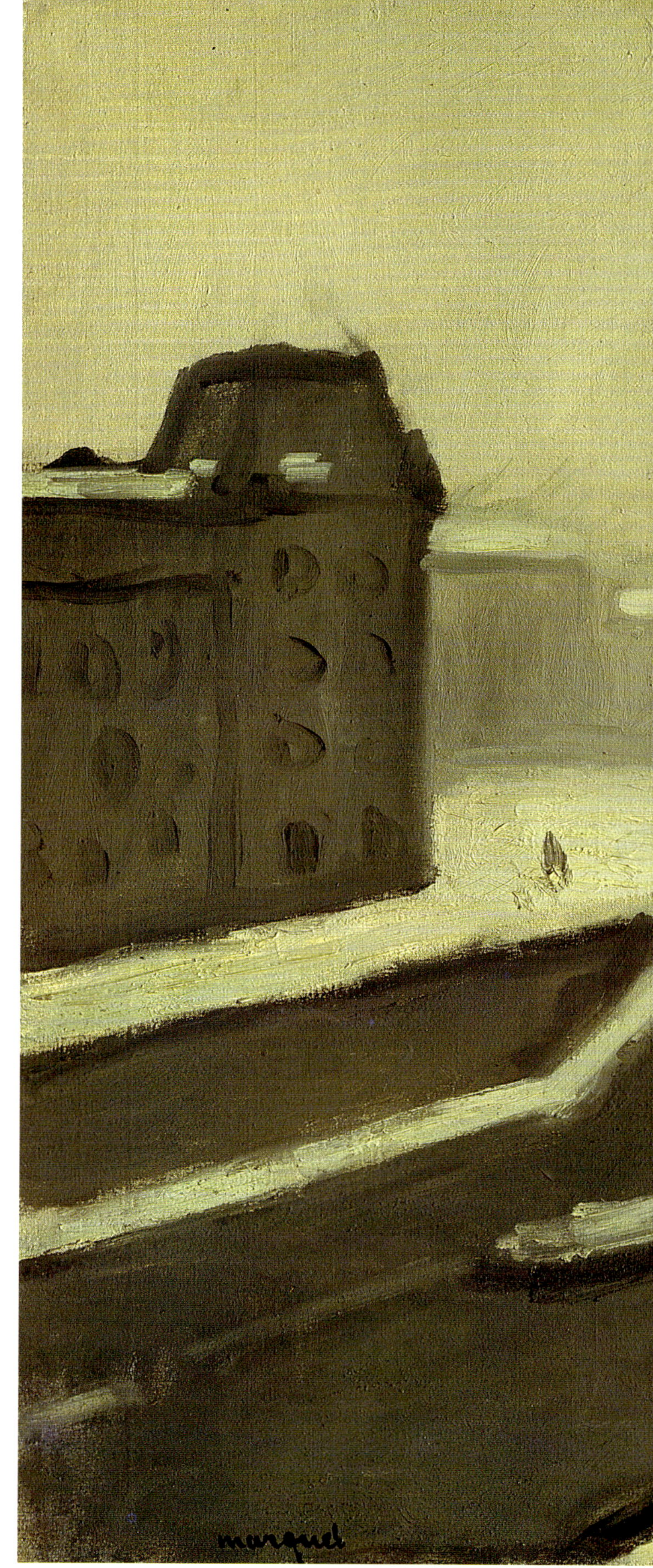

NOTRE DAME DE PARIS IN WINTER
1908
Oil on canvas. 65 x 81 cm.
Signed bottom left: *Marquet*.
Provenance: Galerie Eugène Drouet, Paris;
Sergei Shchukin collection, Moscow;
1918, Museum of Modern Western Art,
Moscow;
from 1948, The Pushkin Museum
of Fine Arts, Moscow.
Inventory No. 3292.

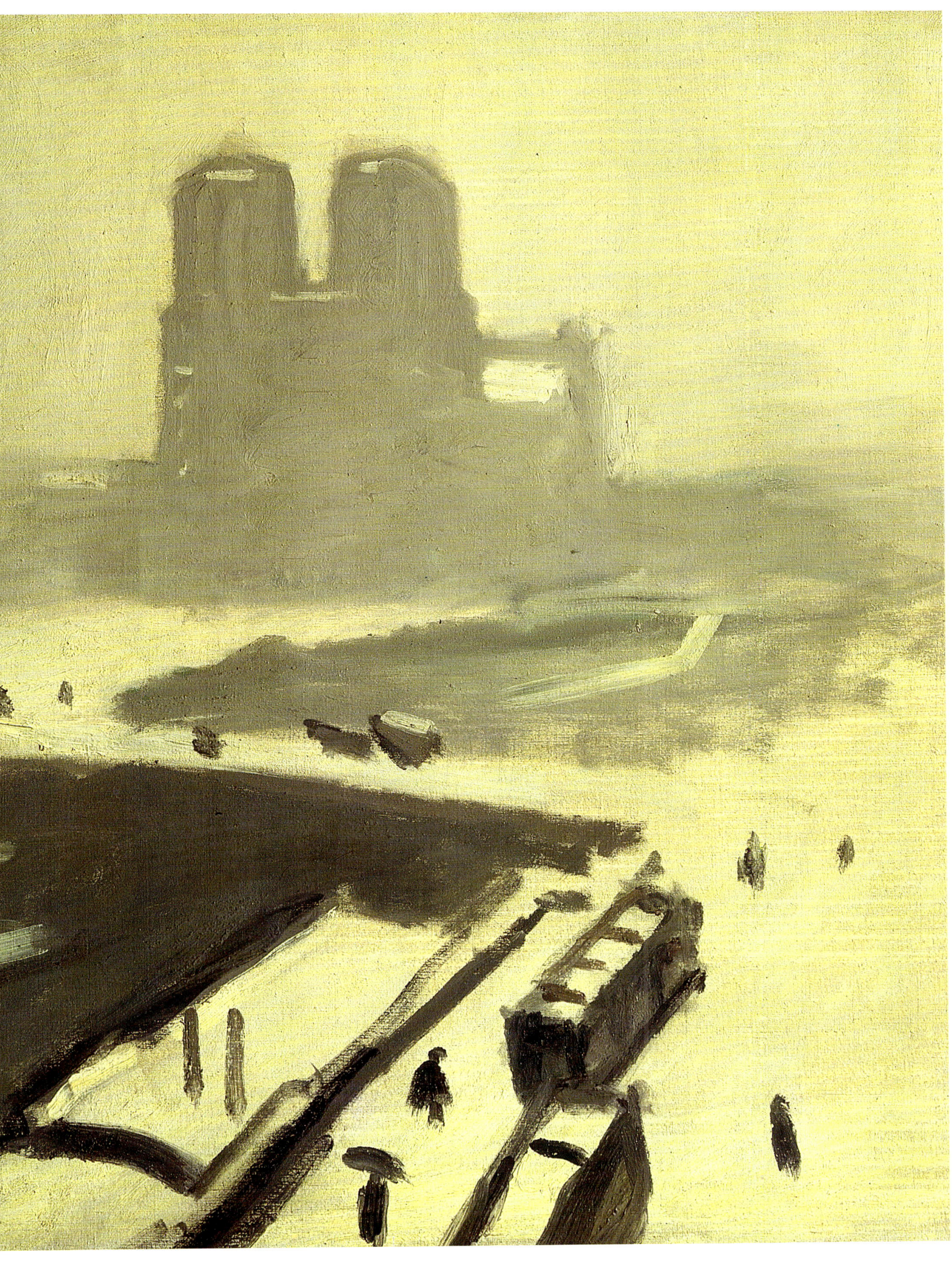

NOTRE DAME DE PARIS IN WINTER
Detail.
The Pushkin Museum of Fine Arts, Moscow.

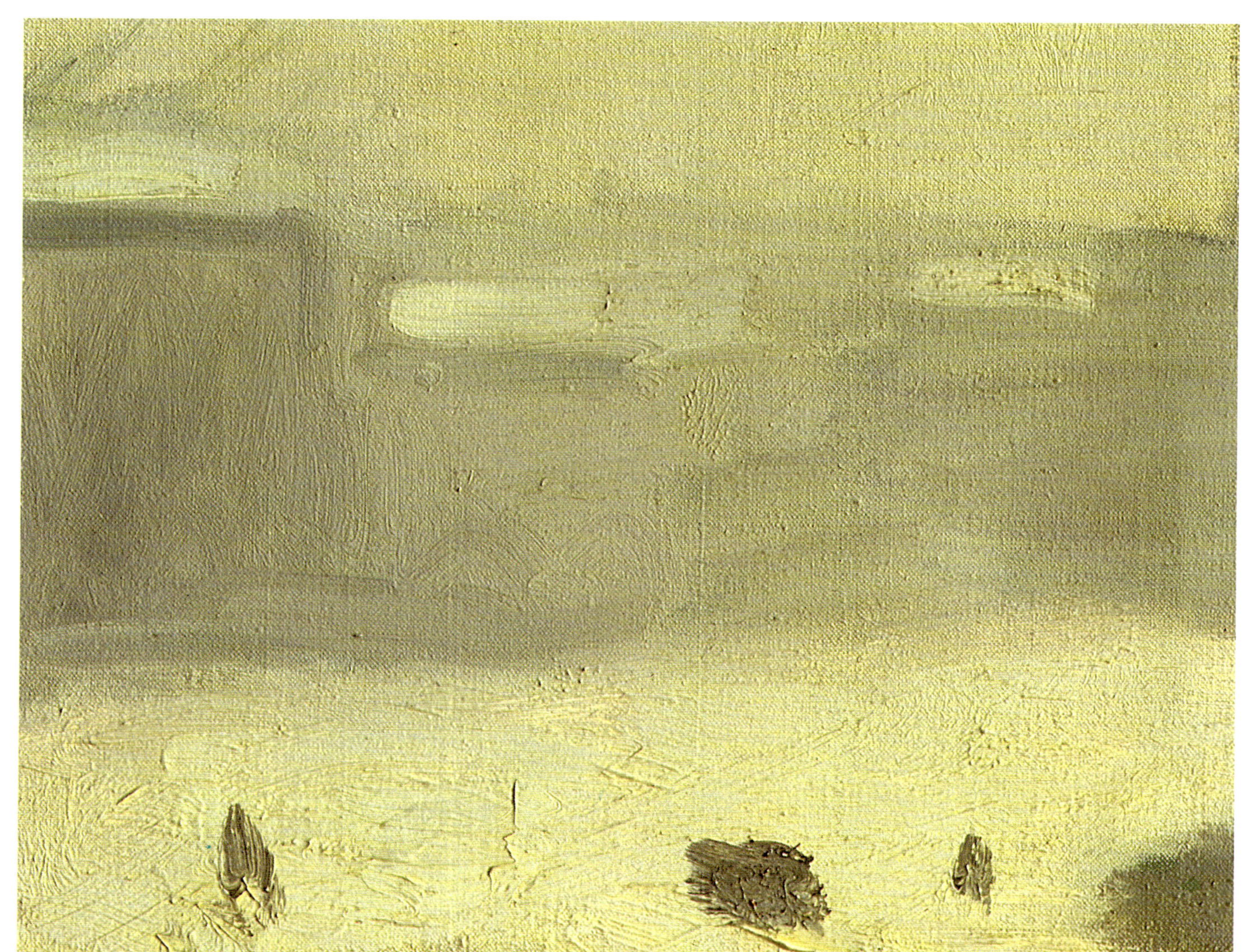

NOTRE DAME DE PARIS IN WINTER
Detail.
The Pushkin Museum of Fine Arts, Moscow.

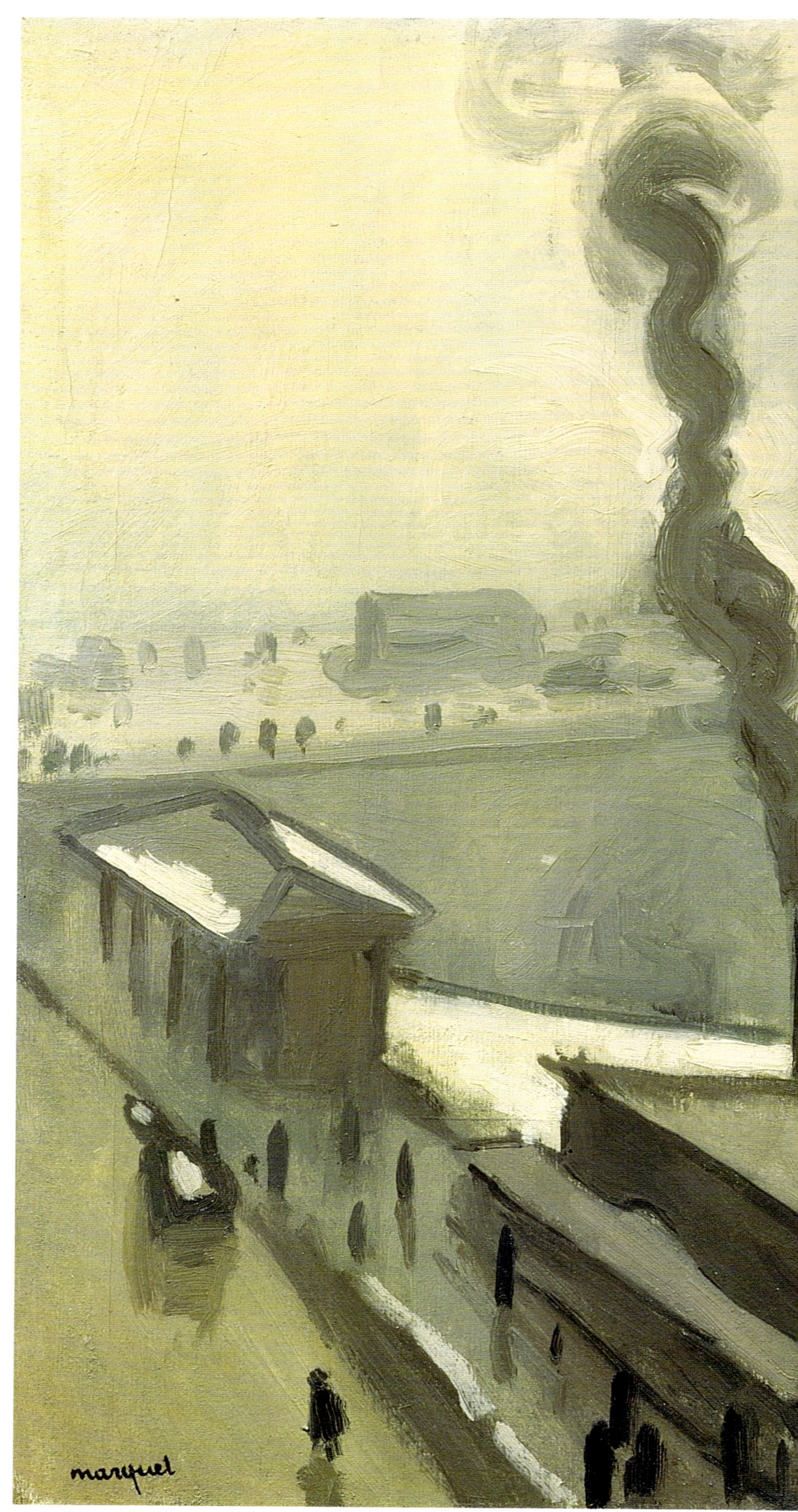

THE PONT SAINT-MICHEL
IN WINTER
1908
Oil on canvas. 61 x 81 cm.
Signed bottom left: *Marquet*.
Provenance: Galerie Eugène Drouet, Paris;
Sergei Shchukin collection, Moscow;
1918, Museum of Modern Western Art,
Moscow;
from 1948, The Pushkin Museum
of Fine Arts, Moscow.
Inventory No. 3293.

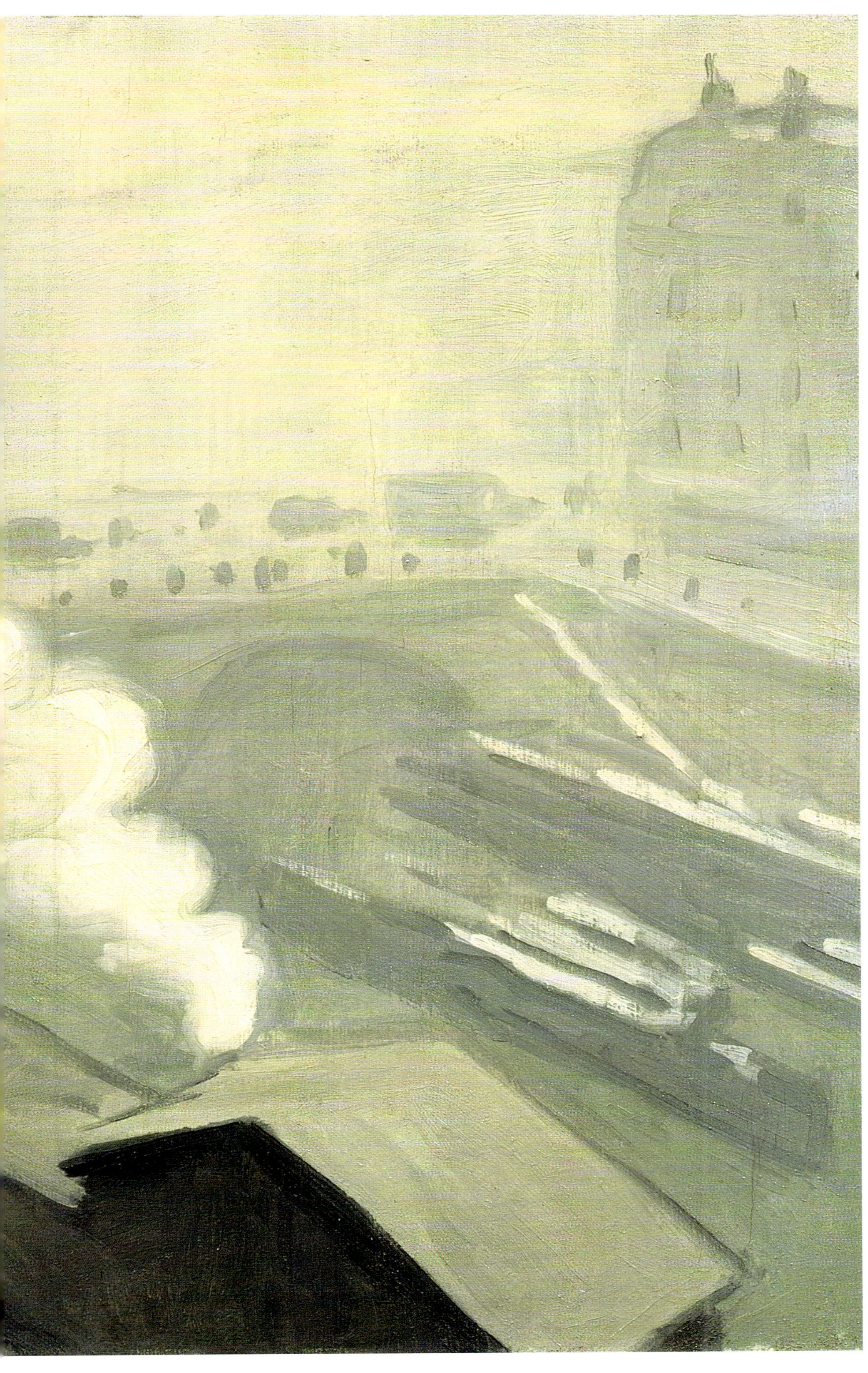

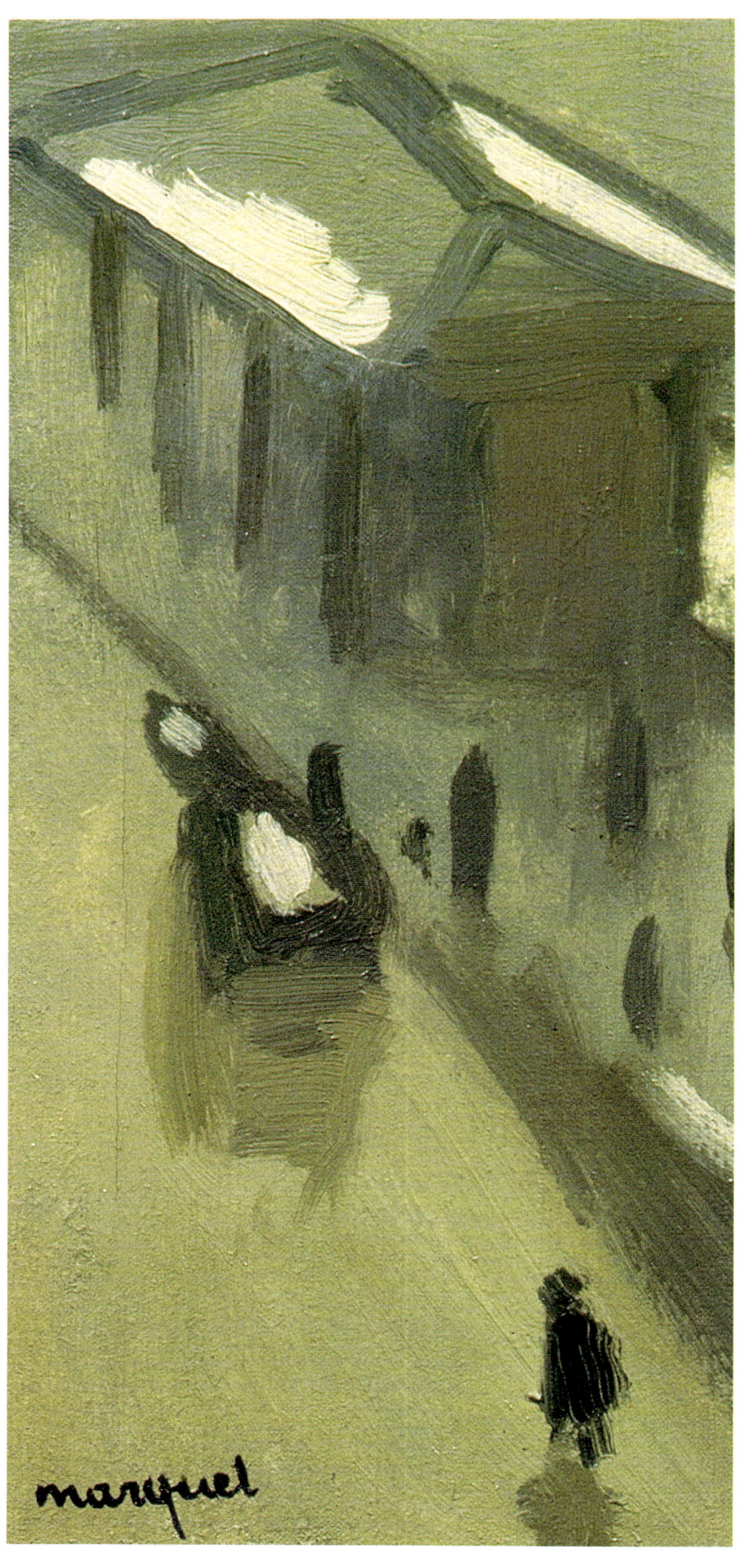

<u>THE PONT SAINT-MICHEL
IN WINTER</u>
Detail.
The Pushkin Museum of Fine Arts, Moscow.

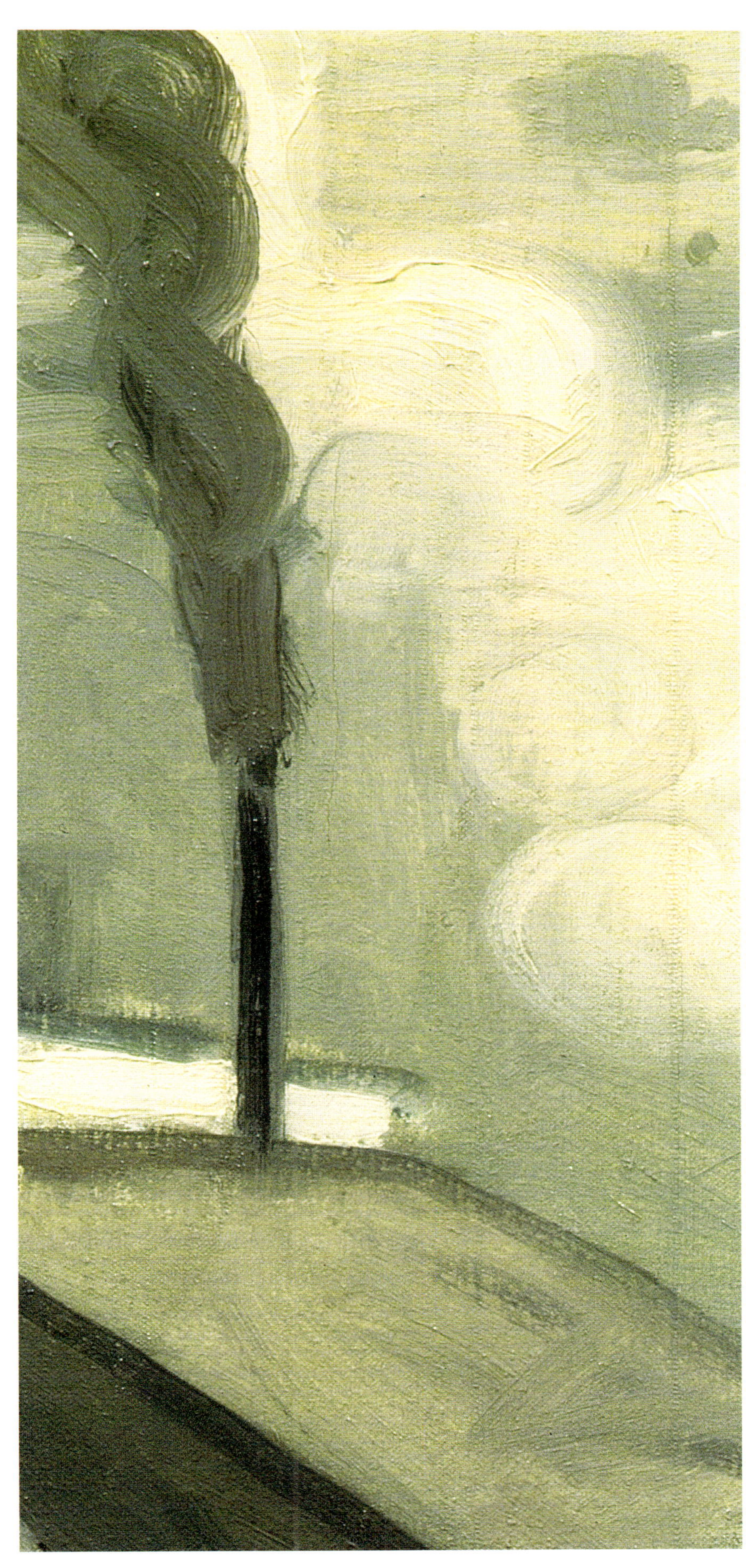

THE PONT SAINT-MICHEL
IN WINTER
Detail.
The Pushkin Museum of Fine Arts, Moscow.

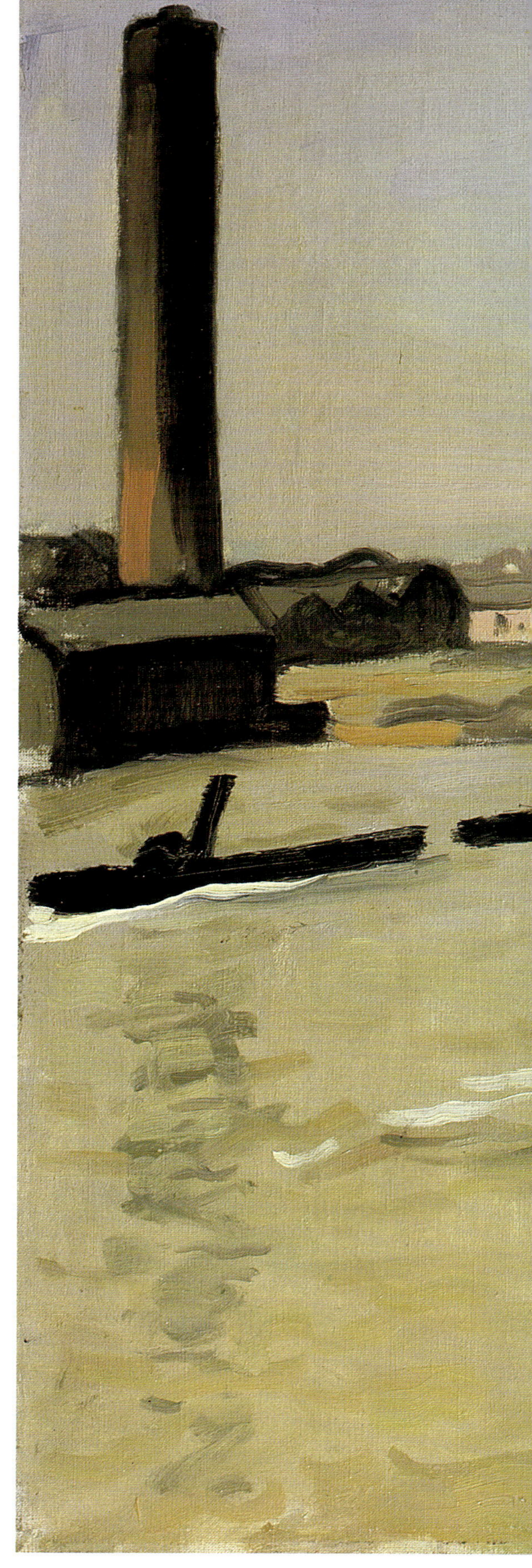

THE PORT OF HAMBURG
1909
Oil on canvas. 65.5 x 80 cm.
Signed bottom right: *Marquet.*
Provenance: Galerie Eugène Drouet, Paris;
Sergei Shchukin collection, Moscow;
1918, First Museum of Modern
Western Painting, Moscow;
1923, Museum of Modern Western Art,
Moscow;
from 1948, The Hermitage, St Petersburg
Inventory No. 8907.

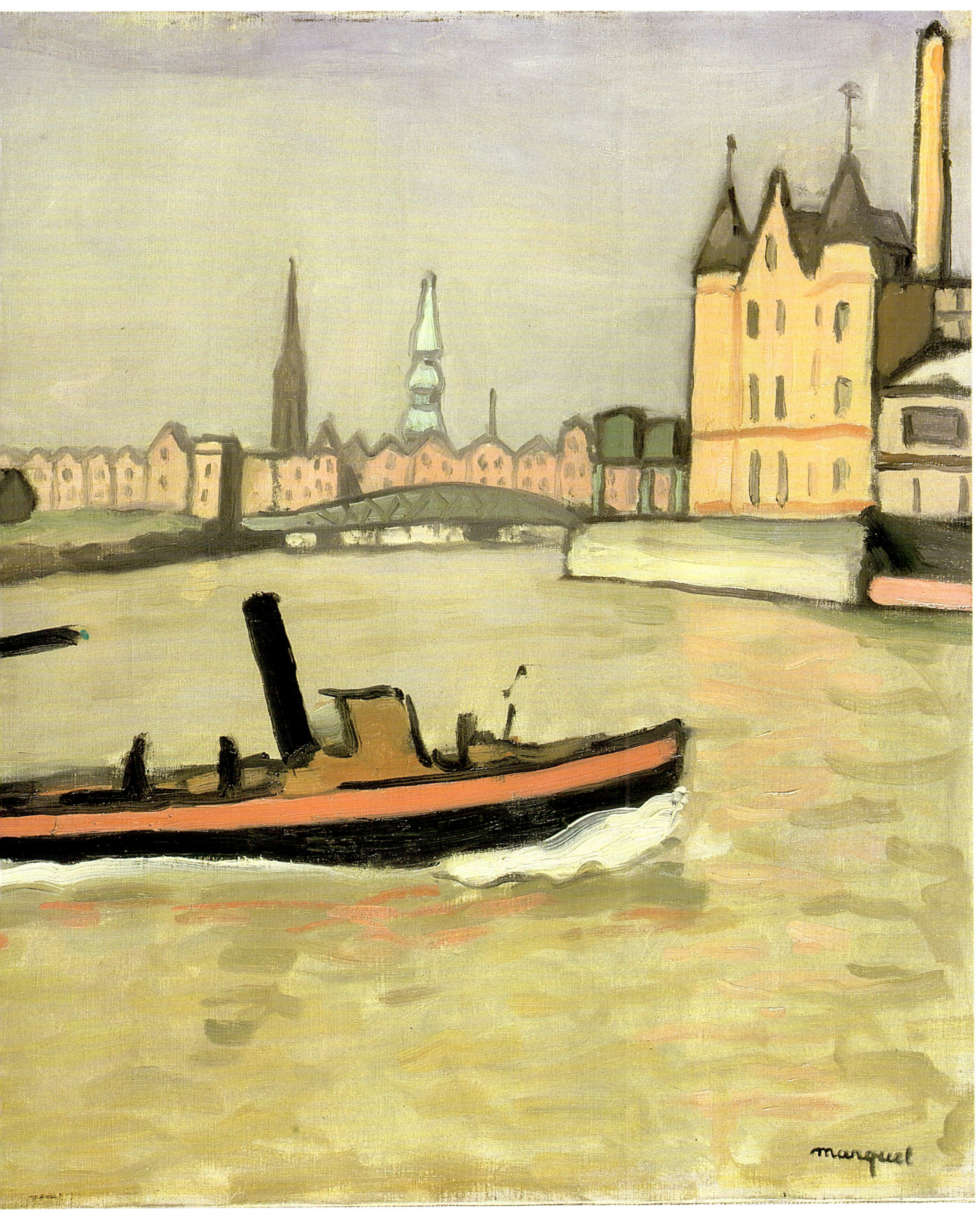

marquet

THE PORT OF HAMBURG
Detail.
The Hermitage, St Petersburg.

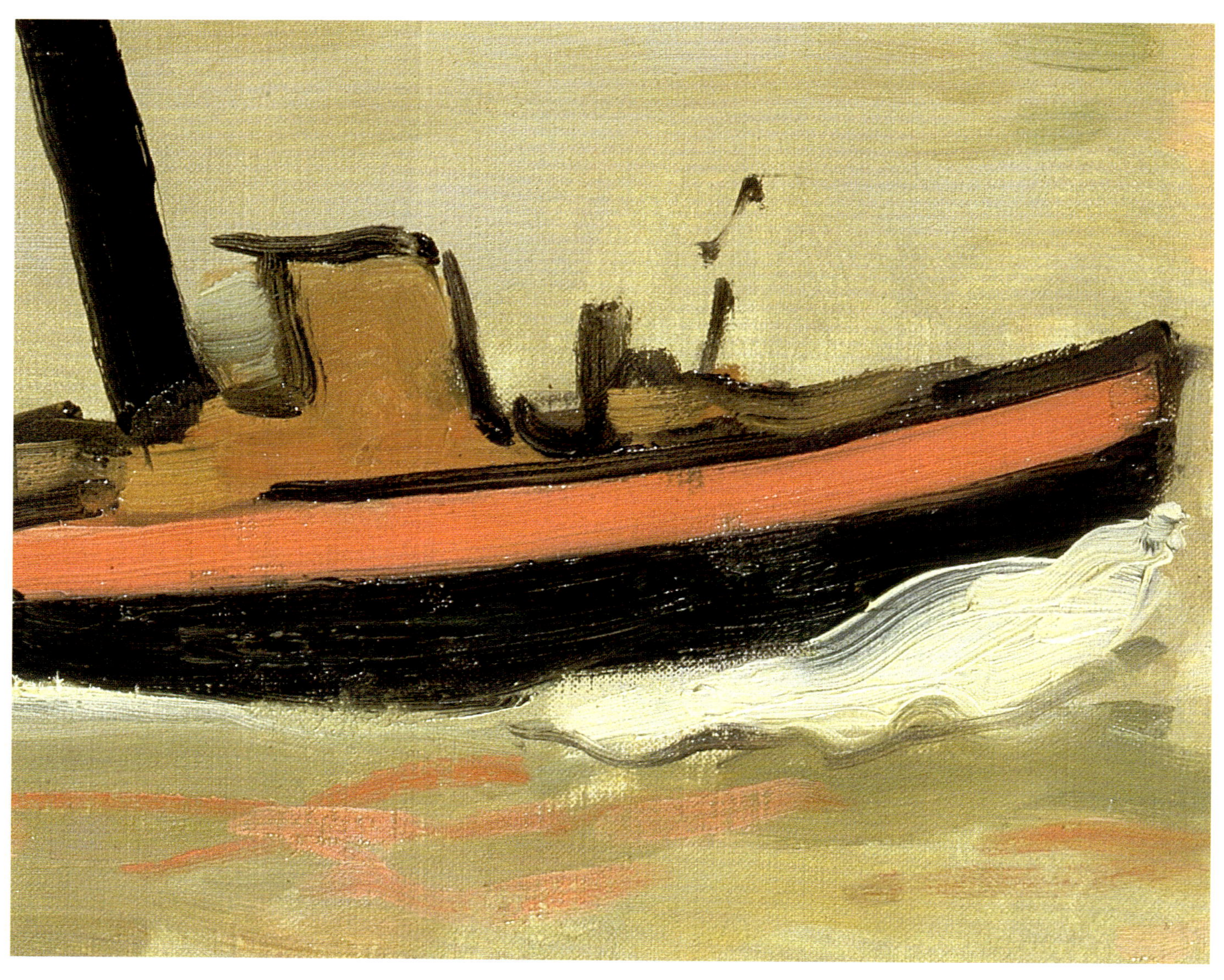

THE PORT OF HAMBURG
Detail.
The Hermitage, St Petersburg.

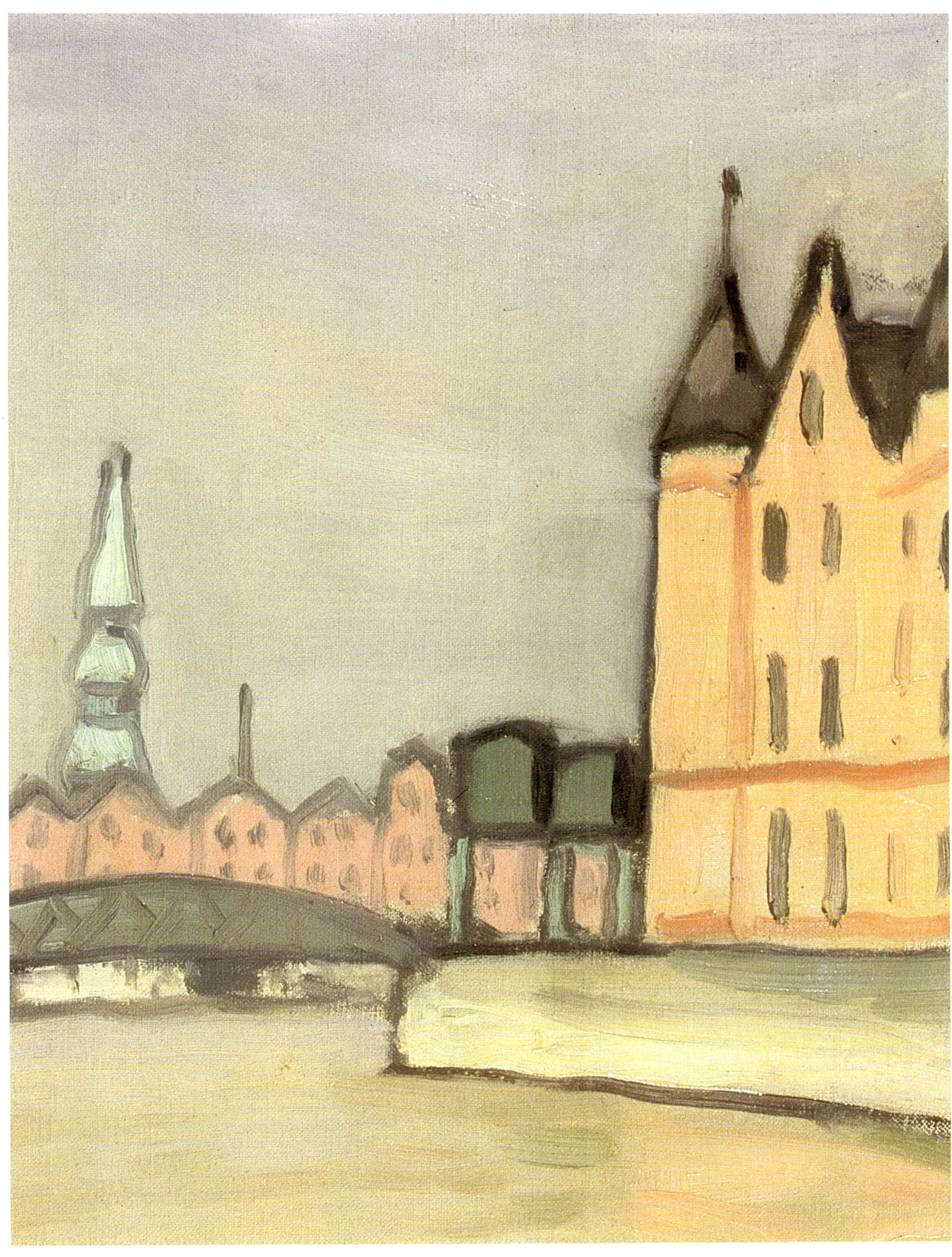

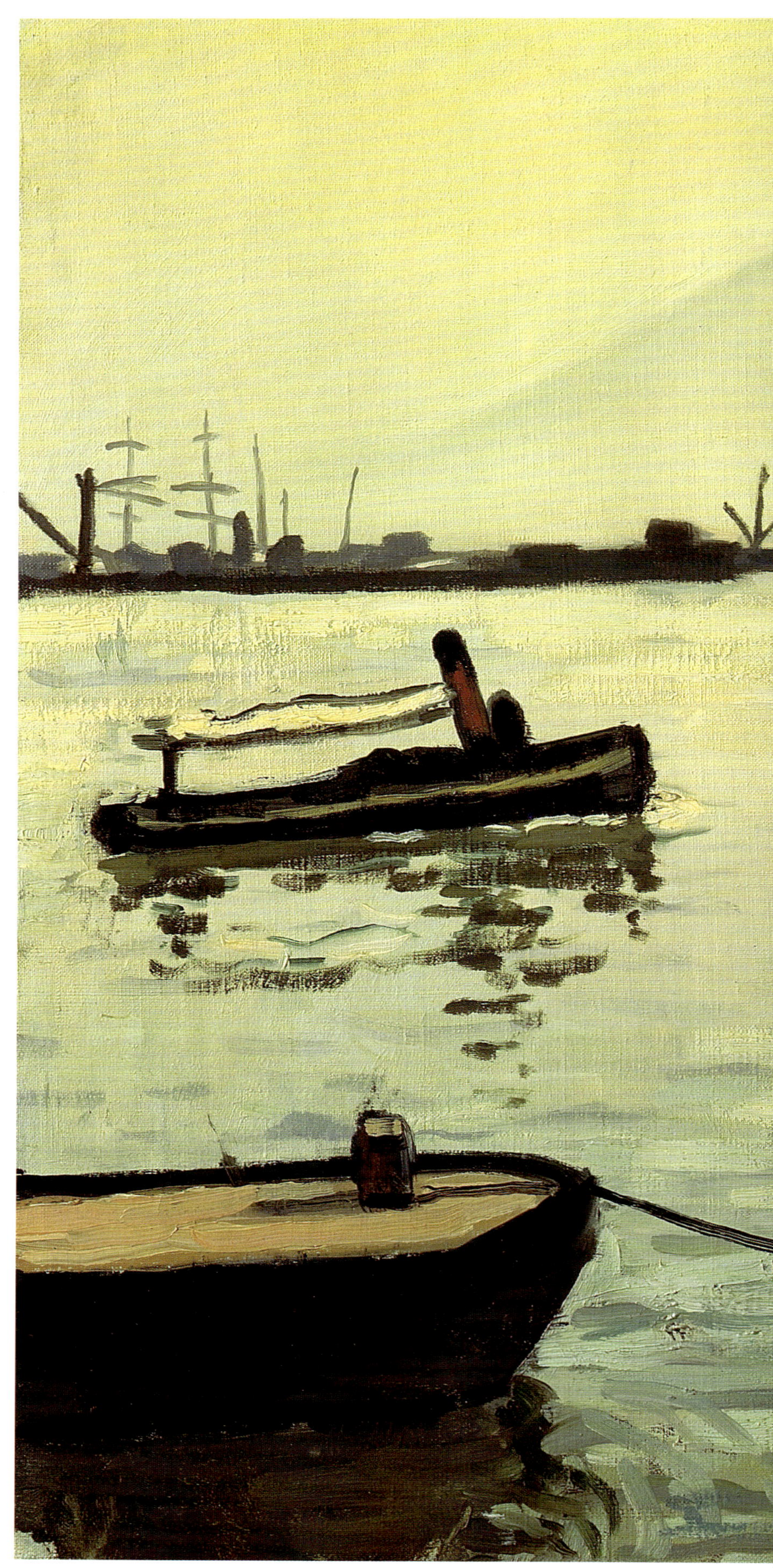

VESUVIUS
Ca. 1909
Oil on canvas. 61 x 80 cm.
Signed bottom right: *Marquet*.
Provenance: Galerie Eugène Drouet, Paris;
Sergei Shchukin collection, Moscow;
1918, Museum of Modern Western Art,
Moscow;
from 1948, The Pushkin Museum
of Fine Arts, Moscow.
Inventory No. 3294.

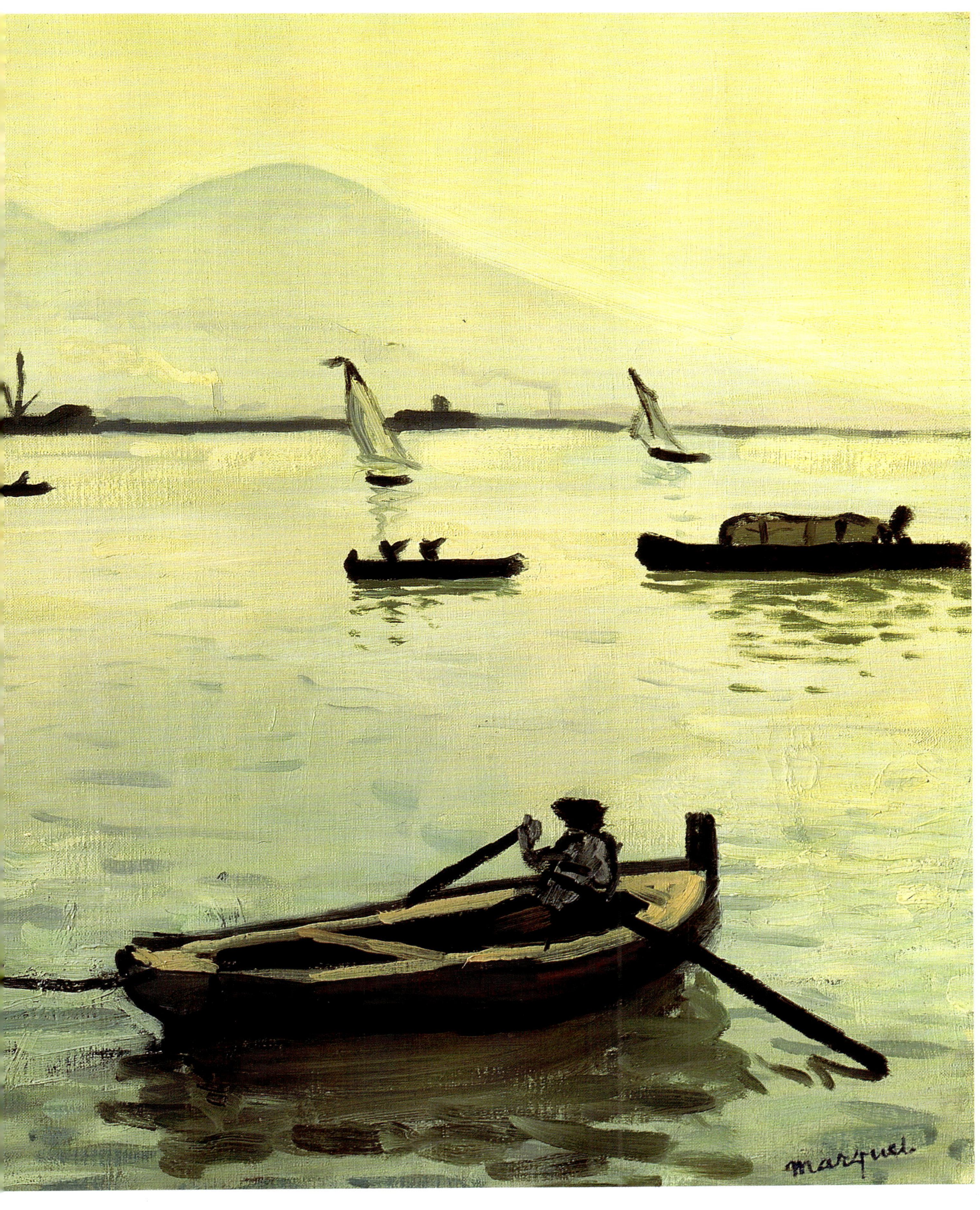

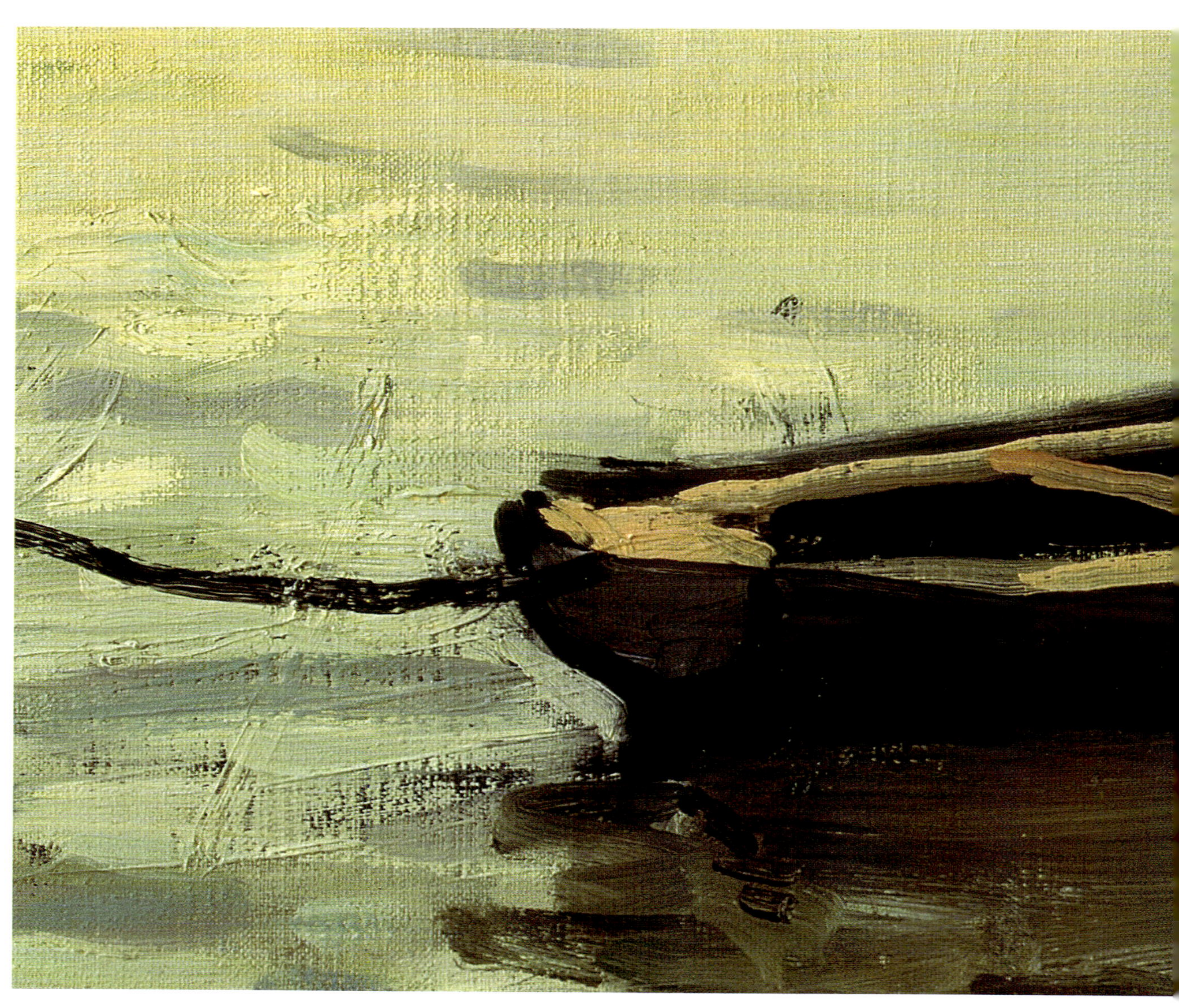

VESUVIUS
Detail.
The Pushkin Museum of Fine Arts, Moscow.

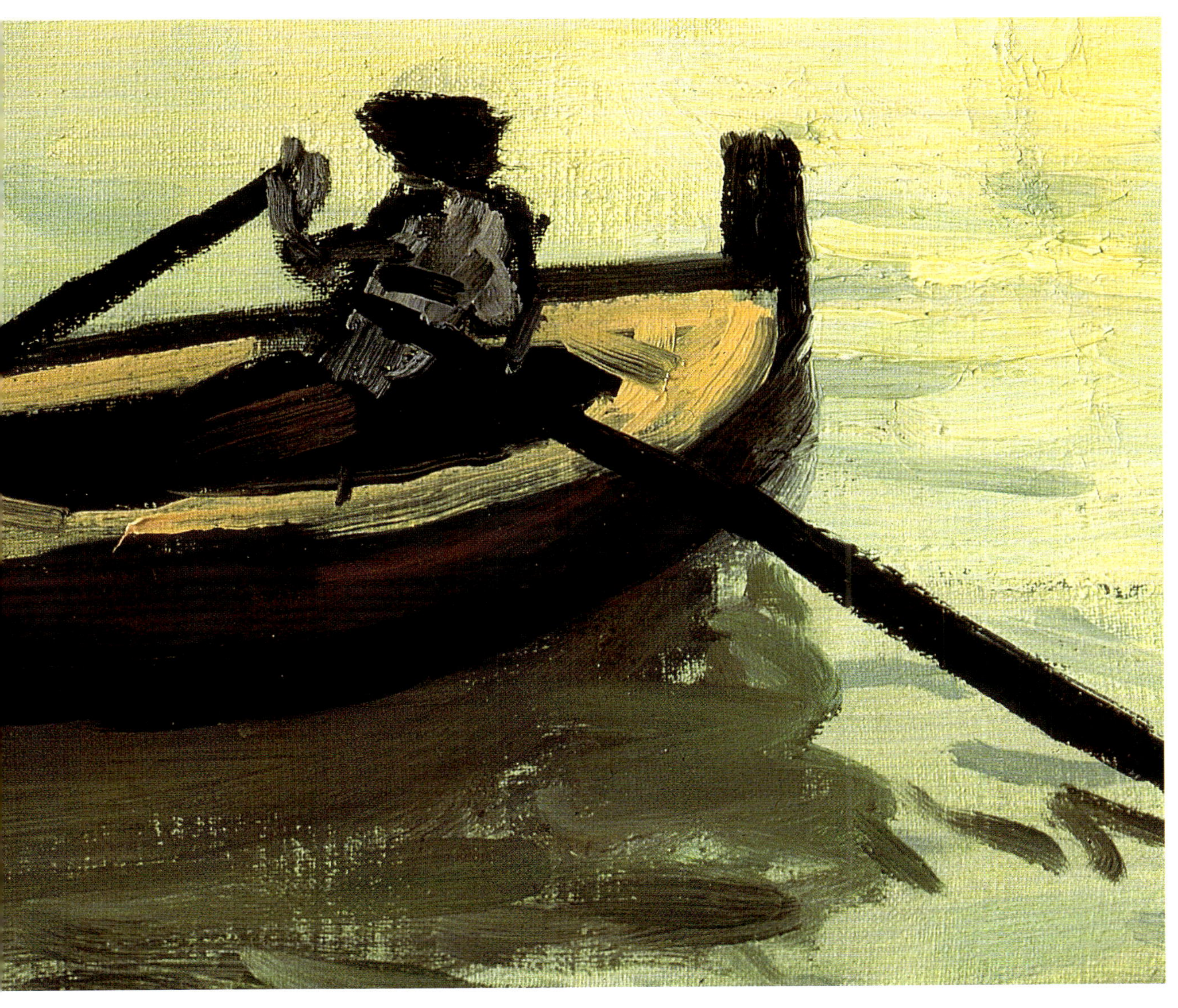

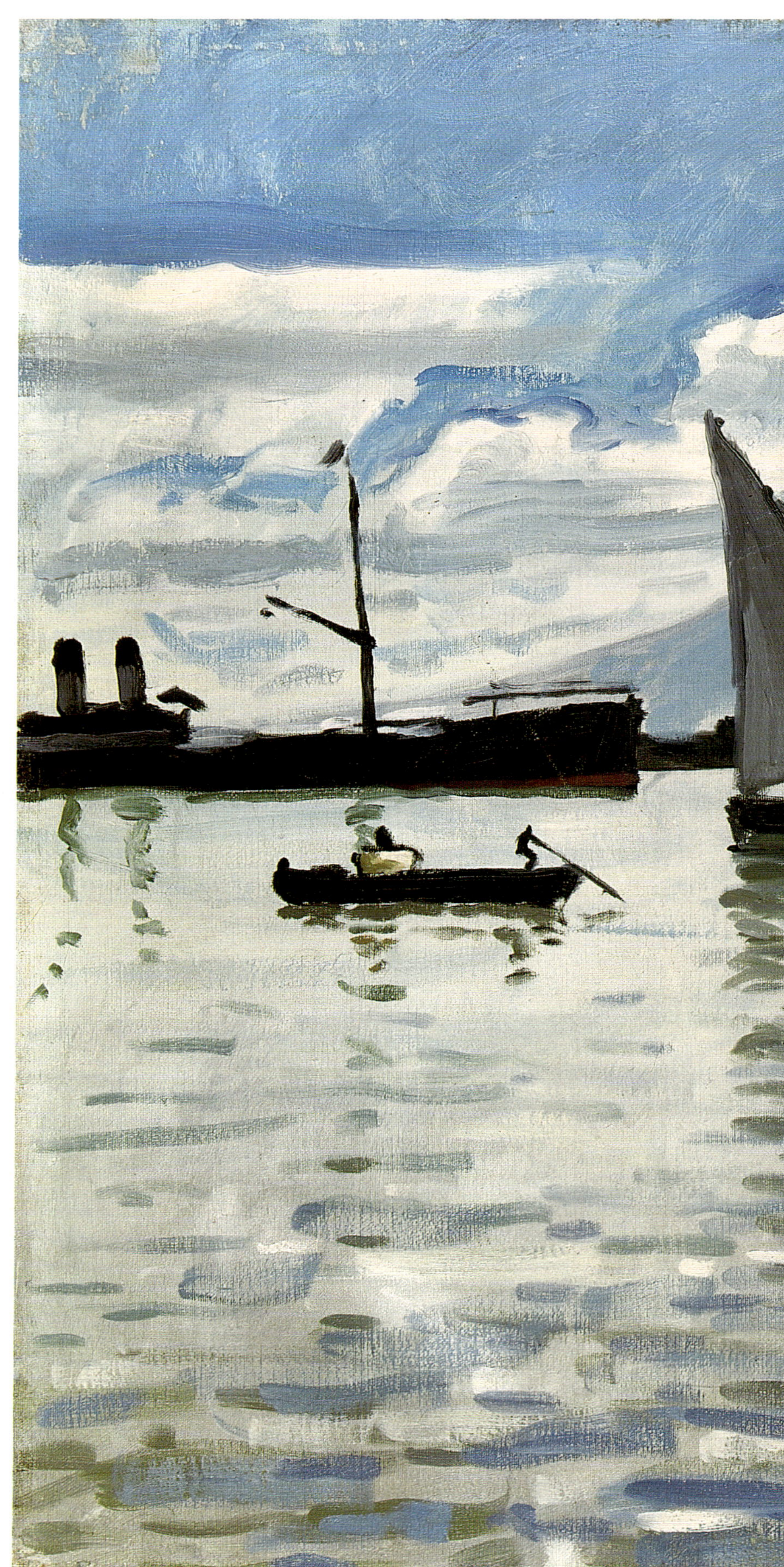

THE BAY OF NAPLES
1909
Oil on canvas. 62 x 80.3 cm.
Signed bottom right: *Marquet*
and dated in ink below: *1909*.
Provenance: Galerie Eugène Drouet, Paris;
1913, Ivan Morozov collection, Moscow;
1918, Second Museum of Modern
Western Painting, Moscow;
1923, Museum of Modern Western Art,
Moscow;
from 1948, The Hermitage, St Petersburg
Inventory No. 9150.

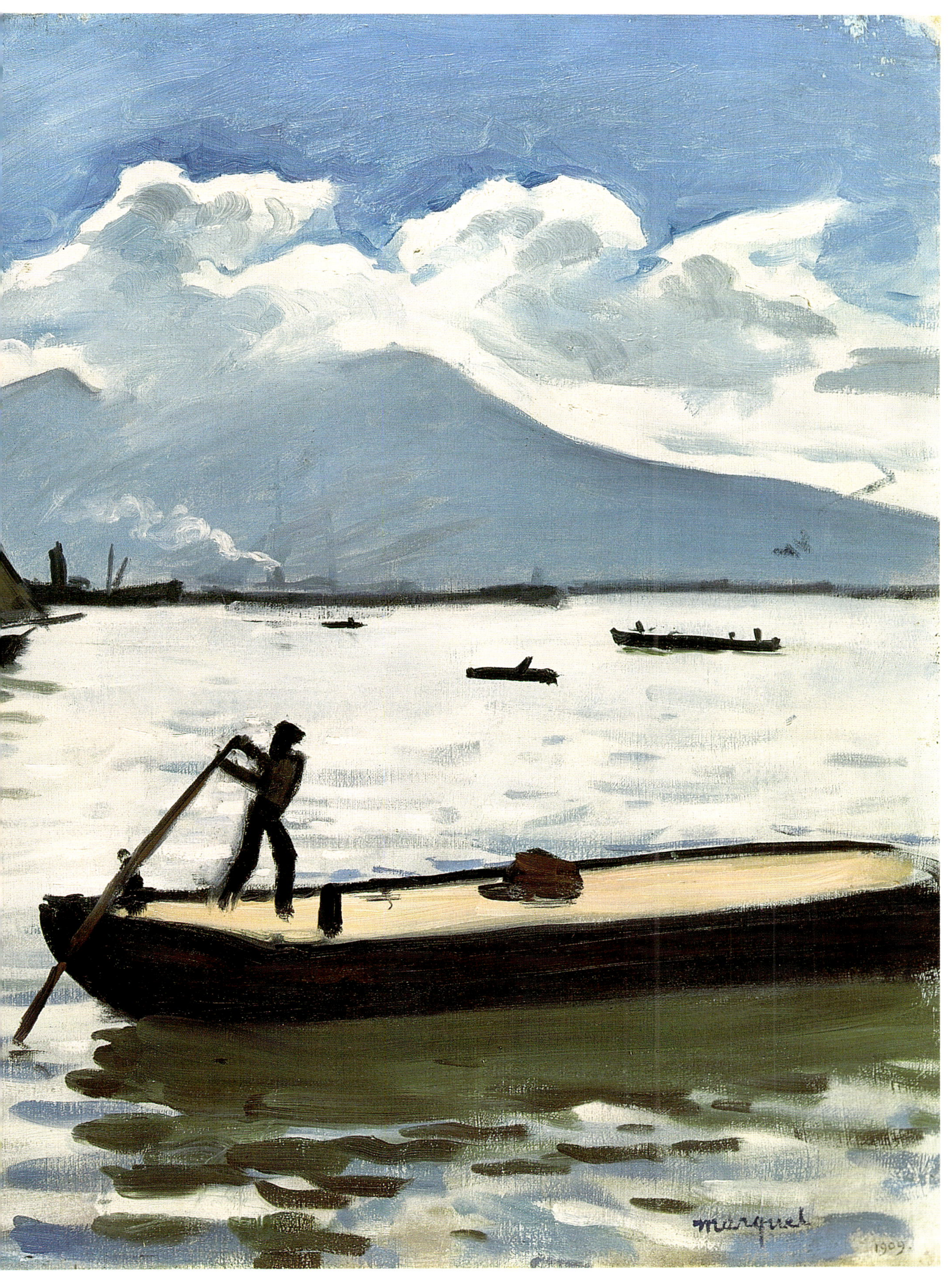

marquet
1909

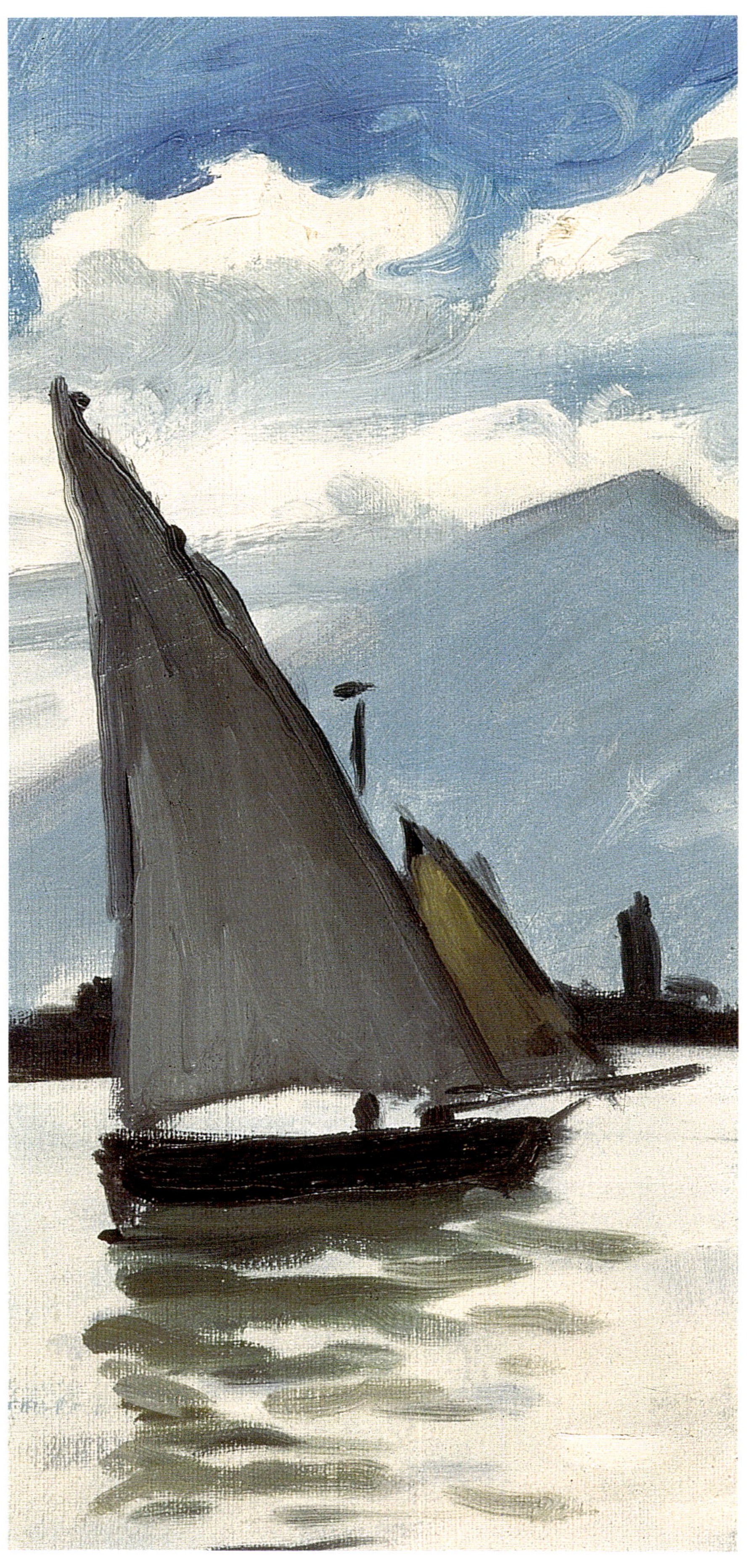

THE BAY OF NAPLES
Detail.
The Hermitage, St Petersburg.

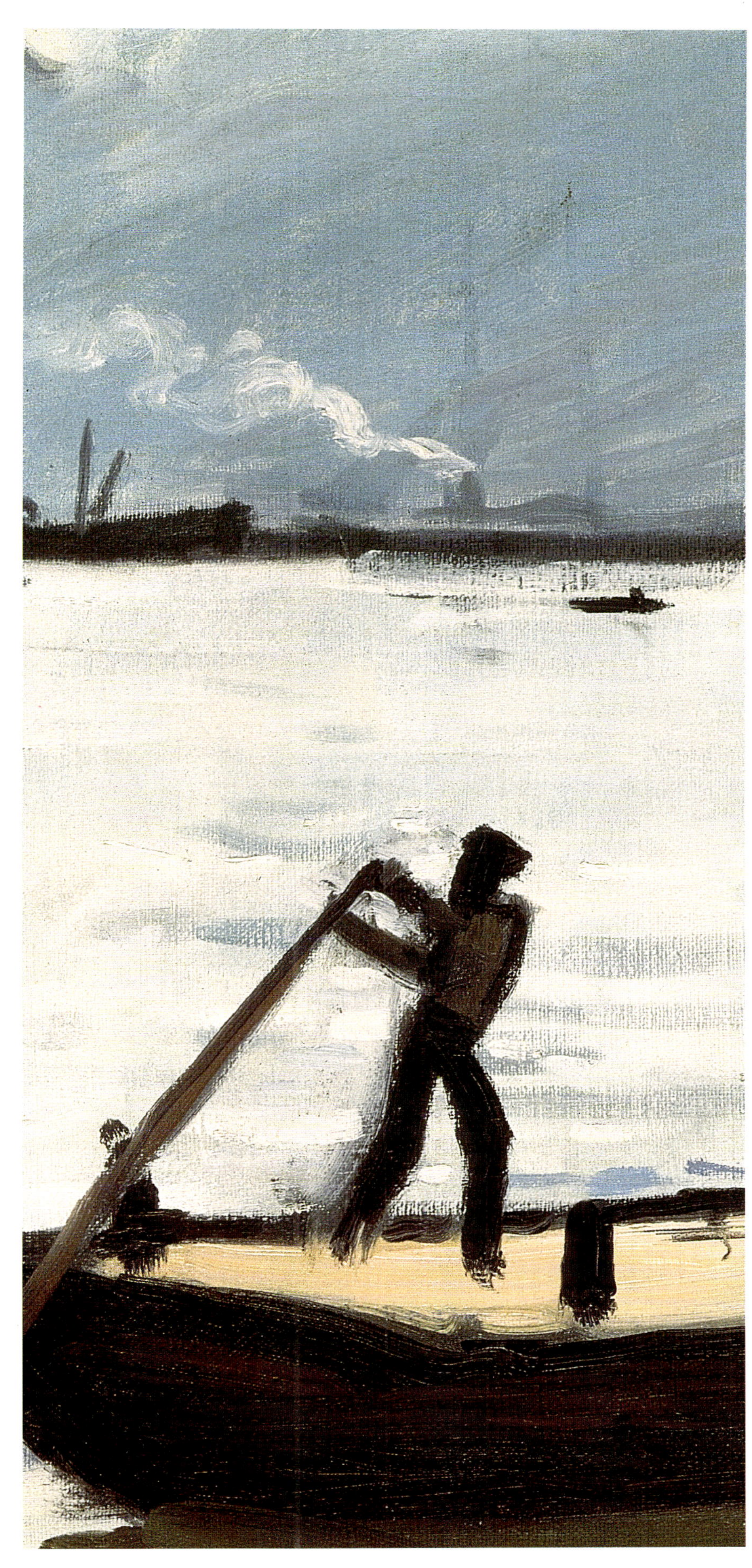

THE BAY OF NAPLES
Detail.
The Hermitage, St Petersburg.

RAINY DAY IN PARIS
NOTRE DAME
1910
Oil on canvas. 81 x 66 cm.
Signed bottom right: *Marquet*.
Provenance: Galerie Eugène Drouet, Paris;
1911, Ivan Morozov collection, Moscow;
1918, First Museum of Modern
Western Painting, Moscow;
1923, Museum of Modern Western Art,
Moscow;
from 1930, The Hermitage, St Petersburg
Inventory No. 6526.

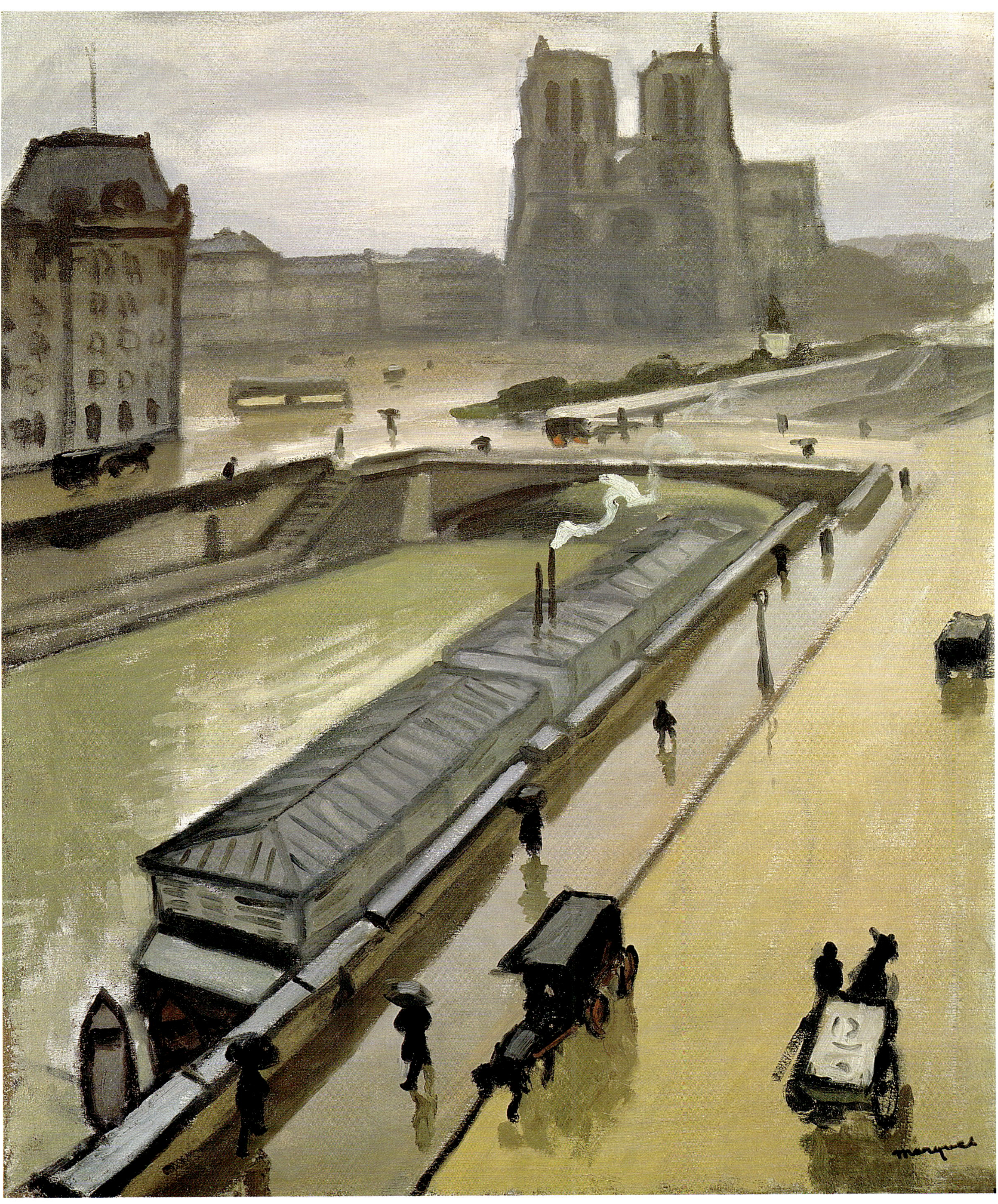

RAINY DAY IN PARIS
NOTRE DAME
Detail.
The Hermitage, St Petersburg.

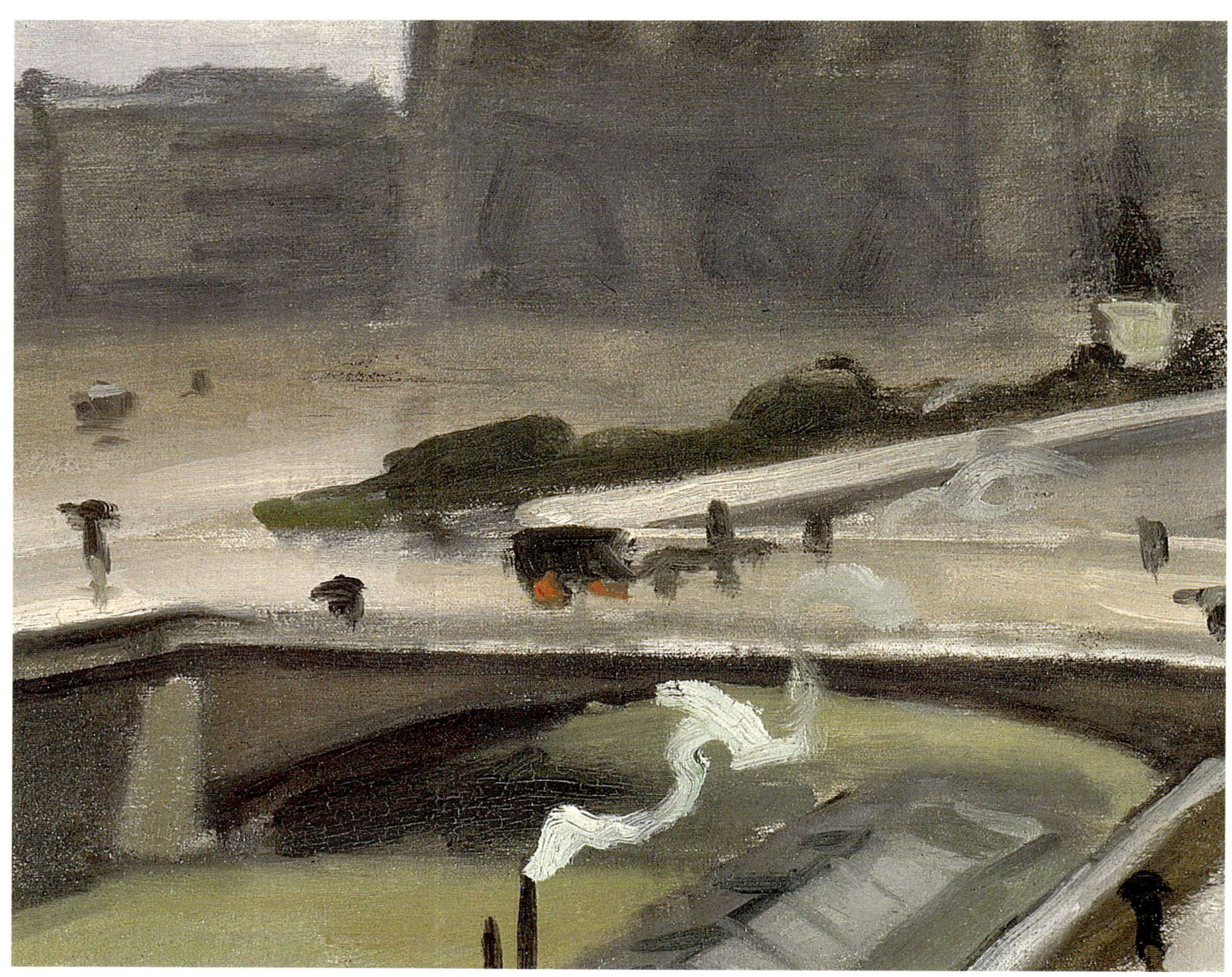

RAINY DAY IN PARIS
NOTRE DAME
Detail.
The Hermitage, St Petersburg.

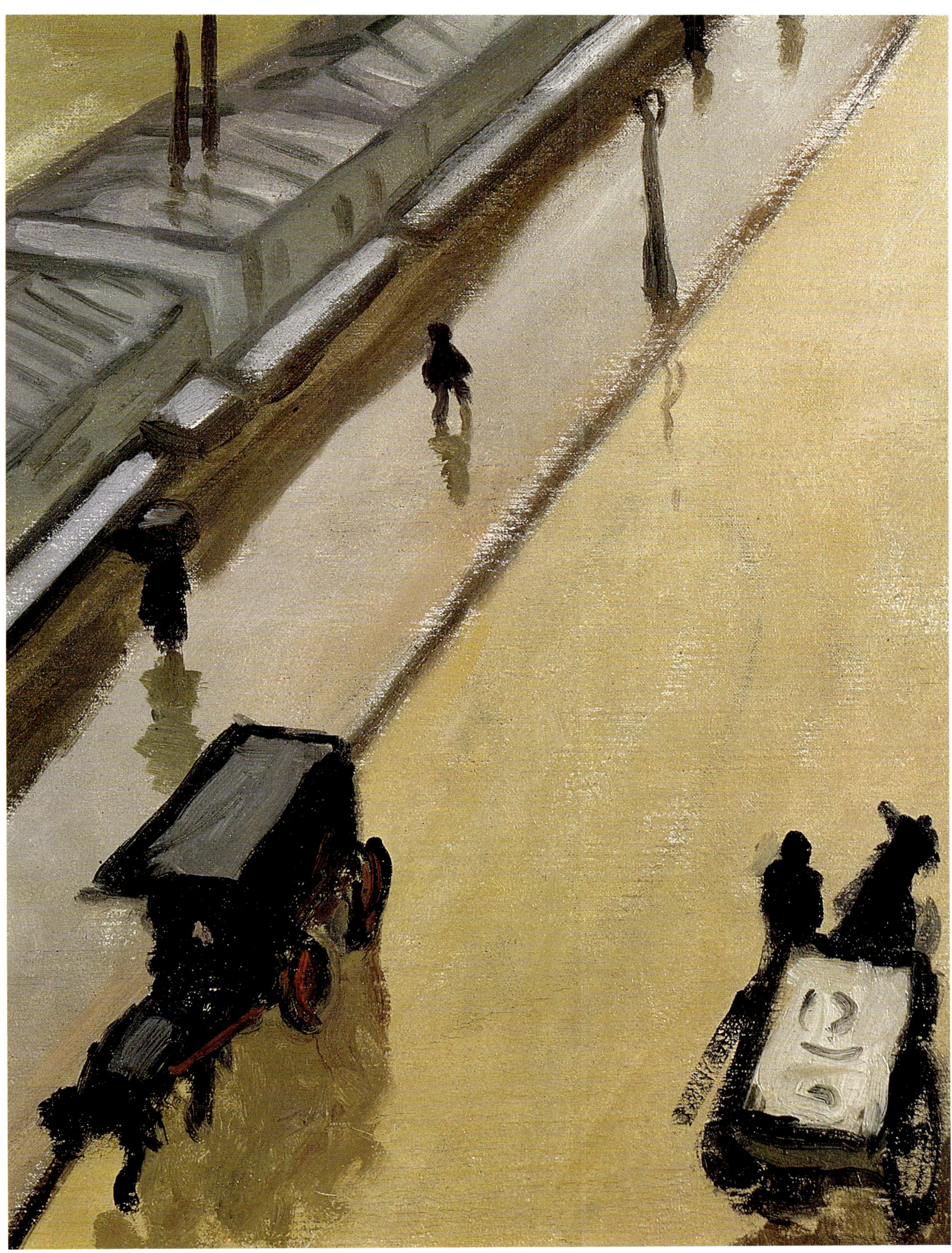

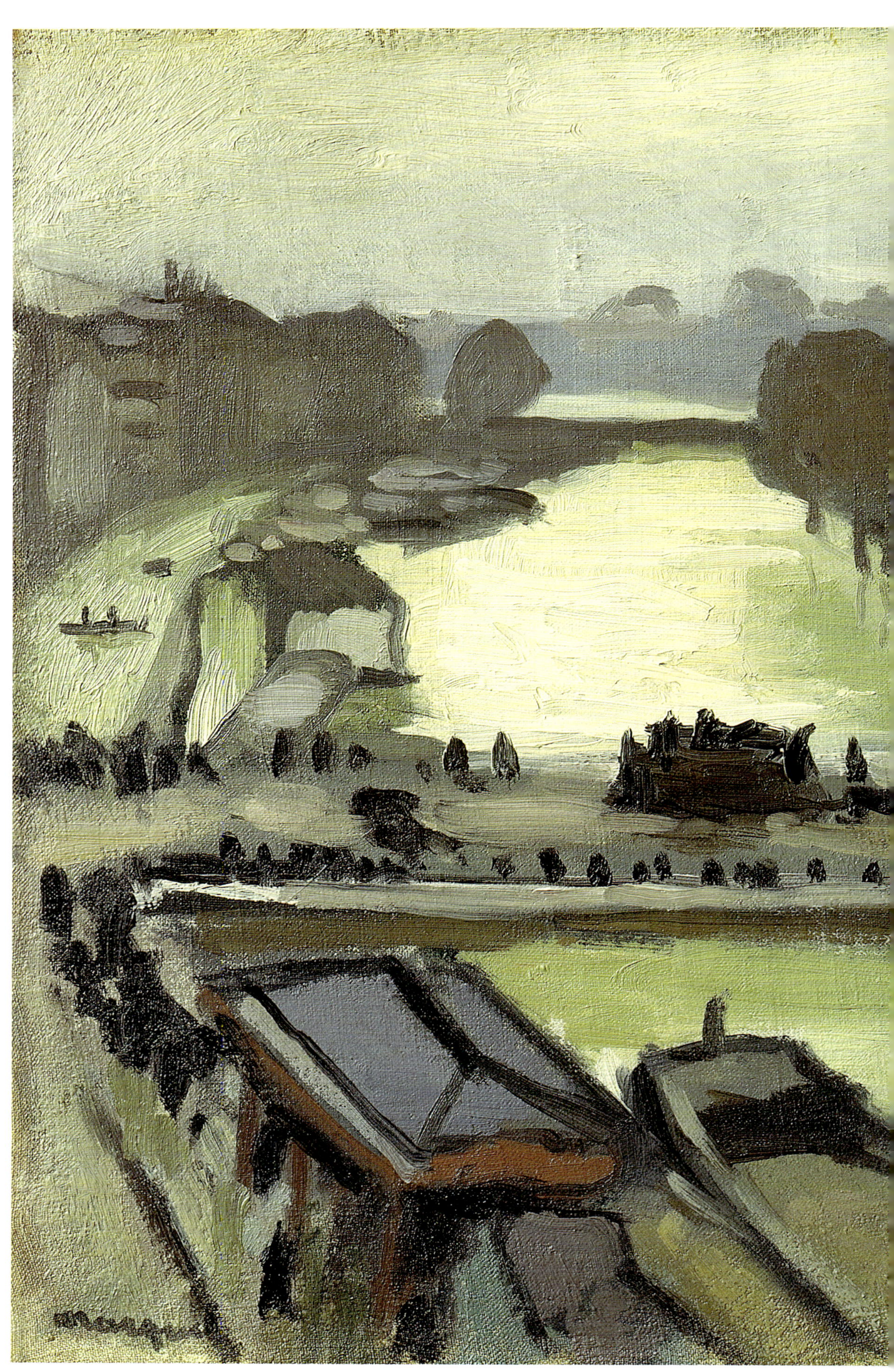

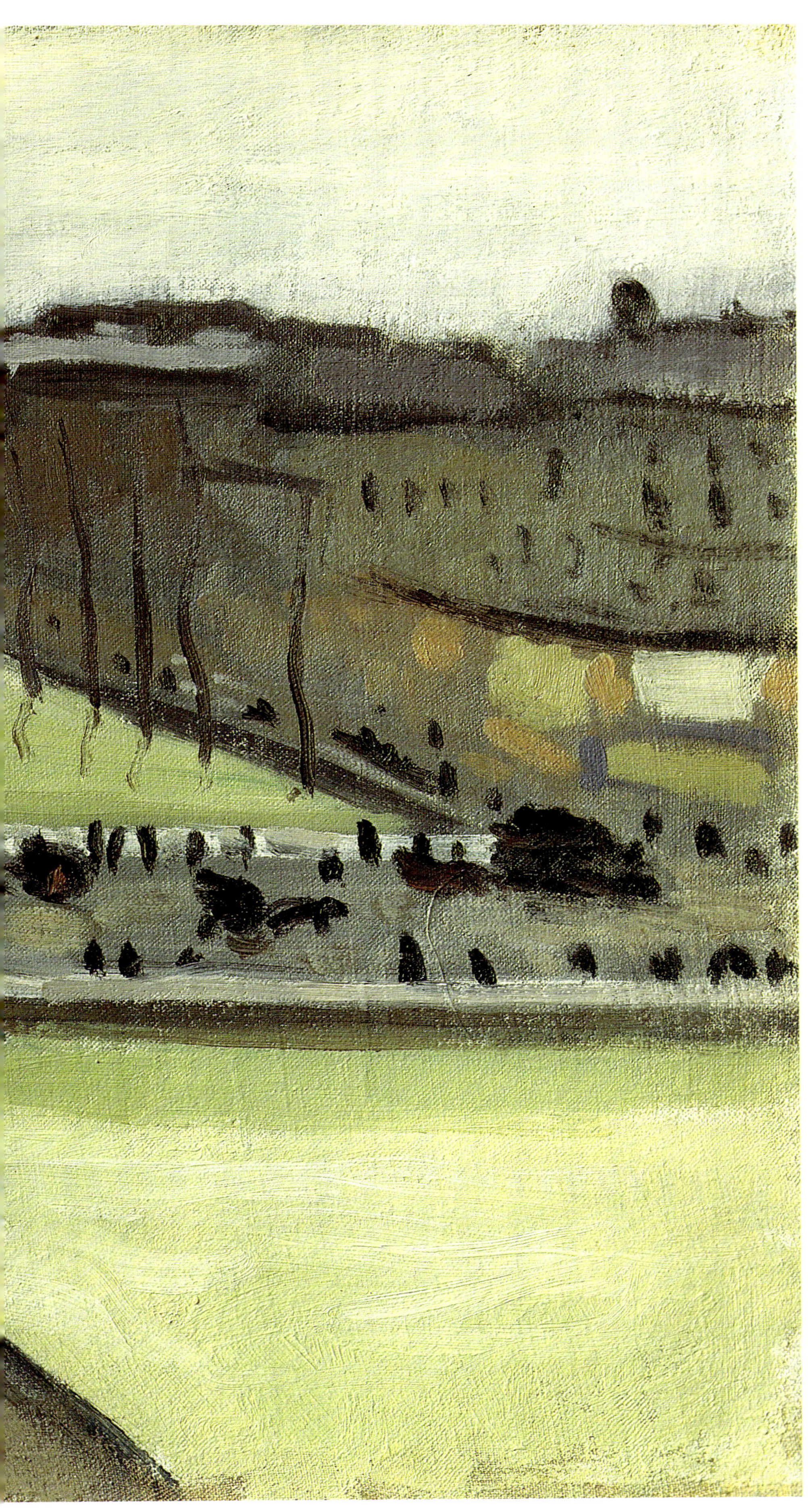

FLOOD IN PARIS
Ca. 1910
Oil on canvas. 33 x 41 cm.
Signed bottom left: *Marquet.*
Provenance: Galerie Eugène Drouet, Paris;
Sergei Shchukin collection, Moscow;
1918, Museum of Modern Western Art,
Moscow;
from 1948, The Pushkin Museum
of Fine Arts, Moscow.
Inventory No. 3290.

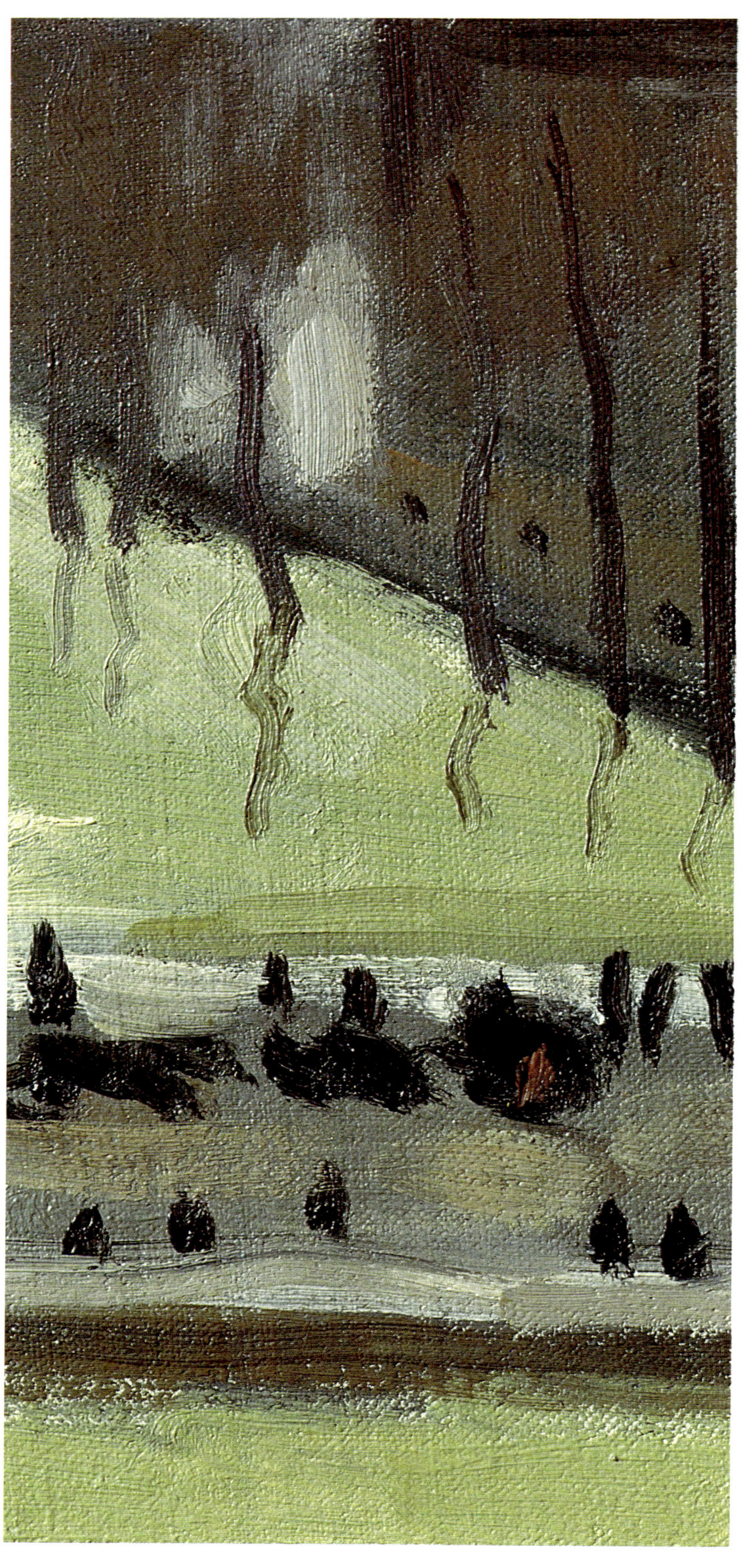

FLOOD IN PARIS
Detail.
The Pushkin Museum of Fine Arts, Moscow.

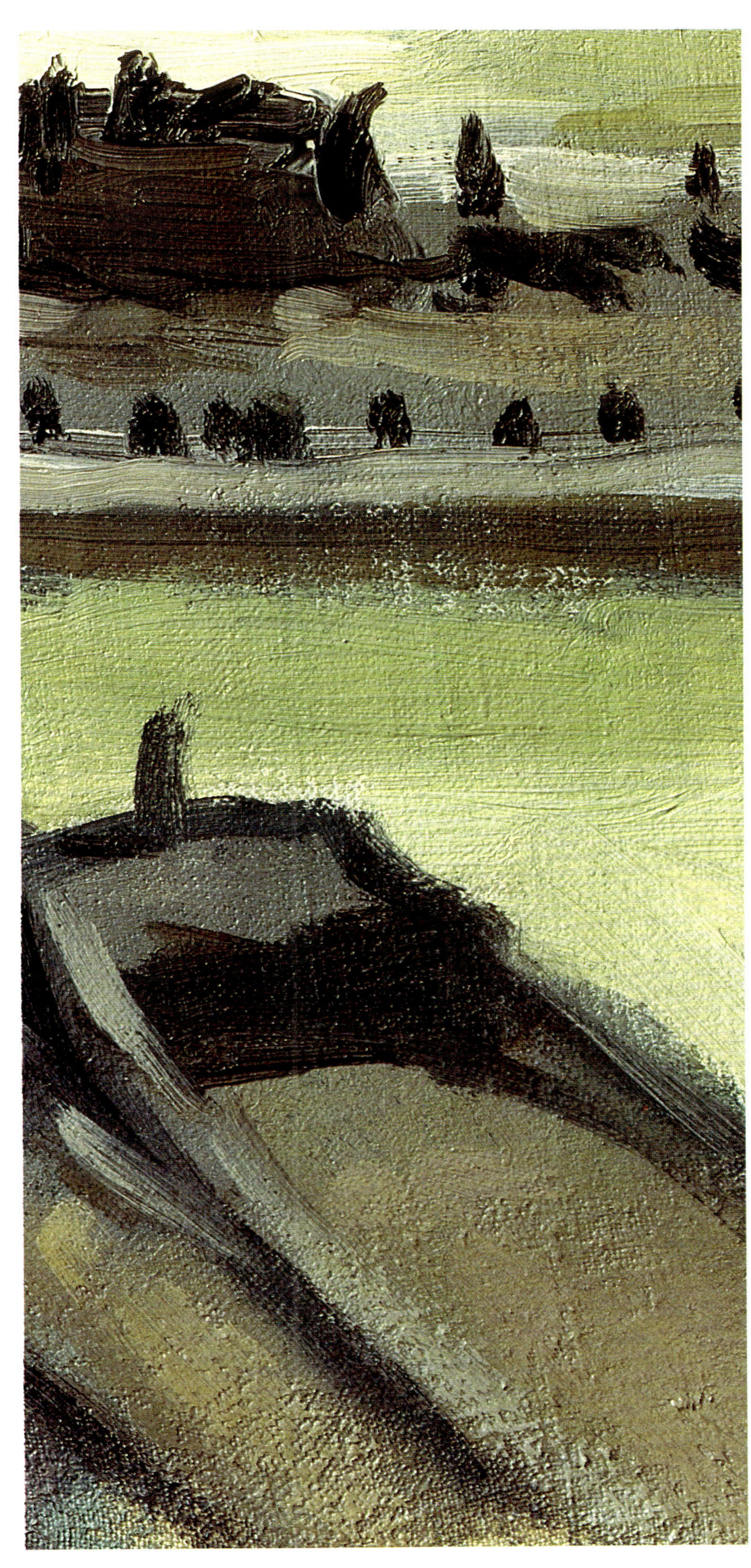

FLOOD IN PARIS
Detail.
The Pushkin Museum of Fine Arts, Moscow.

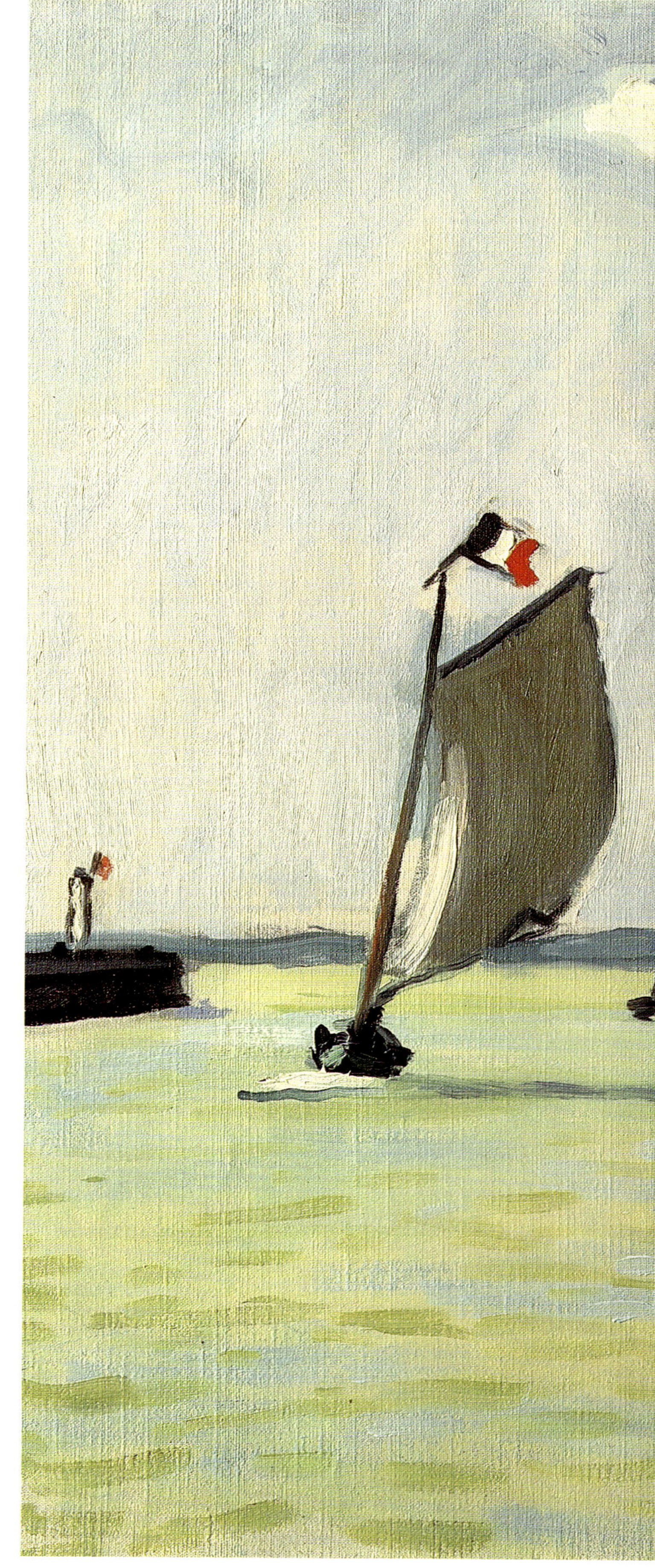

THE PORT OF HONFLEUR
Ca. 1911
Oil on canvas. 65 x 81 cm.
Signed bottom right: *Marquet.*
Provenance: Galerie Eugène Drouet, Paris;
Sergei Shchukin collection, Moscow;
1918, Museum of Modern Western Art,
Moscow;
from 1948, The Pushkin Museum
of Fine Arts, Moscow.
Inventory No. 3291.

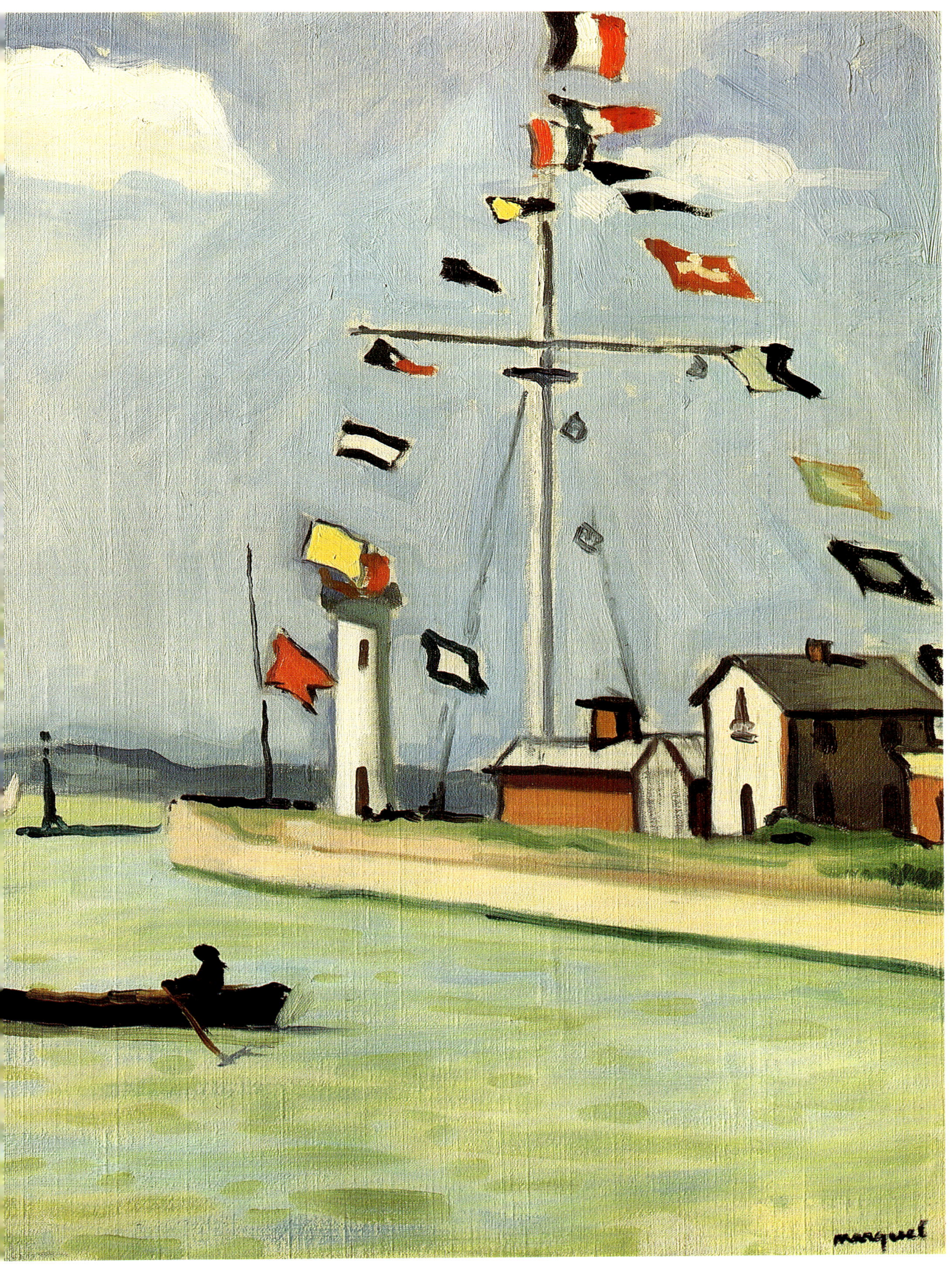

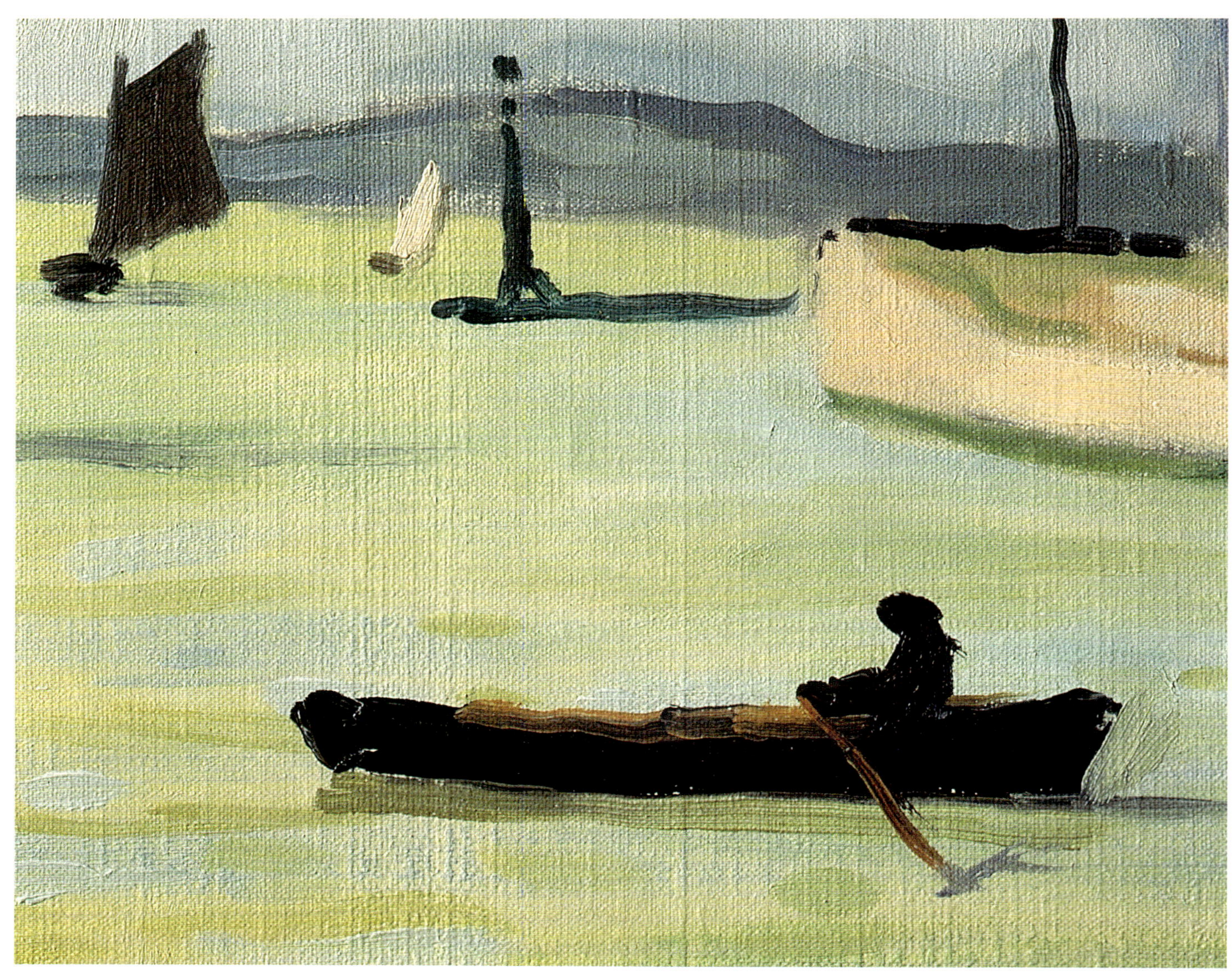

THE PORT OF HONFLEUR
Detail.
The Pushkin Museum of Fine Arts, Moscow.

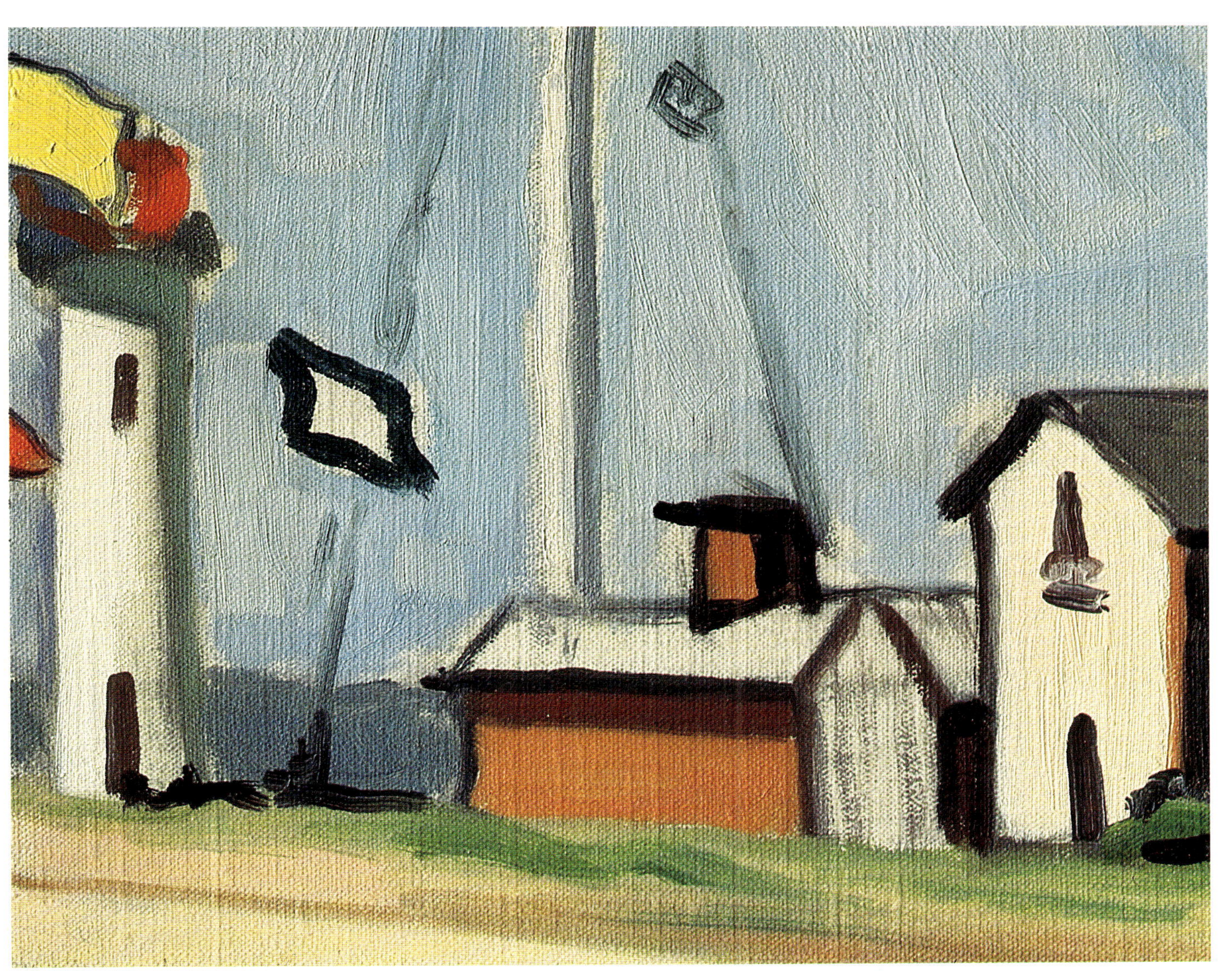

1911
Oil on canvas. 81 x 65.5 cm.
Signed bottom right: *Marquet*.
Provenance: Galerie Eugène Drouet, Paris;
Hans Haasen collection, Petrograd;
from 1921, The Hermitage, St Petersburg.
Inventory No. 4905.

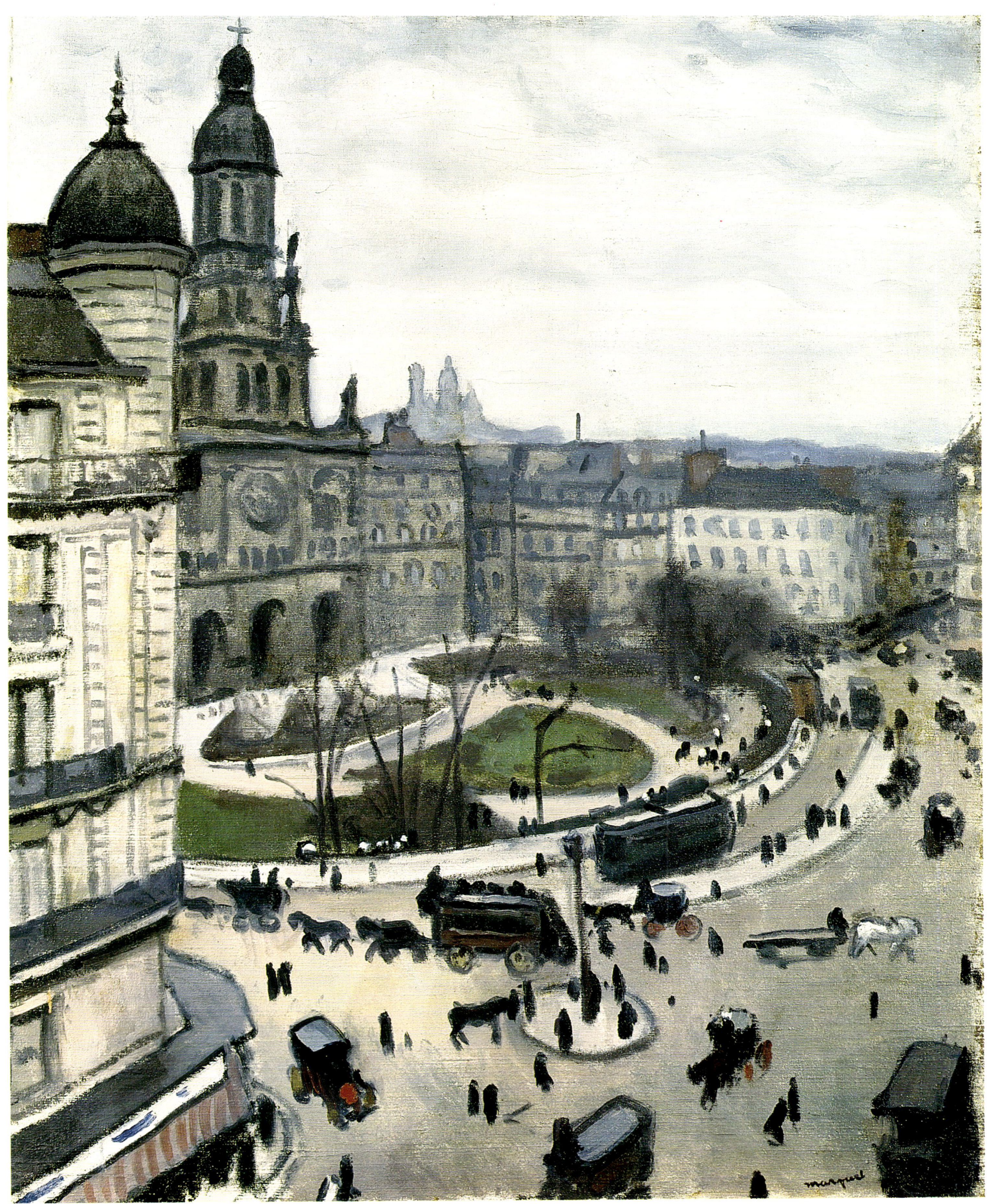

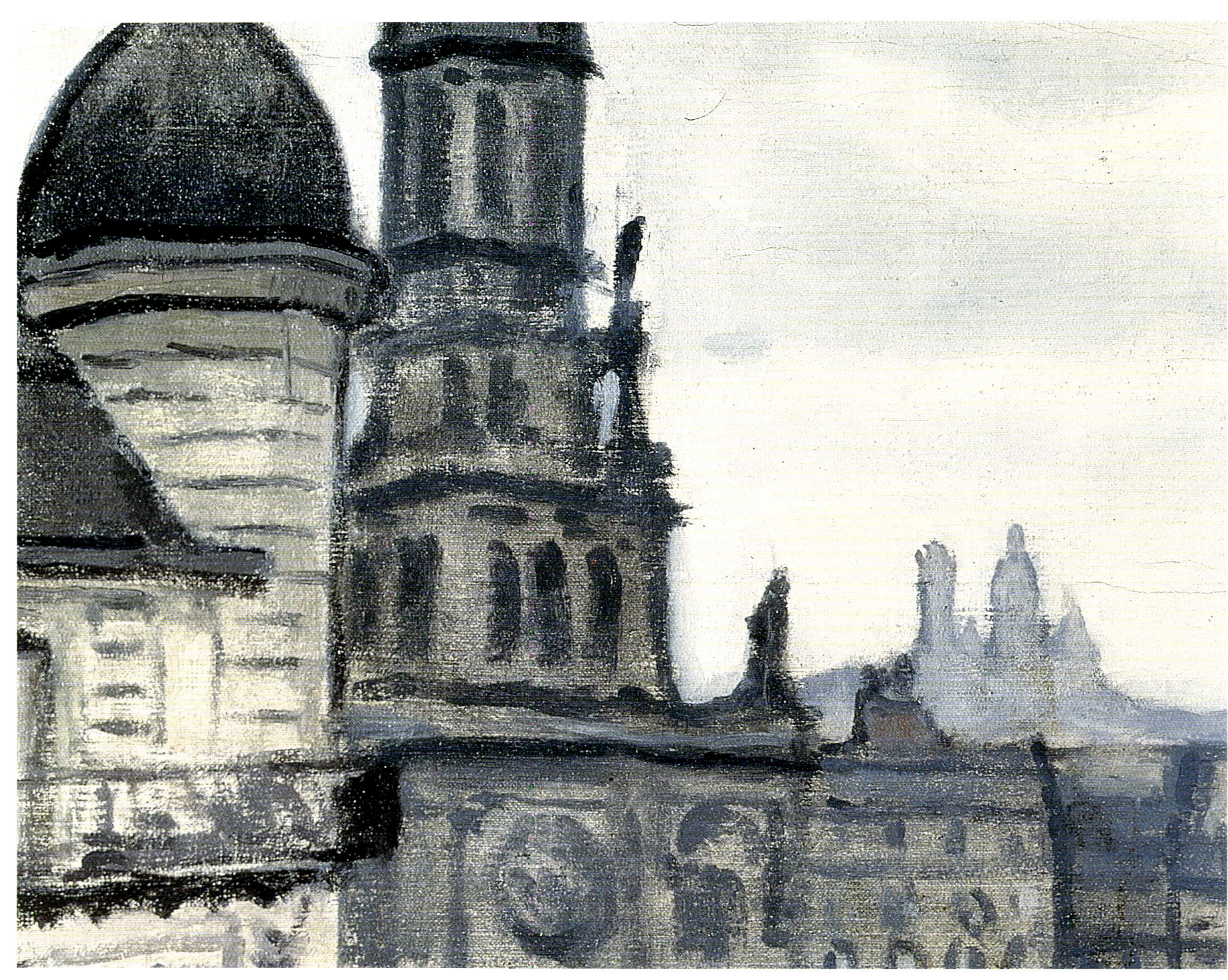

THE PLACE DE LA TRINITÉ IN PARIS
Detail.
The Hermitage, St Petersburg.

THE PLACE DE LA TRINITÉ IN PARIS
Detail.
The Hermitage, St Petersburg.

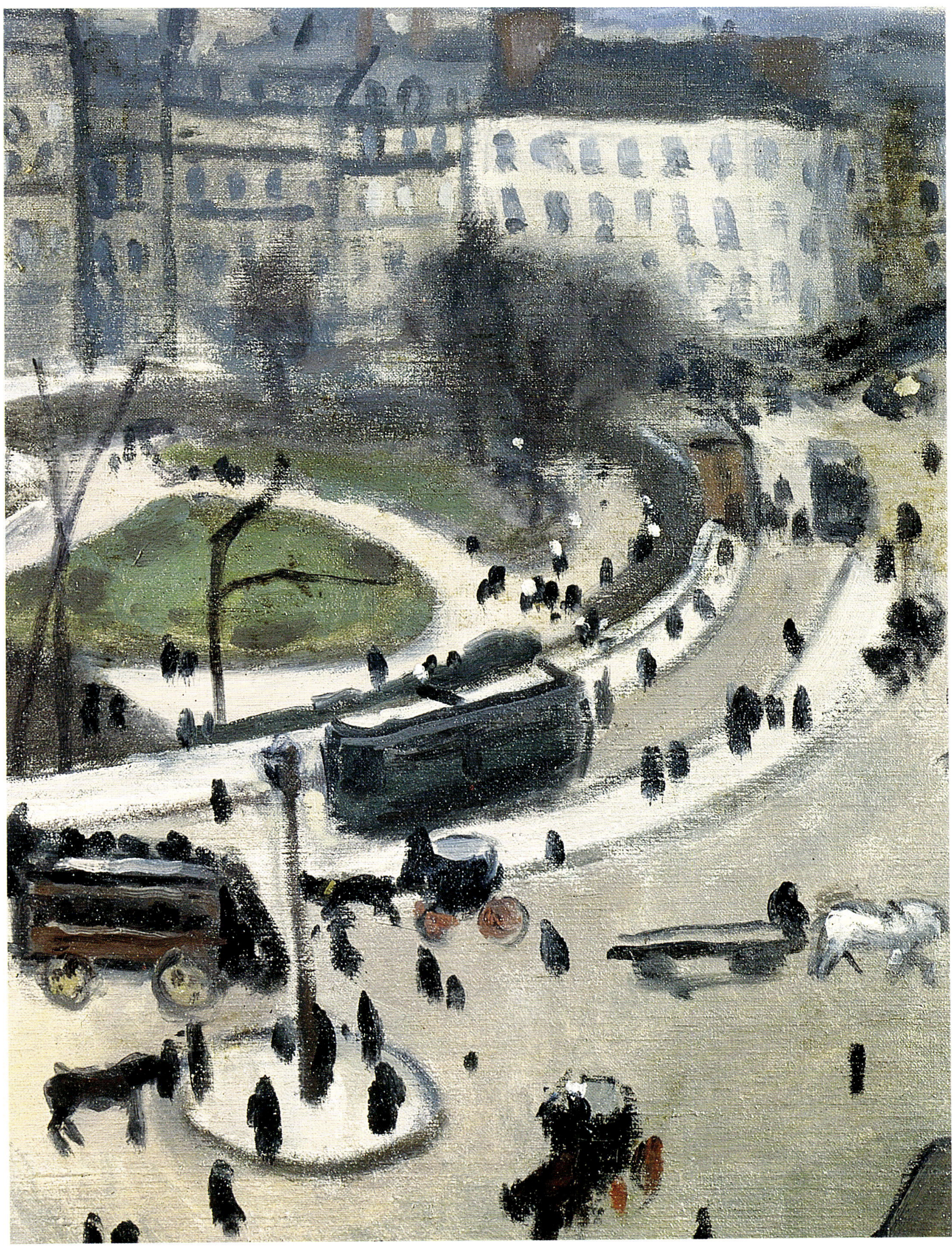

BIOGRAPHY

1875
Born into the family of a railway employee in Bordeaux on
26 March.

1882-1890
Attends school in Bordeaux.

1890
Moves to Paris. Studies at the Ecole des Arts Décoratifs.
Becomes acquainted with Henri Matisse.

1895-1898
Studies in Gustave Moreau's studio at the Ecole des Beaux-
Arts. Paints copies of works in the Louvre.

1899-1900
Works together with Matisse on the Petit Palais.

1900
Exhibits his work for the first time (at the Salon des Indé-
pendants). Paints landscapes outside Paris.

1901
Paints landscapes in Normandy. Becomes acquainted with the
photographer and art-dealer Eugène Drouet.

1902
Begins exhibiting his work in Berthe Weill's shop.

1903
Produces illustrations for Charles Louis Philippe's book *Bubu
de Montparnasse*.

1905
Works on the Côte d'Azur. Is among the exhibitors dubbed
"Fauves" at the Salon d'Automne.

1906
Paints in Normandy with Raoul Dufy. Marquet's father dies.

1907
First one-man exhibition, at the Galerie Drouet. Visits
London. Works in St-Jean-de-Luz. Marquet's mother dies.

1908
Works in Collioure. Visits Italy (Naples). Charles Louis Philippe reviews Marquet's graphic art in *La Grande Revue*.

1909-1910
Visits Naples and Hamburg.

1911
Visits Tangiers together with Matisse. Works in Naples, Honfleur and Conflans.

1912
Works in Rouen. Makes another visit to Tangiers.

1913-1914
Visits Tangiers, Collioure and Rotterdam. Awarded the order
of the Légion d'Honneur, but refuses it.

1915-1919
Work extensively in the south of France.

1920
Publication of the first book on Marquet (G. Besson, *Marquet*,
Paris). Visits North Africa. Becomes acquainted with Marcelle
Martinet in Algiers.

1922
Works in Algeria.

1923
Marries Marcelle Martinet.

1925
Visits Norway.

1926
Visits Tunisia.

1927
Works in Brittany and the south of France. Visits Algeria.

1928
Visits Aswan in Egypt.

1930
Travels to Spain.

1932
Visits Spain and Algeria.

1933
Visits Romania.

1934
Visits the Soviet Union (Leningrad, Moscow, Kharkov, Rostov,
Tbilisi, Batumi).

1936
Visits Switzerland and Italy (Venice).

1940
Leaves France for Algeria.

1940-1945
Lives and works in Algiers. Involved in the Resistance.

1945
Returns to Paris. Works at La Frette.

1946
Visits Davos in Switzerland.

1947
Albert Marquet dies in Paris on 14 June.

157

Man

guel